THE RATIONAL GOSPEL

BOB KING

Copyright © 2024 Bob King.

All rights reserved. No part of this book may be reproduced, stored, or transmitted by any means—whether auditory, graphic, mechanical, or electronic—without written permission of both publisher and author, except in the case of brief excerpts used in critical articles and reviews. Unauthorized reproduction of any part of this work is illegal and is punishable by law.

ISBN: 979-8-89031-976-0 (sc)
ISBN: 979-8-89031-977-7 (hc)
ISBN: 979-8-89031-978-4 (e)

Because of the dynamic nature of the Internet, any web addresses or links contained in this book may have changed since publication and may no longer be valid. The views expressed in this work are solely those of the author and do not necessarily reflect the views of the publisher, and the publisher hereby disclaims any responsibility for them.

One Galleria Blvd., Suite 1900, Metairie, LA 70001
(504) 702-6708

ACKNOWLEGEMENTS:

Thanks to some of the people who supported me as I wrote this book: Leanne King, George Davis, Hugh Hannesson, Jimmy the eye, Debbie Fakes, Alison Dickson, Megan King, Ray and Joan Martin

ISBN: 978-0-9811213-3-4

I hope that people don't confuse my new book title 'THE RATIONAL GOSPEL' with the title of Dennis Prager's book series entitled 'THE RATIONAL BIBLE'. I will preface this by saying that Mr. Prager is one of my favorite author/commentators.

The differences in our books is that Dennis Pager's book talks about the Torah which is the first five books of the Old Testament and the basis for the Jewish religion. In my book I refer to the Old Testament, but I also refer to THE NEW TESTAMENT, which contains the stories of Jesus and His apostles. I also refer to the book of Mormon, which is another witness of Jesus Christ. those books are the main books of scripture In The Church Of Jesus Christ of Latter Day Saints. Thus, Jesus is referred to in the Book of Mormon as the prophesied Messiah and Jesus is the main focus in the Mormon scriptures.

Also included in my book are some quotes from the book of Doctrine and Covenants, which is a book that I consider to be very inspirational.

My personal area of interest, however, is as a minister in my own Christian church. A minister is, basically, someone who serves other people. Dennis Prager and I might differ on some issues, but mostly our political and social philosophies are very similar.

I think that Dennis Prager is an icon in the world of respectable journalism. In spite of that, the power hungry political parties and media corporations have managed to censor his broadcasts because they are not a part of the 'politically correct secular narrative'. This is a travesty of justice to me in a free country that has freedom of speech and freedom of the press enshrined in their national constitution.

Other religious/ political commentators who I admire are Dr. Jordan Peterson, for one. Dr. Peterson took a firm stand a few years ago against the misuse of speech that was promoted by governments who insisted that people should use the 'preferred pronouns' that every person wanted to be addressed by, even if those pronouns originated in the world of fantasy. To not refer to people by their preferred pronouns was deemed to be an offense by government officials and academics and is a violation of some new laws. An accusation like that had severe punishments attached to it.

Politically, I don't care that much for Dr. Peterson's dependency on psychological theories, but I am vehemently on his side politically. I think he should become a politician. Dr. Peterson said in a recent interview that 'nice people' can do more harm than good. He said that 'nice people are not necessarily smart people or virtuous people. They can be used as 'cannon fodder' for the psychopaths of the world, of which there are many.'

He said that psychopaths are experts in turning the apparently good intentions of nice people, like tolerance and all out forgiveness and then twisting those intentions around to become a license to permit many kinds of destructive attitudes. He has worked with psychopaths for many years as a clinical psychologist and he knows them well. He says that they are people who are without a conscience and are also master manipulators. Thus, Dr. Peterson has opened up a new frontier of controversy and I, for one, admire him for it.

Another commentator who I particularly enjoy is Matt Walsh. Mr. Walsh is a devout Christian, but he frequently criticizes some Christian churches for being over-tolerant and not standing up to condemn incidences of sinful behavior. Often he criticizes the kind of behavior that is practiced by young people who are unfortunately 'gender confused'.

To me, anyone who says that there are no foolish people in Christian churches, or virtue signalers, or 'weasels' (as Dr. Peterson would call them), is mistaken. There are enough of those around everywhere.

I would seldom criticize a Christian church or Christians in general, but if I did I would do it for a good reason. Firstly I strongly believe that a Christian church has a moral obligation to support the commandments that are expressed in the Bible. Some churches like to make exceptions to some of those obligations due to having a false sense of tolerance, but that would be betraying one of the purposes of God's that is to call church members to be accountable for their mistaken perceptions.

Some people might accuse me of being intolerant, or even blasphemous, but frankly, I don't care. I believe what I believe, and until an ultimate authority tells me I am wrong, I will stick with my beliefs that I consider rational. I don't do that because somebody told me to do it. I do it because it is mostly from the contexts of my personal life's experiences from which I draw my conclusions.

Some of my other favorite commentators include Ben Shapiro, Dr. Thomas Sowell, Victor David Hansen, and Glen Beck. I like Ann Coulter, but lately she seems to have lost much of her keen sense of humor. That is understandable, given that the political situation in the United States has become quite depressing over the last decade or so.

I name these commentators here because I want to make it clear from the beginning, which side of the political fence I am on. Personally though, I have, in recent years studied the gospel quite thoroughly and I am active in my duties as a minister in my church. Nevertheless, religious beliefs and political beliefs cross paths every day in our modern world. Thus, sometimes it might become necessary for us to explain the moral justification for whatever beliefs we have without having to worry about being persecuted for those beliefs.

My church, which is the Church of Jesus Christ of Latter Day Saints, has as its canonized scriptures too. One book is the Bible, including the Old Testament, which includes the Torah. My Bible also includes the New Testament of course, which tells us about the story of Jesus Christ and about His mission in Israel. As well it talks about as His Magnificent Atonement that took place at the end of His mission in Jerusalem.

It is my personal belief that the great Atonement that culminated in Jesus sacrifice on the cross was the event that actually changed the entire spiritual history of the world. That was because it was a sacrifice that gave every person on the face of the Earth the opportunity to partake of Eternal Life in a sanctified Heavenly realm.

If you would like to receive an email copy of this book (an electronic transcript) please mail a check or money order for six dollars addressed to:

BOB KING
P.O. Box 1105
Lumsden, Saskatchewan, Canada
S0G 3C0.
Please include your email address so it can be sent there.

Thank you.

TABLE OF CONTENTS

1. Testimony — page. 14
2. Roots and the Cycle of life — page. 16
   Subtitles: Giving and Receiving; My Roots, What do I want to Become in My Life?
3. Rest and Relaxation at Last — page. 24
4. The Ten Steps to Self Fulfillment — page. 32
   1. **Freedom** *(bob's obbs) Freedom and liberty);*
   2. **Peace** *(Subtitles)*
      a. **Forgiveness**
      b. **forget the bad stuff**
      c. **self-preservation;**
      d. **self-improvement (repentance)**
   3. **Intelligence**
   4. **Courage**
   5. **Kindness**
   6. **Righteousness**
   7. **Loyalty**
   8. **Joy**
   9. **Confidence (faith)**
   10. **Patience**
5. New Wine and Old Bottles — page. 53
   Subtitles: The Three Point Regeneration Process
6. The Need For A Prophet — page. 64
   Subtitles: The Holy Ghost's; Jacob Chapter 5
7. Gentle Sparks from Heaven and Wildfires from Hell. — page. 79
   Subtitles: Obsessions (Wildfires)
8. Seduction and the Shattering of Realities — page. 90
   Subtitles: A Good Shattering; Shattering by Deserting a Friend; Only two solutions; Fight Back
9. When the Demons Come After You — page. 106
10. Flowers Were Meant To Give Away — page. 116

11.	Evil Spirits	page. 118
12.	My Secret Love	page. 129
13.	The Six Realms Of Time	page. 138
14.	An Old Friend	page. 148
15.	It's all about Obsessions	page. 164

    Subtitles: Negative Issues, Swatting Mosquitoes, and God's Job; Repentance is a Gift; It's All About Obsessions; Saddle Soap?; What Have We Learned?

16.	Bob's Obbs #1	page. 186
17.	Faith, Hope and Charity	page. 194
18.	In Appreciation of True Artistry	page. 207

    Subtitles: Lets Appreciate Good Art, Good Core Values and Freedom; Encouraging Young Artists; Serious Sex and Novelty Sex; Standards of Entertainment; Evil Spirits and Porn

19.	Anatomy Of A Smile	page. 227

    Subtitles: Give Them A Chance To Remember; Remember the Shining Moments; Kay Kay; Yipee, A Good Thought has Arrived; Nurse Jen

20.	No Beer	page. 243
21.	A Spiritual Overview	page. 245

    Subtitles: Spirituality and Being Clean; Freedom of Religion; An Unseen World; Liberty, Bondage and the New Covenant; Organized Religion; Religion Causes Wars?; The Salt of the Earth; Spiritual Roots; Good and Evil Spirits; How to Spot An Evil Spirit; Religion and Spirituality; The Problem of Evil in the World; Absolute Morality and Relative Morality; Evil Forces and levels of Understanding; Levels and Being Above Board; Wisdom and the Comforter; Good Religion and Bad Religion; Religion and Knowledge; My Soul and its Inclinations

22. Drugs   page. 313
     Subtitles: A Religious 83 Year Old Man's Experience with Morphine; A Horrific Phone Call; Is There Anything Wrong with Wanting to Feel Good?; Murderers Among Us.

23. A Betrayal and The Spirit of Gentleness   page. 324
24. Nothing God Can't Do   page. 333
25. The Descending Order of Faith   page. 336
26. Always Consider Context   page. 342
27. Bob's Obbs #2   page. 353
28. The Final Gathering   page. 364
29. Little Changes and The Big Change   page. 374
30. The Man You Call Your Dad   page. 377
31. My Testimony Revisited.   page. 381
     Subtitles: The Brides and the Bridegroom
32. GRADUATION DAY   page. 386
33. Evidence of Real Hope and Prophesy   page. 397
34. Letters From a Friend   page. 403

Opening page

THE RATIONAL GOSPEL

Some of the printing in this book is in larger print. Good Spiritual principles are printed in large print and sometimes in capital letters. Details are printed in smaller print.

"Most of the writing and the editing that I did for this book took place at my temporary home of Muchmor Lodge in the city of Regina, Saskatchewan, Canada. I would like to thank the people and the staff there for the support that they gave me." – Bob King

No part of this book maybe reproduced, stored in a retrieval system, or transmitted by any means without the written permission of the author. Published by: Armchair Publishing © July 31, 2023

The Bob King You tube channel is:
https://youtu.be/EMT5qnjTvHo

For information about this and other products please email: bob.sandwiches@gmail.com

I love to write; I like to write about potential solutions to world problems and personal problems. Writing about these things keeps me sane. I also like to write about the many good things that go in life, writing about those things keeps me happy.

- *Bob King*
2023

I am a man who has made many mistakes in his life so I would not hold myself up as an ideal advisor to anyone who is looking for good moral path to travel on the way to achieving a totally fulfilling life.

In any case, and in all humility, I would to offer some simple advice to those who struggle. I call these twelve principles the Bob King <u>'Besures'</u>.

1. Be sure to establish your exact priorities and in accordance with higher spiritual laws.

2. Be sure to take time for rest and relaxation.

3. Be sure to take time to exercise your body and get some fresh air.

4. Be sure to exercise your mind with creative writing, even journal writing. Write about things that will require you to display your personal ingenuity and check back on those entries as you progress in cementing your philosophy.

5. Be sure to keep your sense of humor and display it when you can.

6. Be sure to keep good company.

7. Be sure to let your children and your loved ones know that you care about them.

8. Be sure to help other people who need help.

9. Be sure to establish your philosophy of freedom and independence in your own mind.

10. Be sure to remember to pray because God wants to be involved in your physical and spiritual healing, and that is what He does best. Plus, the influence of the Holy Ghost can actually help you to see everything more clearly.

11. In matters of discernment, be sure to evaluate what discerning thinkers are most interested in and how they behave. You may judge the principles that people live by, but don't judge the people.

12. That last one applies in the same way to evaluating non-discerning people too, or people who just follow the crowd. Evaluate what principles and what behaviors they are most interested in, and again, you may judge the principles that they live by, but don't judge the people.

I hope you enjoy my book   - Bob King

1. TESTIMONY (2p.)

(Subtitles: A Testimony of the Truth)

I believe that ALL people should integrate ALL of the true principles of the gospel that they know about, into their personality. If they do that then that person should automatically know the correct way to proceed in life. That is what I call an integrated belief system. It is also a <u>rational</u> belief system.

Stop looking for answers to important questions so that you might impress people, when you have already found those answers.

Stop showing your skill at showing tolerance when certain things can make you very angry and you may not be as tolerant as you claim to be.

Stop mulling over every little thing for hours on end. Say what needs to be said and even expand on it if that feels like the right thing to do.

The prophets in the Bible and in the Book of Mormon knew exactly what needed to be said and they said it. As a result everyone who took their words to heart benefitted and their lives changed for the better. That is what we all need to do. Have faith in what you already know and practice your articulation of it.

A TESTIMONY OF THE TRUTH

Sometimes the glory of the truth can get buried beneath an abundance of words. But understanding simple truths is still a great thing. Be assured of that and feel confident about expressing those truths.

Start by gaining a <u>TESTIMONY</u> of simple truths, by the Spirit of the law. Then let us give all the glory unto God, who is the great Dispenser of truth. And let His love shine in your hearts, either in your old age, or in your youth.

2. ROOTS, THE DIVINE CYCLE OF LIFE, AND WHAT I WANT TO BE (8p.)

THE DIVINE CYCLE OF LIFE

Life consists mostly of giving and receiving. Sacrifice is the ultimate form of giving, while gratitude and appreciation are the ultimate forms of receiving.

There are four basic objectives that we all need to learn to give and to receive in order to become fulfilled as people. All of those things are inter-related. I, personally, call these four directions 'The Great Cycle of Life' Those things are, as illustrated below are:

9 o'clock- God (or truth),

12 o'clock- Purpose (or knowledge and wisdom),

3 o'clock - Love (or joy),

6 o'clock – Peace (or beauty and Security)

These four things are the ultimate good things. The word '<u>purpose</u>' relates directly to the word 'knowledge', or 'wisdom'. The word '<u>peace</u>' is related to the word 'beauty'. These things are connected and they might make up a circle, or cycle, that looks something like this:

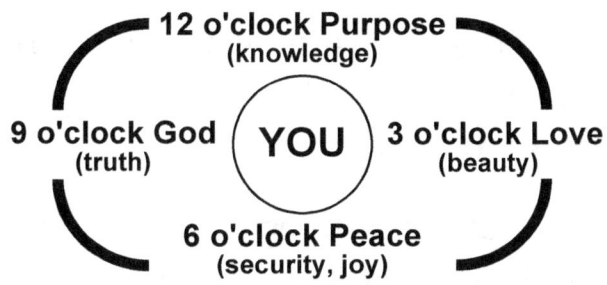

1. **Truth, or God**, is the beginning and the end of the cycle. This would be the NINE o'clock position. our Great God is the beginning of all truth and the end of all truth. God wants us to receive Him and of our own free will, and as our Creator and a wise Being who has a plan for us. He wants us to obey righteous Laws so that we can be a part of His Eternal family and live fully within **The Divine Cycle of Life.**

2. **Purpose (meaning, wisdom, intelligence)** If our momentum in this cycle is going forward in a clockwise motion then we will proceed to the category of **purpose or meaning or intelligence**. Going forward in a clockwise motion, we then Knowledge or wisdom. We need knowledge in order to perceive God and love to be able to feel joy. and perceive our purpose in life. God wants us to be wise.

3. Love. Love is truly beautiful. We need love life so that life can have good meaning for us and in order to come to know God and to love life and to come to know our purpose in living. If you do not have love, seek diligently as to where you might find it. God wants every one of us to be able to give love and to be able to receive love in the purest of ways. .

4. Peace. Peace is a sure <u>knowledge</u> your life is good. We need peace in order to have <u>joy</u> and <u>love</u> and to have a <u>purpose</u>. If you feel you have no purpose ask yourself if you

THE RATIONAL GOSPEL

really have love. God wants us to be peaceful and wants us to promote peace. Our Spiritual Father (Creator) is the lynchpin (or hinge) for all this.

As you can see, these four things are all inter related. These four things should be both given and received. Truth has elements of beauty and love and purpose in it, but we need knowledge to know where we can find those things. It is the same with each element in relation to the others. They are all things that we, as humans, need to have knowledge of and to and be aware of their presence in our lives.

Are you prepared to give and receive of those four things? If so, I congratulate you and I look forward to seeing how you progress in your life. Just remember to love your God as much as you can and thank Him for His patience as He tries to fulfill your Eternal needs and waits on you.

MY ROOTS

My grandfather was named James King Sr. He was a man who partially raised me, and we were pretty close. He was a Scotsman and a devout Christian and an expert gardener to boot. He was also, to his credit, a teetotaler.

When he was a young man, World War Two was just breaking out in Europe. Grandpa loved the idea of freedom and wanted to defend his freedom loving country which was Scotland, so he enlisted in the British army.

Because he was a Christian and a pacifist, my grandfather did not want to shoot a gun and kill other people, whether those people were unrighteous or just misguided, So instead, he became a stretcher bearer whose job was to carry wounded soldiers from the battlefields. During war BEING A stretcher bearer has just as much danger and risk as any other position in the army, if not more.

He lived through it all though and after the war, was over he and his wife, Jean, moved to Canada and started their life as a farm family in Manitoba. They named their first child James, who was my father. They moved to the city of Winnipeg a few years after that where my grandfather got a job as a male nurse at the Deer Lodge hospital, which, at the time, was a hospital for war veterans.

In the meantime, they raised five children together. My own father (James or Jimmy) had a number of jobs after World War two was over, but after some time he settled into a job that he loved. That job was as a musician and an orchestra leader. He gained a lot of notoriety in that job over the years. Unlike my grandfather, my father was not a teetotaler, but he became very successful in the music business. My mother, Faye Armitage King, was a stay-at-home housewife and she was very good at it.

My Grandpa also strongly believed in <u>unity</u> among Christians. At the time there were many different Christian sects in Canada and for some strange reason they did not get along as well as they should have. As a result of that, he and my grandmother joined the United Church of Canada and became very active in it. The name of the church says a lot about it. I picked up many good things from that church, but those things did not really have a lot of permanent 'staying power' with me. (*Shame on me.*)

When I got older, I went to university, where I studied English and philosophy. I got married, and then I got divorced, and along the way, I developed a friendship with a friend named Al. His last name was Cohol. Maybe you have met him.

Musically, I learned how to play the guitar and the bass I also started performing and began to write songs. My songs turned out to be fairly popular with people who were in my age group. I also did some acting in a few travelling theater groups.

I needed to make some money to continue my education, so at one point I ended up playing the bass guitar in a comedy show band called Kornstock. I found that enjoyable and I played with that band for five years and I wrote more songs. Most of my songs were of a comedic nature and many of my songs were geared for children.

Later on, I did more recording and I put out about fifteen albums of original songs over the years. As a musician, I got more diversified in my performing and in my song writing. I began performing a lot for children in schools and I also taught an interactive, self-made songwriting course for elementary schoolchildren for students in grades four to six.

That was a good job that I enjoyed working at and I actually recorded many songs that the students and I wrote together. It culminated when I won an award for the best children's album of 2005 from the Western Canadian music awards.

Two of my songs sold over one million copies apiece, but I won't go into that right now. I am more interested in the spiritual songs and stories that I am presently writing. So I will proceed.

WHAT DO I WANT TO BECOME IN MY LIFE?

"What do I want to become most in life?" I asked myself when I was younger. At that time, I did not really know what I wanted to do, so I waited for some good opportunities, but I would say that the thing that interested me the most was music.

At the present time I might say that I would like to become a good father to my family and a productive worker in society. I might also say that I want to work towards the idea of helping to implement justice in the world. That is <u>not</u> because I relish the thought of being a lawyer. It is because, over the years I have come to understand God better and to love Him. I have also come to know that God loves justice, and I want to be more like God for now and for the future.

I think that God would approve of that ambition. I also think that life has given me many present examples of <u>injustice</u> in this world. Perhaps that is so that I will come to know more about injustice and that might be so that I can be better at fighting against injustice on a higher level, and as well, be an advocate for true justice. That might be called <u>'true learning'</u>. In any case, I just want to help create a 'just society'.

Is that selfish?

No. That is because the promotion of justice is how I express my gratitude to God. God wants us to be grateful. The test of gratitude is embodied in whether or not we have learned a true principle from something we experienced, even if it was something distasteful. I thought that when we learn good principles of truth, or get 'true learning', we will become grateful, and then we can put those principles to good use in our 'fallen world'.

This world of ours is more than ready for justice and more than ready to accept 'people who choose to do the right thing'. I want to do that because I simply want to be a more intelligent person in the future than I am right now. In other words, I want to love 'justice' like God loves justice.

God is powerful but he uses his power for righteous purposes. Therefore I want to be powerful, but I want to be powerful in His way. That is because God might sometimes decide to forsake His power for the sake of being righteous, or merciful or charitable. An example of that is the way he handled the torturing and murder of his only begotten Son during the great Atonement. He did not come down and obliterate the enemies of his Son, even though he could have easily done that. He knew, I would guess, that his children would be better off learning a higher principle, particularly the law of sacrifice. Thus, I want to be righteous too and even offer up a sacrifice, if that is necessary. Again, that is because I want to be like God is.

God also wants us to be loyal and loving. Therefore, He must be loyal and loving himself. I want to be like that too, because I want to be like Him.

Our Father also wants us to be merciful. Therefore I want to be kind and have mercy on others so that I might be like him. I also want to be forgiving and avoid thoughts of personal pride like God does.

God loves intelligence. He wants to bring order out of chaos by intelligent means. Therefore, I want to love intelligence and order because I want to be like He is. I also want to love 'simplicity' for the same reason.

> **"my soul delighteth in plainness."**
> **- 2 Nephi 31: 3**

Thus, it is not all that complicated. These desires of our God's are good and they are also, plain and simple. If God's desires are plain and simple, then I want my desires to be plain and simple too. That is why we say simple things like 'choose the right'. Again, I say things like that because it makes total sense and because I want to be like Him.

Perhaps the biggest reason that I love God so much is because I know that we are all His Spiritual children and that He loves His children and He strongly desires that we should learn as many good things as we can in this stage of our lives.

Thus, He wants to raise us as all so that we will come to know what love really is, and what peace really is, and what joy really is, and what our purpose really is.

Besides those things, He wants us to know who He really is, and who His Son really is, and who our Spiritual comforter and our advisor (the Holy Ghost) really is. He also knows that teaching us these things will not be a 'walk in the park'.

3. REST AND RELAXATION AT LAST (8p.)

Subtitles: 'But seriously folks'.

"I'm out to have some Double U and double U", said my brother David, who was at that time, quoting one of his personal heroes. That hero of his who was also a cartoon character and was a normally soft spoken man named Elmer Fudd.

Elmer Fudd was a character who was often seen on cartoons produced by the Warner Brothers company, the company that also produced Bugs Bunny and many other characters.

Elmer also had a slight speech impediment. Elmer once said the following words while he was on a sojourn into the woods to experience the beauty of nature:

"Ahhh", he said, "west and wewaxation at wast".

Yes, Elmer was a soft spoken man, although perhaps a little deficient in his word pronunciation. Nevertheless, he always made sure he carried a big shotgun under his arm. He did not believe in going out in the woods defenseless. Little did Elmer know though, that when he went out into the woods there was a 'wascawy wabbitt' named Bugs Bunny waiting to mischievously disrupt his plans. The rest is cartoon history.

When I was younger, I decided to seek a career as a musician and songwriter, which turned out to be a career that I worked at for many years and in which I had varying amounts of success. Nevertheless, it brought me much satisfaction and I have no regrets about it.

A career as a writer and entertainer can be fun, but there is a certain lifestyle involved in that that can be testy. It can be a lifestyle that can have many 'proverbial bumps' on the 'proverbial road'. I have had some disappointments in my career, but it has always been a policy of mine to be accountable for my decisions and my actions, whether they work out well for me or not. All in all, I did okay.

I am a crippled man now, mainly because of a debilitating stroke that I suffered about ten years ago. I could call myself a victim of fate because of that, but I don't do that. I won't hold anyone else responsible for my misfortunes. I know now that when I was younger, I neglected the benefits of living a healthy lifestyle and I never really took good care of myself properly..

Besides that, there are some good things that I have actually learned from my challenges, and I would guess, that I even more things that I have yet to learn about how to deal with the 'hardness of life'.

Nevertheless, I will still be strong about stating my opinions, as long as I am confident that they are well thought out. I also make it a point to refuse to knuckle under to someone else's unreasonable demands and/ or to their idealism.

I have the inner tenacity to stand up for righteous beliefs and I don't really understand why some people have a belief system that is not well thought out at all. I also recognize that I must resist certain bad tendencies in myself that I nurtured in my past. I did some foolish things back then, things that did me no good, but I have always maintained the skill I have on the fine art of 'relaxing'.

I don't want to brag, but I would say that my ability to 'rest and relax' is well above the norm. I think that I should receive a few accolades for that because, after all, I have worked very hard at it. Yes, I think I might even say, Like Mr. Fudd would also say, that it is good to be able to say to myself, **Ahhh, 'west and wewaxation' at wast.**

In any case, life is sometimes difficult for me. At present, I sometimes I feel like I am caught in a 'rat race' with a bunch of other rats. Some of those rats may be 'nice' rats and some of them may be not so nice. In any case, I feel, at present, that I've got to get away from all that. I seek an escape of some kind to get away from the 'nose to the grindstone mentality', that so many of my cohorts enjoy.

To be totally honest, I don't really like 'work' very much, but I don't apologize for that. I suspect that I was born that way. So I am content to blame the genes of my mother and father for that and then proceed to and let it go. I am not lazy, but am confident that I do have a rather nice looking nose, despite the fact that there have been a few incidents in my life where a rogue grindstone almost cost me some disfiguration of my nostrils when my nose got too close to that grindstone. That is one reason why I like to spend as much time as possible enjoying the simple pleasures of 'west and wewaxation'.

Besides that, please don't ask me about the scar I have under my left nostril. It's none of your business and the grindstone that caused it is now in a garbage dump somewhere with absolutely nothing to grind except air. That is kind of a shame because, from what I understand, there is no market anywhere in the world for 'ground air'.

Nevertheless, I proceed with my life as a writer and I think that I usually have a positive influence on my readers. Specifically, my readers they seem to appreciate my views on the value of 'rest and relaxation in life. Some people claim that relaxation skills are no big deal, but I would beg to differ. I have always found enjoyment in relaxing and I do believe that it has made me a more positive person. I don't let the hustle and bustle of a busy world get me down. Whenever I get stressed, I just go out into the woods and blast a few 'wabbits' and I automatically feel better about my life.

And I don't worry about the rabbits. In the cartoon world that I live in, the rabbits always come back to life in the next frame and life just goes on as it has always has gone on.

I still appreciate good humor though. As odd as it might sound, a weird character like Elmer Fudd always makes me laugh, and by doing so, he actually gives me hope for the future.

To get out of my previous mindsets will take a 'change of thinking' for me. It is not easy to change patterns of thinking that I have lived by for many years, but I have confidence that a positive attitude is definitely a good thing.

Sometimes, making a living out in the world seems like a 'rat race'. However, if you share your life with 'ratty people', your environment can become a part of you. You can ignore it for awhile, but you should know that you will probably need to discard certain habits and customs and attitudes that enabled you to feel comfortable inside that 'rat realm' for so many years.

We can tolerate the nasty habits of other rats, but sooner or later, we must face up to the fact that 'wats and wabbits' are both varmints and our world would be better off without them. I know that this is not a popular opinion. I know it because I mentioned it to my psychiatrist, and as a result of that, he said that he doesn't want to see me anymore.

That 'hunter's realm' is basically a realm of selfishness, not necessarily one's own selfishness, but someone else's selfishness that was imposed upon you as they exercised their 'rattiness' over you. Those 'ratty' feelings could have been imposed on you by yourself, or by another person, or by a group if people, who have various 'rat like' qualities. But whatever the source was, those 'ratty' social realms are not good places to live in, nor do they offer much opportunity to 'just wewax'.

Thus, it seems to me that serious, and unencumbered, rest could be the best solution for me and you during moments of stress. Thus, I say, enjoy your relaxing moments and give thanks for them.

Getting good rest on a continual basis has always been a part of me, but I fear that I have ignored that part of me for a long time and recently, I have come to realize that I have sorely missed it. Thus, I believe that I will pay 'that restful part of me' another visit, starting today. I believe that it is now time for me to take that old shotgun down from the rack.

So can I make a silk purse out of a wabbit's ear (as I think the saying goes)? More importantly, can I now find true happiness when I am NOT a part of the 'Wat Wace'? Can I find true happiness out in the great outdoors with the birds and the bears and the deer and those rascally rabbits? I say, 'YES', I CAN DO IT.

So, personally, I believe that I need to relax again at this time in my life. I need to reset my desires for peace, without giving in to depression or anxiety, or conspiracy theories. No, I will not do that. I am still able to stand on my own two feet and smile for the camera.

And getting back to Mr. Fudd for a moment, I have some serious questions about him that I would like to have answered, such as, "was Elmer really a worthy mentor for me or my children, and was he really a good role model?" Another question is, "Is it a good policy to always use a shotgun to settle disputes?"

The Warner Brothers company never bothered to discuss Elmer's personal life at all, but I can't help but wonder about a few things, like: "was there a Mrs. Fudd in the picture?" We know that one's families are an important part of our happiness. What would Elmer have to say about that?

Also, "Did Mrs. Fudd have a speech impediment similar to the one that Elmer had?" And, "Did she have a good head of hair?" Never mind. Those things are quite irrelevant. Families, however, are very important, so I ask: "Did Elmer have children? What were their names? Were they well behaved and obedient to their parents? Did Elmer believe in child discipline?"

Those things don't matter much to me because that is Elmer's business and not mine. But the main topic here is rest and relaxation and the importance of those things. I can only assume that Elmer, if he was indeed the patriarch in his family, would teach his children about the importance of 'rest and relaxation' in their lives.

***

BUT SERIOUSLY FOLKS

In our church, we regard Jesus Christ himself as the head of our church and we seek personal revelations and guidance from Him through prayer and also by the power of the Holy Ghost who is able to dwell within us and speak to our understanding.

A friend of mine, who is also a preacher, asked me a question a few years ago about the nature if the Godhead, or as he might call it 'the Holy trinity'. i quoted one of my favorite scripture writings to explain my thoughts on that.

> *"The Father has a body of flesh and bones as tangible as man's; but the Holy Ghost has not a body of flesh and bones, but is a personage of spirit. Were it not so, the Holy Ghost could not dwell in us."*
>
> *- Doctrine and covenants130: 22*

My friend was a good man and he still is a good man, but I found it unusual that, being a preacher himself, he did not yet understand the nature of the Father, Son and Holy Ghost, which is a big part of the central principle in the gospel.

Seriously again, in our church, we also have twelve apostles who have been ordained to do special work under the guidance of our prophet, who is himself guided by our Lord who is Jesus Christ.

One of my faviorite speakers in my church, and also one of my favorite apostles is Elder Jeffrey R. Holland. I will quote Elder Holland Elder Holland below on the subject of rest and relaxation:

> *"Fatigue is a debilitating fact for all of us. We all get tired. We all need a vacation no matter how brief or inexpensive it might be. Certainly this is the reason that God ordained a Sabbath".*
> *- Jeffrey R. Holland*

Chapter 4.

THE TEN STEPS TO SELF FULFILLMENT (21p.)

SUBTITLES:
1. Freedom
(bob's obbs) freedom and liberty
2. Peace,
four sub steps to peace
    a. forgiveness,
    b. forget the bad stuff
    c. self-preservation,
    d. self-improvement and repentance
3. Intelligence
4. Courage
5. Kindness
6. Righteousness
7. Loyalty
8. Joy
9. Confidence (faith)
10. Patience

Recently, I wrote that peace is freedom and freedom is peace. I wondered, at the time I said that if people were to consider those two great things first, would it provide enough encouragement to motivate people to strive for success in their lives by seeking those two things? Was success really that simple? Was that formula really enough to make the equation complete? On further consideration I decided that it was not enough. So I added eight more principles.

Note: You may notice that I put the principle of freedom ahead of the principle of peace. There is a reason for that.

The reason is that freedom must be earned and that will take courage and wisdom to earn it. If freedom is not earned, but is dictated according to a government controlled agenda, then it will not work and peace will never happen.

Step one: **FREEDOM**

> *"If you don't appreciate freedom then you could spend your whole life in bondage. If you don't appreciate <u>peace</u>, you could spend your whole life in turmoil and chaos."* – Bob King

> *"Of all tyrannies, a tyranny sincerely exercised for the good if its victims may be the most oppressive. It would be better to live under robber barons than omnipotent moral busybodies. The robber baron's cruelty may sometimes sleep; but those who torment us for our own good will torment us without end for they do so with the approval of their own conscience."*
>   - C.S. Lewis

FREEDOM AND LIBERTY

Bob's Obbs – (Bob's observations on freedom and liberty)

> **"Proclaim liberty throughout the land." – Leviticus 25: 10**

"You can't be happy if you are not free. In today's world there are many evil forces, seen and unseen, who seek to take away the freedom of individuals and cause them to decrease their free agency and, accordingly, shrink their spirits and their spiritual potential, so that they will become slaves to the powerful ruling class."

"The opposite of freedom is bondage. Bondage means being controlled by forces outside yourself, and even sinister forces that abide inside of yourself. Bondage limits a person's growth and their potential. It shrinks their free spirit."

What is freedom? What is liberty?

"I define freedom as 'having the opportunity' to choose good. I define liberty as knowing exactly what your legitimate God-given parameters are and then choosing to live within them without any outside interference. Anything outside of those parameters and universal laws will end up chaotic."

"Chaos, or anarchy, might sound like freedom, but it is not. Chaos will eventually come down to the law of the jungle, which means that ninety-nine per cent of the population will eventually become enslaved and brought into bondage."

"Because I was once a non-Christian myself, I think I know a little about where non-Christians are coming from. On the other hand, most non-Christians, having never been converted, do not have a clue where I am coming from. That is understandable, but I figure that any commentaries on the important aspects of life are usually more revealing when a person has seen things from both sides of the spectrum."

In the Rational Gospel we have a policy that says, "We should take truth from wherever we can find it. We have studied the doctrines of various religions and we cannot accept them all because they often contradict each other. Howerver, we have accepted the individual principles from each one that are the most cohesive, most intelligent, most practical, most spiritual, and the ones that make the most sense from beginning to end."

"Freedom and bondage are basic elements of life and of the human spirit. Thus, my opening arguments and my presentations of evidence will be in favor of liberty, which is the most practical form of freedom. Bondage, is the opposite of freedom and liberty and has nothing to do with those two things. I will be analyzing those two basic elements in this book. That covers not only the physical elements in life, but the unseen spiritual elements as well."

"Basically, Spiritual factors differ from material factors because they are Eternal factors, whereas the things of this world are temporary factors and do not last. Therefore, logically speaking, spiritual things should be of more concern to us than temporal things because they are of an Eternal nature and are of Eternal worth."

"Some of the forms of personal bondage that I write about, like addictions and depression and false ideals, are very common in today's world. Some solutions to spiritual issues may be offered by commentators, but I find most of them lacking. Thus, I rely more in a spiritual perspective and I also look for some kind of **spiritual authority**, which implies the existence of an omnipotent Creator and knowledgeable servants of that Creator. I have found that any viable solution for earthly problems and that presents a deterrent for human bondage, always has a religious component to it."

"Everyone should try to get the big picture in life because if you do not have it, you will get the small picture or a series of small pictures. The devil also sees the big picture. That is because his ambition is to become greater than God and he knows that God sees the big picture. Thus, he wants to follow suit in his own way."

"While I say to people 'let freedom reign' in political affairs, let me be clear that there are some things that I consider to be more important than freedom. One of those things is honor. Freedom can sometimes be used for good or bad, but things like honor, compassion, decency, etc. can only be used for purposes of good."

"Nevertheless, for us to have honor, **we must have the freedom to make honorable decisions.** We must also be free and be able to act of our own accord and not be forced to act in a certain way by any governing bureaucrats, who really should have no authority in dictating the moral standards of private citizens."

"Seek the will of God in all things and then have the courage to act in your free decision. Wisdom comes first. Courage comes second. Hopefully, they will both come at the same time."

"One of the freedoms that many addicts often ignore is the **'FREEDOM TO STOP'**. This is especially true of people who have any kind of addiction. An addiction can be to a substance, like drugs or alcohol or tobacco. Or it can be an obsession to a mindset or to another person's will, or to a political ideal, or to a personal habit, or to a **game** of one kind or another. Addictions are powerful things."

"Some addictions can kill you. Many men and women will actually choose **death** over the choice to stop indulging in a bad habit even if they know their habit or obsession is a bad thing. That is how powerful an addiction can be. If a person chooses death over a habit that has a small amount of gratification in it, that is their decision, but they should know though, that indulging in such a habit is **unwise.** If they realize that, and have a healthy respect for wisdom, They should, then, have the will and the inner strength and the intelligence to **STOP IT.**"

If they choose not to stop it, they will be choosing death (or compulsion) and denying the power of liberty and of wisdom. When a person denies those things that will be the time when negative consequences will come into play. People should be aware that consequences to decisions, be they positive ones or negative ones, can be **permanent**."

"Many people who I have met have stopped their addictive behavior, so I know that it can be done. As a religious person, I believe that a soul can enter into various realms after their physical death. One of those realms might be the Heavenly realm, but there can be other realms as well. Finding and choosing a positive realm by which you can commit yourself to freedom is a good thing and a wise thing **if** that person is **prepared** for what might come their way in the other various realms of the Eternities. Preparation is a large comp[onent of intelligence."

"Like all of us, the soul of an addict will go to another realm of one kind or another, after their body dies. If their soul should go to a bad realm, it is possible that they may undergo torment. Without a doubt, that will be a painful and frightening thing. That is because a soul can regain cognition, or intelligence over time and to some degree in the afterlife.

This is due partly to the grace and compassion of our Heavenly Father and also to the existence of **'angel teachers'**, who will teach the souls of all people who have prepared for that 'new learning'. It is not guaranteed however that the ordinary soul will accept' that new learning. Some souls may have the mortal ways of thinking that they experienced in their mortal life **'embedded'** in their character. If such 'thought habits' should be embedded in their character, then the trajectory of their 'soul mind' will be fixed and permanent. Thus, the ability to actually change, or repent, will not be possible."

When that happens their spiritual mind will begin to examine their life more closely using their spiritual memory banks. Because the spirit can be a mighty force when it is taught using proper doctrine. More sure knowledge will also be available to them and thus, they can come to more exact conclusions than they ever would have come to in their mortal state.

Coming to those accurate conclusions will not guarantee that the person will 'make good' on making those necessary changes. That is because the person themselves will be physically dead after their mortal life is over and there is some question as to whether any new thought will become embedded in their character. That is because their old ways of thinking will still be in control and might be impossible for a 'new way of thinking' to enter in to the person's mind.

Even if that opportunity did enter into the person's mind, there is still some question as to 'would the person be cognitively capable of 'taking the solution to heart' and exercising it?

Thus, it will not be a sure thing that positive change will happen. If the acceptance of gospel principles does not happen then those deceased souls could be forever 'stuck' in their old ways and habits that they formed in mortality.

This is a natural consequence of a person, or a soul, continually accepting the old ways of thinking instead of accepting the 'new ways of thinking'.

Then people will then realize that their decision to live a clean life or a rebellious life was their own decision one hundred per cent. That will be something that, try as they might, they will not be able to deny it. Therefore, they will be accountable for the things they did and for how things turned out for them.

A person may not fear any retribution for what they did in mortality, but I would guess that such is something that might cause their eternal soul to worry, even worry endlessly. Would that bring on permanent anxiety? My, what a horrible concept.

Evil is here, and the consequences of aligning one's self with it can be permanent. Thus, it must be fought against because it seeks to hold all people in some kind of bondage.

In these times, it seems that the devil's tactics are ones that are designed to trick us and tempt us into meaningless pursuits like carnal acts of all varieties. Thus, after a while many of us will no longer have our free agency to decide which paths we should take. Thus, most of us will just throw up our hands and let someone else decide the right way that we should go.

One might not see that as a 'forced' bondage, but nevertheless, it is still bondage because the opportunities to make righteous choices will, simply, not be there anymore.

Step two: **PEACE.**

Peace comes to a person when the truth becomes sought out by that person and known to that person and accepted by that person. Another vital factor in having peace come to you is the realty of feeling **love** in your life. Love could be described as the ultimate value in life. Learning about love could be the same thing as 'learning' about the ultimate value in life. Sounds good to me. Count me in. That is why, in the first two commandments of God's ten commandments, the word 'love' is featured prominently.

I am not talking about the love that is presented in dime store novels. I am talking about <u>ultimate forms of love</u>. That kind of love not always possible without intelligence and understanding. The same goes for courage as it pertains to freedom and liberty, courage is essential for both freedom and peace to be established. To elaborate further, freedom is not free. It must be earned. Freedom, or liberty, is not always going to happen without the element of courage. Neither is peace. Both courage and wisdom will be necessary in order that freedom and peace might actually happen.

We have learned from history that a great prize like liberty must be <u>earned</u> and will probably not happen without a fight. That fight might also be an ongoing one. The main infractions of freedom in today's world are the infractions that violate 'freedom of speech' laws. I am referring mostly to the powers that be violating our rights to free expression on the internet especially. In Canada, where I live, Facebook is one of the prime violators in that regard. They censor any words that stand in opposition to the leftist thinking that dominates all of our public information sources. These sources give out biased information through government bureaucrats and by the media servants of those governments and by the academics and self interest groups that are influential in our country.

Thus, excellent conservative thinkers will be shut down and not allowed to give their opinions regarding very important matters, or even on minor matters. They will also censor anything else that they want to just on a whim, including censoring many religious posts that try to explain the actual nature of the Spirit and the actual nature of mortal life and the actual nature if working for a Holy cause that would greatly benefit the whole world.

This kind of freedom is a comment on censorship at the community level and in the national level. Whether you are left wing or right wing, censorship of honest opinions is a travesty of justice and it should be purged. That is because the first casualty in this perversion of the truth is the truth itself and, unless some kind of divine intervention happens, or a revolution, that will be the main cause of the inevitable disintegration of our society.

***

Four Sub-steps to Peace

1. **Forgiveness.** Forgiveness towards someone who has done you harm might seem like the hardest sub-step to do,

but it is actually one of the easiest steps. One reason that it is easy is because it will actually give you a feeling of relief that you are no longer feel resentment to another person and that you can dismiss all ill feelings towards that person or those people. This will give much more space where you can let the positive aspects of life become foremost in your mind.

2. **Forgetting the bad stuff**.

Forgetting the bad stuff is more difficult than forgiving the perpetrator of the bad stuff, but it is still essential to your peace because it clears the pathway to that peaceful state that most of us desire to partake of. That pathway can be littered with stumbling blocks that will hamper our progress on the road to the treasured feelings that peace can bring to us. Thus, we must keep in mind certain aspects of correct behavior such as, "*To err is human, to forgive divine."* (Alexander Pope) Or *"To gain an understanding of another person's actions we will need to "walk a mile in their shoes"*.

This applies to forgetting about our own mistakes as well as forgetting about the mistakes of others.

> *"This is the covenant that I will make with them After those days, saith the Lord, I will put my laws into their hearts, And in their minds will I write them; And their sins and iniquities will I remember no more.*
> *Hebrews 10: 16,17 KJV*

If it is good enough for the Lord to say it, it is good enough for me to hear it.

3. Self-Preservation

The third sub-step is what I call SELF-PRESERVATION. This is a defensive maneuver. It applies to the preservation of dignity for one's self as well as the preservation of dignity and love for the people close to us.

This can be the reason why the third sub-step could be the most difficult one. It is because that preservation that I speak of must be <u>constant</u>. We can forgive another person for their bad actions, but we must never forget the bad <u>principle</u> of what happened during the incident that made you feel wronged.

This principle of forgetting the offending person but remembering the malice that was involved in it is to prevent ourselves from falling into a similar trap in the future.

As an addendum to that, I would say that I know that my fiercest fight will end up being with myself. My greatest battle will be to conquer that part of myself that desires to follow my worst inclinations.

4. Self- improvement and Repentance

> *"A smart person knows there are certain places in the world where they should not go. A wise person knows there are certain places, even <u>within their own minds</u>, where they should not go. "*   - Bob King

Some non-religious people do not like to hear the word 'repent' mentioned at all. Why? It is mostly because of a distrust of religion. To each his own, I say, but we must be careful not to 'throw the spiritual baby out with the unclean

THE RATIONAL GOSPEL

bathwater'. I say that because the act of repentance is actually a great gift given to us by our loving Heavenly Father and we should be grateful for it. When we repent we seek for truth and where the truth is found, that is where a person's strength can be renewed.

> *"But they that wait upon the Lord shall renew their strength; they shall mount up with wings as eagles; they shall run, and not be weary; and they shall walk, and not faint"*
> - Isaiah 40:32

The word repentance means nothing more than exercising a positive change in a person's life. So what is wrong with that? On the other hand, accepting a philosophy of self indulgence IE: 'If it feels good, do it', is nothing more than a pernicious lie.

I say that it is the highest of ambitions for a person to want to be the best person they could be, both for their own sake and for the sake of others. As Jesus pointed out, it is hypocritical for a person to try to remedy a speck in another person's eye when they totally ignore a log in their own eye.

Recently, I was watching an interview with the psychologist Jordan Peterson on the topic of transgenderism. It was about certain people who were in favor of the idea that sex surgery was something that could be beneficial to a young girl who 'got an idea into her head' that she was really a little boy. Thus education administrators, and even surgeons, often accept the idea that surgery would be beneficial for that young girl. I hold a different opinion.

Dr. Peterson is big on collecting data about such decisions and he says that, from the letters that he receives that come from men and women who receive this surgery, and accepted the philosophy that goes along with it, is that the general results are that the patients are usually filled with regrets about their transition.

In any case, it is too late to go back and reverse the process. Thus he says that children are too young to be allowed to make such trauma inducing decisions. To me, Dr. Peterson seemed to be more militant about this issue than on any other issue that he talks about these days. I think it is nice to see someone take a strong stand in issues that can lead to permanent damage in a human being. .

I was talking to a friend who agreed with Dr. Peterson who said that the surgeons caught committing such acts should be put in jail. I will only say that I am personally in favor of that notion. Dr. Peterson also called the surgeons and medical administrators who support this notion are nothing more than 'butchers and liars'.

That is strong language. Using another analogy, and I know that this is not provable, but I know that a former Prime Minister of Canada, namely Pierre Elliot Trudeau, once called passionately for Canada to be a **'just society'**. Despite his son Justin's immature behavior and his idiotic quotes, (see *"When we kill our enemies, they win"*, I have a sneaking suspicion that if Pierre Elliot Trudeau really believed in justice, he just might be prone to agree with Jordan Peterson's opinion of the modern day surgeons in today's world. When Pierre Trudeau was alive however, this issue did not exist, so we will rally never know what he would have thought of it.

Dr. Peterson also spoke up on another issue that made 'the woke people bristle'. That was when there was a parallel

---

THE RATIONAL GOSPEL

movement that said that there should be a law that states that 'conversion therapy' even when performed by professional psychologists, and with the full consent of a homosexual who <u>want</u> to change, should be against the law.

Furthermore, that law said that anyone who used conversion therapy on a man or a woman who desired to partake of it should either be arrested or heavily fined. Many ordinary citizens did not really understand how lawmakers were literally forcing certain people <u>not to have their desire fulfilled</u> because their doctors and were prohibited from helping them under the threat of prosecution.

Thousands of busybodies who had no understanding of sexual issues or freedom of speech issues or freedom of choice issues signed petitions demanding that voluntary conversion therapy be outlawed. In many places conversion therapy was outlawed and it is no longer practiced in those places. Such is the so-called wisdom of those modern day busybodies who have fallen for the 'woke lies' that are in our midst.

I would not be at all surprised if those people tried to pass another bill that actually made repentance, which is an act of self-correction, against the law. Perhaps it might one day happen that priests or pastors could be arrested for accepting confessions from some of their parishioners.

My topic in this essay was being unable to forgive and forget wrong doing and that letting bad ideas invade our minds can impede a person's progress for decades and beyond, but it is far more beneficial, and <u>easier</u>, to be positive and faithful and forgiving. So let us apply those four sub-steps into our psyche every day.

***

Re: personal growth and repentance.

The president of the Church of Jesus Christ of Latter day Saints is Russell M. Nelson. President Nelson recently said that it was good for a person to <u>repent</u> every single day. A friend of mine found this a little confusing. My friend said, "I live a pretty good life and try to obey the commandments. Do I really need to repent every single day?"

My reply to him went thusly:
"We live in a tainted world. Because we live in a tainted world, we will probably become a little bit tainted ourselves, whether we intend to be or not. Repenting every day gives us the opportunity to 'clean the slate' as we begin each day. It also allows us to 'cover all the bases' and connect with our Heavenly Father. Thus, I think that president Nelson's quote was very appropriate.

***

After some consideration, I figured that there are eight other principles missing from this 'self-fulfillment equation'. They are: intelligence, courage, kindness, righteousness, loyalty, joy, confidence and patience.

Step 3. INTELLIGENCE (wisdom); develop understanding and Intelligence. If you do not know exactly what I am talking about here you will need to study it out, even using Christ as your exemplar.

> ***"The glory of God is intelligence, or light and truth - a fullness of which can be obtained by mortal man only through obedience to eternal laws."***
> ***- Doctrine and Covenants 93:37***

THE RATIONAL GOSPEL

Step 4. COURAGE Be fearless and try to instigate good ideas in your life and in the lives of other people within your circle of influence, and mainly through the sacrifices that you willingly make.

> *"Courage is resistance to fear, mastery of fear - not absence of fear."*
> — Mark Twain

> *"Courage is not simply one of the virtues, but the form of every virtue at the testing point."* – C.S. Lewis

Step 5. KINDNESS. Be kind (including have civility and charity, also have love for other people and have respect for yourself.)

> *"Do things for people not because of who they are or what they do in return, but because of who you are."* - Harold S. Kushner

Step 6. RIGHTEOUSNESS. Practice honesty and goodness whenever and wherever you can.

> *"Therefore do not worry saying, 'What shall we eat?' or 'What shall we drink?' or 'What shall we wear?' ... For your heavenly Father knows that you need all these things. But seek first the kingdom of God and his righteousness and all these things shall be added to you."*
> - Matthew 6: 31-33

Step 7. LOYALTY.

"The strength of a family, like the strength of an army, is in its loyalty to each other." -Mario Puzo

Practice loyalty and <u>devotion</u> to a righteous cause. The main 'cause' that I speak of is the love and loyalty you have for your Creator. Also, be thankful for that opportunity and do what you need to do to make your loyalty known to your Heavenly Father.

Step 8. JOY.

"Men (and women) are that they might have joy."
- 2 Nephi 2:25 (Book of Mormon)

Find delight and joy in all of these steps. This has to do with our very purpose in life. That means to be 'joyful' in the truth. Living by unexplained and vague 'community standards' is a ruse. Thus, appreciate your freedom because a way of life that emphasizes freedom is the forum where your rewards will 'click in'. There is joy there. A person will never experience joy when they are being held in bondage of any kind.

When devilish forces are able to stifle people's intelligence and their knowledge of reality, then that will be a sign that joy will dwindle and that the end of freedom will soon come after that. Therefore, fight against those 'bad ideas' when you can, and do so with 'joyful' confidence.

Step 9. CONFIDENCE (Faith)

Valuing freedom, and striving for it, is the first step to gaining confidence. I define freedom as '<u>having the opportunity to choose good</u>.' Liberty means knowing exactly what your legitimate God-given parameters are and then choosing to live within them without any outside interference. Thus, you will gradually come to know the difference between right and wrong.

Don't ever feel too proud of yourself or be too boisterous. That will just inflate your ego. In the other hand, don't underestimate yourself. Don't be afraid to be pleased with yourself for the good things that you have thought and expressed or written in the past, and the good things you have <u>done</u> in the past, and the good things that you are doing in the present. If you are a good thinker and have honorable ambitions then you have probably justified yourself more than you know. Accept that justification and the blessings that go with it. That is something that will give you confidence.

> *"Love and truth, people you can find in disguise anyplace or anytime, but you can just say so long once confidence is gone. Cause nothing matters anymore."*   *- Brownie Magee*
>
> *"As soon as you trust yourself, you will know how to live."*
>   *- Johann Wolfgang von Goethe*
>
> *"Religion should <u>not</u> be an unsolvable puzzle with*

answers given to us only in past times. It is about the present relationship we have with the living and Eternal force of creation. With faith and confidence in Christ, we can discover that."
– Bob King

I am getting old. The vultures that feed upon people's lack of mental sharpness are circling above my aging brain as I crawl through this increasingly hot desert that is life. Fortunately, I know where there is a healthy supply of water and it is accessible to me. I am talking about 'living water' and I hope that you, too, have been so blessed with the knowledge of its whereabouts.

That makes nine steps so far on the road to fulfillment. I added one more. It is patience:

Step 10 Patience.

"Let us not become weary in doing good, for at the proper time we will reap a harvest if we do not give up." *– Galatians 6:9*

Do not condemn those people who seem to be incapable of completing any of those first nine steps, because they basically, 'know not what they do'. Allow people, as God does, to have their own time in which to learn and grow.

Sometimes some people will succumb to the temptations of the devil without a fight because they fear the devil's power. There is another way to resist him. That is to simply <u>'wait him out'</u>.

The devil knows his time is limited in this life. He does not have much time left. On the other hand, if you are a follower of Jesus, you will have an eternity waiting ahead of you. That was His promise and his promises are true.

HAVE PATIENCE. WAIT THE DEVIL OUT AND HE WILL EITHER RUN IN FEAR OR ELSE WILL EVENTUALLY JUST PERISH IN HIS OWN CORRUPTION.

RIGHTEOUS PATIENCE CAN MEAN RIGHTEOUS WAITING. THAT ALSO MEANS WAITING WITH FAITH. YOU CAN GET REWARDS BY WAITING WITH CONFIDENCE AND WAITING WITH HUMILITY AT THE SAME TIME. PRAY TO THE FATHER/CREATOR WHO MADE YOU AND ASK HIM TO GIVE YOU STRENGTH AND WISE COUNSEL. HE WILL DO THAT IF YOUR MIND IS OPEN TO IT. HE DESIRES THE BEST FOR YOU AND HE WILL GIVE YOU MANY BLESSINGS WHEN YOU ASK FOR THEM.

***

Chapter 5

5. NEW WINE AND OLD BOTTLES

"Neither do men put new wine into old bottles: else the bottles break, and the wine runneth out, and the bottles perish, but they put new wine into new bottles and both are preserved." - Matthew 9: 17

I have finally learned the meaning and the wisdom of the metaphor that Jesus used about putting 'new wine into old skins'. It took a long time. The symbolism is fairly simple to understand when seen from a distance or in hindsight, but it is harder to understand when it is happening in the present. The immediacy of it all often does not work in our favor because there are long-term solutions involved and many people are more interested in short term or immediate solutions. Long-term solutions always involve principles of right and wrong. Right principles last over time, wrong principles don't last over time.

The vast majority of counselors and therapists say that the problems their clients need help with come from issues that are grounded in the past. Past trauma, past perceptions, past experiences, past relationships, etc. Some would put the figure at 80%. Some would put it even higher.

When I was twenty years old I met a young woman when I was working at a fishing lodge in Northern Ontario for the summer. She was very pretty, and I remember being quite smitten at the time. At the time I was working away from home and commuted back to my home in Winnipeg occasionally. As far as romance in my life went, I had intentions for this other girl at the time who lived in Winnipeg. She happened to be drop-dead gorgeous and I somehow felt my ambitions were locked in, or committed, to her. Looking back, I see that I was mostly caught up in a delusional way of thinking where I gave my imagination far too much liberty. I was a terrible dreamer. I was also pretty inexperienced at that age.

I pushed the relationship to my beautiful fishing lodge girlfriend or my 'new wine' girlfriend further to the point where I was on the emotional doorstep of having to decide whether or not to make a serious and long term commitment to her. That scared me.

The home of the girl from the fishing lodge was in the opposite direction from me, about five hundred miles away from my home. And soon my summer job would be coming to an end, so I was in a quandary. I was put in a position where I needed to decide whether to pursue the relationship or not. I knew such a commitment could have led to marriage and even though I felt very comfortable with her, that notion had not been in my plans. The woman had not been part of my previous life, including my social comfort zones and my ambitions. It was hard to fit her in to my understanding of the world and my present circumstances at that time. She was 'new wine' to me, but I was used to my old bottles and things just did not seem right.

One night, after I returned home to Winnipeg, I remember being in a car and talking to a friend about this young woman, at least I thought he was a friend. He really wasn't. He was a crony I used to hang out with. I have not seen him in forty years now. That friend was an interesting character who had more experience with women than I did. Looking back though, I would say that he was entertaining, but definitely lacked morals and was quite ignorant about meaningful things. Nevertheless, he was 'fun guy' and a part of my old context. He was like one of the old bottles. When I told my friend about my new girlfriend, he was fairly flippant about the situation. Looking back, that was understandable because he was in fact just as stupid as I was, maybe even more stupid. In many ways we reinforced each other's ignorance.

In his own way, he suggested that I move on in my life. Looking back now, I think that paying heed to his words was a foolish thing to do, but that was not his fault, but it was I, myself, who foolishly, paid heed to him. It was really my fault that things fell apart.

I decided I could not put my new wine into an old bottle. I was just not ready to get rid of my old bottles. I ended up dismissing the notion that that beautiful woman and I could become united as one. She was fresh and beautiful, but she was far away, and I chose the comfortable old bottles over the exciting, but risky, hopes of sipping new wine on a permanent basis. Yes, I chose my old contexts as opposed to building new contexts, and I look back on that now as a foolish thing to do.

I can only see clearly the principle in that situation many years after it happened. It is too late now. Those have got to be the saddest words there are in life – 'too late now'.

I suppose my 'new wine girlfriend' might not have made my life perfect, but I will never know what might have happened. I only know that I remember that time fondly, but with some painful regret about my decision. It still have regrets after all these years.

THE NEW WINE CANNOT BE BROUGHT BACK. SHE IS OLD WINE NOW, WHEREVER SHE MAY BE. I HOPE SHE IS HAPPY AND EVEN FORGIVING. IT IS ONE OF MY BIGGEST REGRETS THAT I TRIED TO PUT NEW WINE INTO OLD BOTTLES, BOTTLES THAT HAVE SINCE DISINTEGRATED.

A FURTHER PROBLEM HERE IS THAT CHOOSING OLD BOTTLES OR WINESKINS CAN BECOME A HABIT IN OTHER ASPECTS OF LIFE TOO. I IMAGINE THERE WAS NO SUCH THING AS PSYCHOTHERAPY BACK THEN, BUT THERE WAS SUCH A THING AS GOOD ADVICE AND THIS IS ONE EXAMPLE OF IT, EVEN THOUGH IT IS BASED UPON MY OWN REGRETS. IN MY OLD AGE, I SEE THAT CONVERSATION WITH MY EX-FRIEND AS A VERY ASTUTE ONE THAT AFFECTED MY LIFE AND PROBABLY SUCH A THING HAS AFFECTED THE LIVES OF MANY MEN AND WOMEN BOTH IN OLD TIMES AND IN MODERN TIMES.

A good example of this principle is when a person becomes interested in the gospel of Jesus Christ. They might perceive upon hearing the message that it that is a perfect way to find peace in families, nations and in the world. It is also a way to bring joy and meaning into their own lives. The problem is that they will need to store this new wine, or new way of thinking, in a way that will stop it from spoiling, (Yes, wine can spoil.) and new bottles will need to be called for.

People can become accustomed to drinking old wine in old bottles. By that I mean they are always using old ways of thinking that coincide with old habits and familiar situations that they feel comfortable in dealing with. One of the faults that I find in many people that I meet is that they simply find it difficult, often even impossible to change their customary ways of thinking.

In the case I just talked about, a prime example of using old bottles from the past as a framework for any 'new wine' that might come into our life. This 'new wine' deserves our consideration. We need to think about the best way to preserve it's sweetness and give it a chance to breathe in the new surroundings that it has inherited. We cannot afford to stuff our pre-formed concepts that we thought about during our younger adolescent years and stuff that new wine into a tired and over used old bottle. Images of 'old bottles' will probably slow down any growth or excitement or passion that the new wine is capable of displaying. Thus, it can be a serious business and we should seek out certain higher forms of discernment.

IF AN OLD BOTTLE SUITS YOUR PURPOSES, THEN, BY ALL MEANS, KEEP IT AND APPRECIATE IT. IF YOU ONLY DO THAT FOR THE REASON THAT YOU HAVE ALWAYS DONE IT, YOU MAY NEED TO DO SOME MORE THINKING. A TIRED OLD BOTTLE WILL PROBABLY BE 'UNSUITABLE' FOR FACILITATING A NEW AND EXCITING FORM OF GROWTH. WE SHOULD RECOGNIZE THE TIMES WHEN AN OLD BOTTLE HAS OUTGROWN ITS APPEAL OR USEFULNESS.

Old bottles and lifestyles might be incompatible with new wine, so people might reject the new wine out of hand. They might fear that they will lose their friends and family and be left alone to negotiate the making of new bottles, something they are not used to doing. So they MIGHT abandon the idea of new wine, using whatever excuse, and stick to the old wine in the old bottles. Regrettably, I am somewhat familiar with that mindset.

Too often the people will opt for the old wine and the old bottles because it is more convenient. In those cases, it is easier to just use old bottles, which are a person's old thought patterns and familiar social contexts. Is that a problem? Maybe and maybe not. I personally think though that might be a sign that it is time to GROW UP.

The profoundness of this short scripture from Matthew, that I quoted in the beginning, is evidence for that to me now, but I don't think the symbolism is often grasped as much as it should be. It wasn't obvious to me until many decades had passed. In the meantime I have learned over time those words of Jesus' are profound words about choosing to live in the past too much. Some people might say that decisions made in youth, or even in our early adulthood years, are not that important and they don't matter very much. Not true. On occasions in my youth, I dismissed new learning out of habit and it affected me for the worse.

When it comes to wisdom, Jesus has shown Himself to be the master once again. The savior received his knowledge from the Father, and so He became very wise. Some of us may have other 'new wines' in our lives today that we could investigate and benefit from, but refuse to do so because they seem to exist in new bottles (new contexts) that we are unfamiliar with. That good new wine, just might contain a better belief system and might be just what we need to be happy, but we are creatures of habit and I suspect that that has always been so.

IT IS ONLY THE NEW MAN OR WOMAN, OR THE 'BORN AGAIN' ONES, WHO CAN MAKE THE TRANSITION TO A RIGHTEOUS AND FULFILLING LIFE BY OUR DESIRE TO LEARN NEW AND PRODUCTIVE HABITS. WHEN WE JUST MAINTAIN OLD HABITS THAT ARE UNPRODUCTIVE, WE WILL NOT BE PREPARED TO LEARN THE ART OF BOTTLE MAKING AND PRODUCE NEW BOTTLES THAT WILL STORE THE EXCITING KNOWLEDGE THAT IS WITHIN THE NEW WINE.

BRIGHAM YOUNG SAID SOME THINGS ABOUT REVELATION. HE SAID THAT IF YOU GO INTO A SACRAMENT MEETING WITH A GOOD ATTITUDE AND YOU ARE ACCOMPANIED BY THE SPIRIT, YOU WILL HAVE REVELATIONS POURED UPON YOUR HEADS LIKE WATER. HOW MANY OF US ARE FEELING GOOD AND SLIGHTLY WET ON A GIVEN SABBATH MORNING?

HOPEFULLY, MANY OF US WILL FEEL THAT WAY, BUT HOW MANY PEOPLE FEEL COMFORTABLE WHEN THEY ARE DRENCHED WITH A BUCKET OF COLD, NEW WATER? THAT MIGHT NOT BE AN APPEALING THOUGHT IN THE PRESENT MOMENT, BUT IT CAN BE INVIGORATING. THE PRESENT MOMENT CAN HAVE MANY GOOD THINGS TO OFFER IF WE ASK FOR THEM AND WATCH FOR THEM. IT IS, AGAIN, ALL ABOUT LEARNING, AND LEARNING HAS MANY FACETS TO IT.

Jesus said that we should never put new wine into old bottles lest the bottles break and the new wine runs out. He said this more than once so it must be important, but it was obviously said as an allegory or a parable, so it is up to us to figure out what it means in our own lives.

The world is an acidic place. As any health food expert will tell you, acidic food or liquids are not good for you. They will do harm to your body. Alkaline foods, however, are good for you and promote good growth.

Stress, fear, guilt, resentment, ill feelings do not feel good. Those are acidic feelings and too many of those feelings are not good for your vessel. They scratch up the inside of the bottles, even cause holes to appear in the vessels that are your minds and bodies. This can cause the alkaline substances, or the good feelings/ new wine, to run out of your vessel and spill on the ground. Spiritually speaking, this new wine might be seen as containing virtuous things like love, forgiveness, joy, virtue, etc. What happens when those good things leak out of your vessel? I say that it never ends well.

SO WHAT DO WE DO? WE CREATE NEW BOTTLES. HOW DO WE DO THAT? WE FIRST SEEK THE COUNSEL OF THE GREAT BOTTLE MAKER HIMSELF WHO CREATED ALL THINGS. HE IS THE LORD OUR GOD. WHEN WE CONNECT WITH HIM THROUGH PRAYER AND BY OBEYING THE COMMANDMENTS, HE WILL REMOVE THE GALL OF BITTERNESS FROM US AND ACTUALLY BRING NEW ADVENTURES, POSSIBLY EVEN LOVE, INTO OUR HEARTS.

IT IS ALSO UP TO US TO REMOVE THE BITTERNESS OR ACIDIC THINGS FROM WITHIN US. WE'VE GOT TO LEARN HOW TO FORGIVE MAINLY. IF WE LET THE ACIDIC EFFECT OF RESENTMENT EAT AWAY AT US WE WILL SUFFER 'ACIDIC EFFECTS'. HOLES WILL START TO APPEAR IN OUR BOTTLES AND THE NEW WINE WILL RUN OUT.

WINE, IN REAL LIFE, CAN GO BAD, BUT <u>CAN WE GO BAD BECAUSE WE DRANK SOME RANCID WINE</u>? SOMEONE ELSE MIGHT HAVE EVEN PUT AN ACIDIC SUBSTANCE INTO OUR BOTTLE, BUT CAN WE BE PROACTIVE ENOUGH TO EXPELL SUCH TOXIC SUBSTANCES? WHAT IS THE SOLUTION FOR THAT?

IF YOU ARE FEELING DEPRESSED OR CONFUSED LET ME BE CLEAR THAT YOU SHOULD NEVER UNDERESTIMATE THE POWER THAT COMES WITH <u>PROPER</u> REST. WHEN LIFE BECOMES STRESSFUL, THERE WILL COME A TIME WHEN YOU SHOULD JUST GO TO BED AND NOT GET UP FOR A FEW HOURS. JUST RELAX. I CALL THAT PROCESS AN ELIXIR. IT

COULD BE USED TO GAIN BACK THE OFTEN-ELUSIVE POWER THAT COMES THROUGH 'REGENERATION'.

THE BOB KING THREE POINT REGENERATION PROCESS

"The lord reasons in plainness and simplicity'.
- Doctrine and Covenants 133: 57

My three point regeneration process is very simple. Here are the three points:

1. RELAX.
Stop and smell the flowers.

2. DO THE RIGHT THINGS.
If you had a decent upbringing you should know what the right things are. Do them. If you did not have a decent upbringing, there is still time to learn what those right things are. (You only need to look in the right places to find them).

3. WAIT AND WATCH FOR THE GOOD RESULTS TO COME IN.

The devil also believes that he can wait you out and that, if you do not have a solid belief system, you will eventually succumb to his ways. The Lord's ways always work the best, even though they will happen on HIS time and not yours.

It is good to mix your restful moments or 'inactivity' with prayer. That can usually cause positive activity to happen. That means 'good' activity, so please pay attention to what your spirit is telling you and feel right and humble if you ever indulge in prayerful contemplation. It is a good way to make yourself 'clean'. When making 'new bottles', it is always good to start with a 'clean environment.

Sleep is important. Exercise is also good. Eating right, or even occasional fasting, can also be healthy. Listening to gentle music before bed or conversing with a friend who shares the same beliefs as you is another way to relax. A conversation with a like-minded friend has a cleansing aspect to it. You will be less likely to get unto meaningless ways of thinking when your mind is rested and your thoughts are clear and you are in agreement with the people who matter the most to you.

Saying daily or nightly prayers is another way that you can clean, or wash, your spirit. Enjoy your leisure time while you can. Learn something about the benefits of relaxing, and even learn something about yourself. When that happens, don't sit on it until it fades away. Get up and participate in a new adventure of some kind, even a 'thought adventure'.

There is a time when oversleeping may happen out of laziness or even out of physical exhaustion. Sometimes we need to stabilize the multi-directional effect of tension that we are experiencing. We will need to balance our inner metabolism and bring physical relief to our restless minds. When we are rested, it is easier to get back to our basic belief system that we once treasured.

GOD HAS HIS WAYS OF ALLEVIATING STRESS FROM OUR LIVES AND HELPING US TO HEAL. THOSE WAYS MIGHT SOMETIMES BE MUCH SIMPLER THAN WE THINK AND MIGHT EVEN SEEM UNUSUAL TO PEOPLE WITH PRESET NOTIONS OF PERFECTION. RELAXATION IS NOT 'GOOFING OFF'. IT IS GOOD FOR THE SOUL. WHEN NOT OVERDONE, AND IT IS THE SOUL THAT BRINGS US TRUE DELIGHT AND FEELINGS OF HAPPINESS. IF YOU HAVE WPORKED HARD FOR THE LORD'S PURPOSES, THEN KNOW THAT YOU DESERVE A REST.

FINDING YOUR OWN WAY OF RESTING IS AN EXERCISE (IRONICALLY), BUT THE MAIN SOURCE OF HAPPINESS IS, AS I HAVE SAID, LIVING A GOOD LIFE, VOID OF OFFENCE TOWARDS GOD AND MAN, AND OBEYING THE COMMANDMENTS. ESPECIALLY THE FIRST TWO COMMANDMENTS WHICH ARE LOVING GOD AND LOVING OTHER PEOPLE.

***

GETTING BACK TO THE ORIGINAL QUOTE IN THIS ESSAY, WHICH SPEAKS ABOUT PUTTING NEW WINE INTO OLD BOTTLES, I WILL SAY THIS: THAT QUOTE IS NOT THAT EASY TO COME TO AN EXACT UNDERSTANDING OF IT. IT IS REALLY MUCH MORE SIMPLE TO UNDERSTAND THAN IT MIGHT SEEM AT FIRST GLANCE. I THINK THAT JESUS WAS SAYING THAT WE CAN MAKE IT MORE COMPLICATED THAN IT REALLY IS.

"My yoke is easy and my burden is light".
- MATTHEW 11: 30

***

-

I will give you a few more examples on this topic of new wine and old bottles. I was in a hospital for an operation on my back about six months ago. The nurses were mostly from Phillipino backgrounds and they were quite happy and friendly people. They did their nursing jobs very well, but I noticed that they had a problem with the English language. Their problem was with their pronunciations. They would slip into their old Pilipino accents, Togali, I think it was called and a lot of the time I could not understand what they were saying. It caused a few problems in our communication with each other. A hospital is not a good place to have bad communication. My point is that they were trying to fit their new English terminology into their old Philippino dialect and it wasn't working. It reminded me of putting new wine into old, out of date, bottles.

I would constantly have to ask them to repeat themselves. They didn't need to get a phrase wrong. They only needed to pronounce one letter wrong and I would be lost. That is not that uncommon I have found. I find that it is happening more often even with younger English people; 'mumblers' I call them.

Here is another example that happened last week. It had nothing to do with a I was in a printers office trying to get my book published. The owner of the shop was Chinese and a very nice man. He also had some problems with his language.

At one point he was referring to a 'word file' on my computer, but he didn't use the words 'word file'. He used the word **'water file'**.

What the heck was a water file?

I had no idea what he was talking about. I thought that maybe the miscommunication came because of my unfamiliarity with computer terminology. But no, he was trying to put the new words into his old and natural language.
(New wine into an old bottle.) We straightened it out, but it was a little frustrating for a while.

CHAPTER 6.

THE NEED FOR A PROPHET (12 p.)
Subtitle: The Holy Ghost

I cannot talk about the Godhead without mentioning the vital third part of the Godhead who is THE HOLY GHOST. The Holy Ghost is also referred to as The Holy Spirit and 'The Comforter' in the Bible. Personally, I once heard a man refer to the Holy Ghost as the Chief Communications Officer in the church. That title might be a metaphor, but when you analyze it there is a lot of truth in it.

That is because truth is what the Gospel of Jesus Christ is based upon, from the beginning of it to the end of it. Hence, if a person desires to be a part of Jesus' Holy Kingdom, your own life, including your ultimate righteous desires, must have a connection to truth, even a 'constant' connection to the truth. Like it or not, that will be your main qualification if you wish to be a part of it.

Some words can be subjected to different kinds of meanings, but when a genuine prophet speaks any words we can assume that they will be inspired words and you and I can also get a confirmation of truth in those words by that same Holy Spirit who dwells with in us.

So if this essay is about prophets then why, you may well ask, am I talking about the Holy Spirit who does not have a physical body like the Father and the Son, but is a being of Spirit. Nevertheless the physical appearance of the Holy Spirit, I would think, would be very close to the appearance and manner of the other two members of the Godhead.

"Anyone who has seen me has seen the Father."
– John 14: 9

The reason that I talk about the Holy Ghost AND the righteous prophets in the scriptures at he same time is because the Holy Spirit, and all of the righteous prophets, all speak the truth. That is the connection that they all have. They can tell us what the will of God is either in public or in private. That is their divinely inspired job.

> "That good thing that was committed unto thee keep by the Holy Ghost <u>which dwelleth in us</u>."
> - 2 Timothy 1: 14   <u>(emphasis added)</u>

The phrase "which dwelleth in us" is an apostolic declaration that the Holy Spirit can actually live inside of us and know our thoughts. He can also speak to us and reveal truth to us in a voice that has been described as a 'still, small voice'.

What a wonderful reassurance that is for people who believe.

The Holy Ghost is not just a righteous accessory to God and Jesus. He is a righteous recorder of all of the acts of men and women throughout the history of the world, for both good and evil. . By today's worldly standards that would seem to put the Holy Spirit in a precarious position.

Is it any wonder then that Jesus told the people that a person could be forgiven if they sinned against the Son of Man, but if that person should sin against the Holy Ghost, then he, or she, would not be forgiven in this world nor in the world to come. (Matthew 12: 32)

THE RATIONAL GOSPEL

I will write a lot more on this book about the Holy Ghost and about the Divine Spirit that He is, but for now I will talk more about some characters in the Bible who were obviously human, but who were either selected or chosen to be messengers of the Lord in times when inspired messages were sorely needed because of a lack of truth in the world. Such a time is on the earth now and 'those who have spiritual ears to hear' would do well to seek out those humble people and partake of the knowledge that they are willing to freely share.

"Why am I talking about the Holy Ghost when my topic is about living prophets? The reason in living prophets and the Holy Ghost have the same job. That job is <u>TO TELL THE TRUTH.</u>

Subtitle: Jacob Chapter 5

WHEN I PRAY EVERY MORNING I AM ACCUSTOMED TO SAYING 'LORD I AM THANKFUL FOR THIS DAY'. WHAT I AM REALLY SAYING IS, 'LORD, I AM THANKFUL FOR THE 'OPPORTUNITIES' THAT I KNOW I WILL BE GIVEN THIS DAY'.

I say that because I have settled in to my purpose in life. My purpose in life is being a writer, of songs and stories and articles, including religious articles. I am not just a writer. I am also a commentator. I love commenting most of all on religious matters because <u>I love the truth,</u> AND because I dislike, even hate, untruth or lies or ignorant people and especially ignorant people who claim to have scriptural authority.

I also, love reading the words of the prophets that are in the scriptures. That is because their words will almost always resonate in my mind at random times after I have read them.

I am also an 'idea man', and I often get some of my best ideas by having them come into my mind from exciting and mysterious places. This can often happen as I am lying in my bed in the morning and contemplating the world at large, but it can also happen at any time when the Lord sees fit to give me personal counsel within the caverns of my mind. .

I thank the Lord for the morning sun as well as the morning air and for the birds that sing, etc. but mostly I thank him for those ideas that come into my mind in the morning or late at night, that inspire me to put on my thinking cap and start writing. Those are my opportunities that keep that creative train of ideas rolling down the tracks. I really do work hard at my writing. I do it because I enjoy it and I am grateful that I am often blessed with good ideas. Thus, I thank God for the creative opportunities that are before me each day.

I must say that many of my better ideas don't always come from me, but can come from unknown places, but the seem to come through me and I recognize them by their 'resonating' power.

I do not even know exactly where my special ideas come from, but the tracks for the 'train in my brain' run right past the bedroom window in my house. It does not always come by at the same time of day, but it always comes by sooner or later.

The human mind is often difficult to comprehend and impossible to predict or explain it to others. But I try to 'clear the tracks' from obstructions, because the 'train in the brain' will always come by. That occurrence always makes my day complete and I give thanks for that. I couldn't imagine my day without that inspiration. It has been justifiably called 'the breath of life'.

My faith is secure. My love for certain people is there. My strength is there. My philosophy is sound. Those are the most important things that I treasure, and it definitely helps to have affirmations of those things from the Powers of Heaven. I manage to achieve a state of happiness, or contentment almost every day.

I am discovering though that I am not really a 'day off kind of guy'. I have not been since I was a young boy and I played sports with neighborhood friends. Then we lived 'in the present moment' with the real world all around us and I loved it. This would be as opposed to sitting around doing nothing which has never had any appeal for me.

Now that I am of the senior citizen status, and have experienced many things, I find myself writing down a lot of my experiences. That is because writing is what I love to do the most. Also, I want to write certain things down before I forget them. Who knows, if I forget those things, they might be gone forever.

The attractions of the physical world do absolutely nothing for me except in certain rare moments like when I played sports in my youth. Also, I have exhilarating moments when I am in the beautiful realm of nature, or when I am playing music and singing with talented friends. I cherish those moments as well.

I actually like to 'think', but still, I am aware that I need to avoid the escapism that comes with too much 'fantasy' thinking.

I am getting old and I can get a little entangled in ideas sometimes. I never thought I would get that way, but nevertheless, I am fortunate because I have a come to know certain things in this life that most people never come to realize.

The first is that I know what my purpose is in this life. I came to believe in the divinity of God the Father and in His Son Jesus Christ. Jesus Christ is the 'anointed one'. He is he Messiah and the Redeemer of the world. He is the 'living water' in our lives and He can bring life and light into our lives. I know that He gave his very life for me, and thus, I will never forsake Him. I am also obedient to my Heavenly

Father who, along with my Heavenly Mother, created me in the Spirit.
(For details on our Heavenly Mother read 'THE INITIATION OF A YOUNG SOUL' In my book, REALMS I HAVE KNOWN'.)

I will not go into another long explanation of the Heavenly Mother, mainly because I do not really know a lot about her because she is, for the most part, anonymous. I speculate that that is because she is sacred and should not be talked about by average men and women on the Earth who have a very limited knowledge about her and for good reasons. She simply lives on a more sacred level. Instead I will just ask a simple question of my readers. That question is; If God is my Heavenly Father, and He created me, did He do that by Himself as a lone male, or was there a Heavenly Mother, who remains anonymous, involved in the picture?

Jesus is a special friend, not because he is famous, but because He is an exemplar for me in all things. He is all-wise and He is all good. He is also totally trustworthy, which means the most to me. He is also willing to make sacrifices for me, even ultimate sacrifices. Also, through the power of the Holy Ghost, Jesus can give me revelations. Revelations are, basically, information about the actual will of God that can be delivered to me by the Holy Spirit and given for my benefit and for the sake of my confidence in Him and my confidence in the fact that life is good.

Secondly, I have come to the knowledge that I also have an enemy in this life. He is the devil and he wants to destroy me and also wants to destroy anyone else who would pledge allegiance to God, who is our Father. This knowledge has caused me to advance in my quest to be righteous for the sake of both myself and for the sake of my loved ones and for the sake of the Godhead who sacrifice much so that all of us can prosper and live in peace. The devil is real and he has laid traps for me in the past, some of which have caused me to falter. Thankfully, I have survived them.

Thirdly, I pledge to fight against the devil and his minions and **repent** of the dark and shady memories from my past, through, which mischievous demons have, at times in the past gained entrance to and have secretly observed those unpleasant incidents. Thus, I am grateful for the spiritual encouragement of our ancestors who have had an influence in our families. Many of those ancestors were spiritually strong and had faith in us and supported us spiritually.

These are the three pieces of knowledge that I needed in order that I might be certain about the truth of the Divine plan of Happiness. Included in my ability to receive of that knowledge is my ability to receive revelations, and even receive revelations about revelations. That means <u>knowing</u> when a thought comes into your mind if that thought actually came from God or not.

For example, I was reading the book of Ether with some friends once. The Book of Ether is near the end of the book of Mormon and it describes another ancient tribe who came to North America before the Nephites and the Lamanites. They left a record behind that was eventually translated by a prophet named Moroni who was the same man/angel who hid the gold plates that the prophet Joseph Smith was led to in the introduction to the Book of Mormon.

The Angel Moroni talked with Joseph Smith many times in the body. It started in the year 1820 and the angel's discourses guided Joseph through much danger because the devil knew about the hidden plates of scripture and the devil had many accomplices, human and otherwise, who had pledged to try to take away the plates. Moroni appeared to Joseph many times as a translated being, or in other words, as an angel.

Historically, many people have asked for a sign from God and they usually felt let down when they did not receive a sign. Ironically, there are many signs and prophesies in the Bible and in the Book of Mormon. It only takes efforts by the readers of those books to search them so that they can learn about those very signs that Christians have talked about for many years.

When I first joined the church of Jesus Christ of Latter Day Saints, I read the Book of Mormon in its entirety. A few years later, I began to accept the intelligence and the passion that was in the book. I was studying the Book of Mormon intensely one day during an extra curricular class. The chapter of Ether however, threw me off somewhat.

I noticed at the beginning of Ether, I was not very impressed with the story that was being told. The tribe in the story seemed very primitive to me. The seeming lack of intelligence of the people in the beginning of that chapter was also a concern for me. The language was more primitive and there seemed to be nothing that was intellectual or prophetic about it, that is, up until chapter eight.

Chapter eight was when a prophet entered into the picture. That prophet was the aforementioned Moroni, who actually appeared in the flesh and interpreted the writings that were written to describe the beliefs of the Jaredites. The Jaredites was the name for the main tribe in the book of Ether.

Using an instrument called the Urim and Thummim, Moroni translated the writings that became the Book of Ether. That was when the narrative changed and the new information gave evidence that a prophet was finally at the helm. The story maintained the history of the tribe, but it expanded much more on the spiritual aspects of what happened. Thus, the book of Ether became a book that was recognized as a part of the true scriptures.

This prophet Moroni was the man who interpreted the writings of the Jaredites in the book of Ether and was the same person, or angel or resurrected being, who appeared to Joseph Smith in 1820 after Joseph experienced the first vision in which he had a visitation from God the Father, and Jesus Christ, in the woods near Palmyra, New York.

With the entrance of the prophet Moroni into the book of Ether, I began to see the big differences in the primitive writings earlier in the chapters and the later writings that were written under the direction of the prophet Moroni. From that point on the book of ether became a book that I believe was inspired by God. That was the big difference. Moroni's translations accurately explained the remainder of the book of Ether.

One example of when the lord speaks to the people happened in chapter 12 when God speaks in the first person. He says:

> ***"And if men come unto me, I will show unto them their weakness. I give unto men weakness that they may be humble; and my grace is sufficient for all men that humble themselves before me, and have faith in me, then I will make weak things become strong unto them."*** *- Ether 12: 27*

THE RATIONAL GOSPEL

In any case, that is how the book of Ether inspired me, and how I was inspired by the words and actions of prophets in the Book of Mormon from the beginning of it up until the end of it.

There are other prophets as well who wrote in the Bible that brought the words of God to life, but I used this example from the book of Mormon to show the importance of revelation and the importance of human discernment as we study those sacred passages in both of those books.

Some people ignore the book of Mormon because of the tradition of their fathers, be it Catholic or Protestant or whatever. But I bear witness that God is great and does have the utmost authority to speak to His people and even to all people, and not necessarily by His own voice, but by the voices of His prophets.

> **"What I the Lord have spoken, I have spoken and I excuse not myself..... Whether by mine own voice or the voice of my servants, it is the same."**
> **- Doctrine and Covenants 1: 38**

> *"Surely the Lord GOD will do nothing but he revealeth his secret unto his servants the prophets."*
> *- Amos 3: 7*

And here is a recent quote by the president and prophet of the church **today,** President Russell M. Nelson:

> **"AS I HAVE STATED BEFORE, THE GATHERING OF ISRAEL IS THE MOST IMPORTANT WORK TAKING PLACE ON EARTH TODAY. ONE CRUCIAL ELEMENT OF THIS**

GATHERING IS PREPARING A PEOPLE WHO ARE ABLE, READY, AND WORTHY TO RECEIVE THE LORD WHEN HE COMES AGAIN, A PEOPLE WHO HAVE ALREADY CHOSEN JESUS CHRIST OVER THIS FALLEN WORLD, A PEOPLE WHO REJOICE IN THEIR AGENCY TO LIVE THE HIGHER, HOLIER LAWS OF JESUS CHRIST".

- 'Overcome the World and Find Rest' By President Russell M. Nelson

***

Wednesday, June 7, 2023
Nothing interesting was going on in my mind this morning. I had no revelations come into my mind and I felt very alone. I went down for breakfast. I didn't even say good morning to my friend 'Fog brain' or to the ex-bagpiper who sits beside me at breakfast sometimes.

I went back to bed after breakfast and it was then when I had a revelation. It was concerning Jacob 5 in the Book of Mormon. and it suited the topic in this essay called 'THE NEED FOR A PROPHET'.

JACOB CHAPTER 5

Jacob, chapter 5 contains the words of an Old Testament prophet whose name was Zenos. The name of **Zenos** was mentioned in the scriptures, but for some unknown reason his words were not preserved there. Centuries later, his words were given out for the people called the Jaredites to read in the Book of Mormon. This amazing story is the excerpt.

Jacob 5 presents a very profound revelation that is also referred to s **the 'parable of the olive tree'**. It tells the story about how God the Father, **who is also referred to as the 'The Lord of the vineyard',** became able to forgive mankind, who were His Spirit children, but who had made the mass decision to turn wicked along their way.

The Father was tempted to 'write them off' because of their wickedness. He was talked out of that decision by the intervention of Jesus Christ, who was the prophesied Holy Messiah.

Jesus, who was the loyal and much loved Son of the Father, convinced the Father to give humanity a second chance. The Father, or the Lord of the Vineyard, then decided to save the people from a spiritual fire that was in an earthly sense similar to a very large brush pile fire.

God knew that the people on earth were very wicked and unrepentant and produced 'wild fruit' that was not good fruit. Thus, the brushfire solution, which God had once considered was cast aside. This happened mainly because of the pleas by Jesus Christ as He pled for mankind to be forgiven by the Father. Jesus was also known byother names like the Messiah and the Sacrificial Lamb and the Son of God. Because of the pleadings of Jesus, all men and women were spared from perishing in the 'brush pile fire'.

That, is a truly amazing story and, in my opinion, is the reason why Jesus Christ is referred to in the Bible as our 'Father'.

> *"for behold, this day He has spiritually begotten you; for ye say that your hearts are changed through faith on his name; therefore, ye are born of him and have become his sons and daughters.*

> ***And under this head ye are made free and there is no other head whereby ye can be made free. There is no other name given whereby salvation cometh; therefore I would that ye should take upon you the name of Christ, all you that have entered into the covenant with God that ye should be obedient unto the end of your lives.***
> ***- Mosiah 5: 6,7***

Thus, Jesus actually redeemed us. It is because He actually redeemed us, spiritually, by pleading for forgiveness on behalf of all mankind. The Father, because of His great love for the Son, as well as His own desire to be forgiving, consented to Jesus' wishes to forgive the wicked people. This, to my knowledge is one of the stories that explains why God and Jesus are not the same person, even though they are 'one' in purpose and 'one' in thought. Here is another quote that explains this and it is found in the 'intercessory prayer in the book of John.

> ***Holy Father, keep through thine own name those whom thou hast given me, that they may be one as we are.***
> ***- St. John 17: 11 (emphasis added)***

The idea that God the Father is the same person as Jesus the Son is an idea that I find quite ludicrous. When Jesus prayed to the Father, as He did on many occasions, was He praying to Himself? That makes no sense and both God and Jesus are quite sensible I assure you.

In the book of John, Jesus prayed to the Father and asked Him if Jesus and His apostles could be 'one', as Jesus and the Father are one. He was not asking for Himself and Peter to be the same person or John to be the same person as Himself, but He was asking if Himself and the apostles could be one in purpose and in thought as the Father and the Son are one in purpose and in thought. Thank you Jesus for clearing that up.

AUTHOR'S NOTE: This book is my OPUS and I think that it might be my best book. This particular essay is one of the reasons why I consider the book to be of such importance. There is a lot of symbolism in the words of Zenos, but still, he describes the relationship between God and Jesus and mankind very well.

Chapter 7

GENTLE SPARKS FROM HEAVEN AND WILDFIRES FROM HELL (10p.)

Subtitles: Obsessions (or wildfires)

After all these years I have finally come to the awareness of one the most important facts that I know of. It is that the world is a dualistic place with a lower level and a higher level. The sun still shines on both worlds, but the lower world, mainly because of the lesser understanding of the people there, is basically less virtuous than the higher world.

In extreme cases, one might say that many parts of the lower world are actually wicked and carnal places. That lower world also contains much deception and bullying, while the higher world, which is not a perfect world, the people there usually make an attempt to present themselves as decent human beings and good citizens. They usually try to maintain a certain amount of respect for all human beings.

People, or spirits, in the higher world are mostly respectful of others and that is true about all the people there, be they young or old, male ir female, rich or poor. The people who inhabit that world are usually people who try to live by a higher moral code and believe in liberty. They praise virtues such as justice, truth, fairness, love, charity and decency.

So one might ask, "How can a person make the leap from the lower level, with all of its drawbacks, to the higher level and there partake of the things there that cause their souls to become more benevolent and more joyful."

Here is my answer to that question about making 'that leap'. I think that it will take some effort on each person's part to make the jump, but there is a more important factor involved. That is that it will take a small spark from within us to do it. In other words, it will take a small spark of **'divine influence'** to be the catalyst that will help you or me to 'make the leap' to a higher and more conscientious level.

We humans do not possess Divinity, but our Creator does. That is because He has a divine nature, or a 'good' nature which is also an Eternal nature. Where that nature originated from, I don't exactly know, but I know that He has it. That gives Him, or should give Him, authority over the rest of us, who are His Spirit children.

So what is the nature of that 'spark of inspiration' that we seek so as to receive revelations? It might be hard to 'nail down', but let us explore it a little bit.

A spark always gives off a very small amount of light. A tiny light is not of much use to a person who wants to have control over the amount of warmth and comfort in their environment. A large light however, or a light that is controlled, does have much relevance in our lives, and even a power that could be called a 'divine power' or a power that comes from a higher place. That 'divine power' can arrange for anyone to receive 'Divine inspiration'.

So Divine inspiration will only come through a 'Divine Being'. In our case that source of Divinity comes from our Divine God.

Because we are children of God, as it says in the Bible, wouldn't our Heavenly Father be willing to share that great gift with us, His children? Of course He would.

That would be true as long <u>as long as we were prepared to actually receive that great gift.</u> God, understandably, would probably not be happy if He gave us a gift and we ignored it and let it go to waste. He may not get angry with us, but he probably would refrain from giving us a similar gift as long as we were not grateful for it.

The potential receivers of that gift could be whoever God wants him, or her, to be. Thus, I am also talking about you and me as potential receivers of it, so please don't take my words lightly. It is an Eternal deal, or a permanent deal, that we all seek.

We know that light is a good thing. Without it we would live in darkness and in frigid temperatures. What kind if a life would that be? Also, a larger light is a light that will help us see everything more clearly.

The scriptures tell us that Christ is the light of the world.

> "whatsoever is truth is light, whatsoever is light is Spirit."
> - Doctrine and Covenants 84: 45

> "Spirit gives light to every man."
> - Doctrine and Covenants 84: 46

This makes this more clear is that the quality of light belongs to God. The devil on the other hand, has been called the Prince of Darkness'. A cover of darkness is something that can always be used to keep hidden things hidden.

THE RATIONAL GOSPEL

God knows what that tiny spark can do to ignite a person's righteous desires. He also knows how to use that spark to create a larger fire, but not a fire that is too large. God knows how to feed that fire with the right material so it will expand and He also knows how to control it so it does not become a raging wild fire that can tend to destroy things.

OBSESSIONS (OR WILDFIRES)

"The roads are icy here where I live. Ice is for winter birds like Penguins. Penguins are short - term thinkers. Ice and snow is all they know about. Thus, they are obsessed with it, mainly because It is always all around them. If they are incapable of expanding their personal thinking realms they will never be free. Likewise, pornography and sexual deviancy is for fornicators. Those people are also short-term thinkers because pornography and sexual activities are all they think about. Thus, they are obsessed with it. Pornography is all around them. If they are capable of expanding their thinking realms and doing away with obsessions and addictions, they must do that, or they will never be free."

- Bob King

If a person lives in a well-lit room, that person might not even recognize a little spark when it appears. That is why a Godly person will have the God given ability to discern a good spark that will grow and will light a person's way. This is as

THE RATIONAL GOSPEL

opposed to an evil spark that can end up burning a person's possessions and even set the person themselves on fire.

Again it comes down to **knowing** what constitutes good and what constitutes evil. It also means **knowing** how to channel that knowledge in the correct ways.

I knew a young woman in years past who had a lit of talent as a performer and she decided one day that she wanted to wanted to pursue a life in the theatre. She was also a close family friend and a former music student of mine. She looked forward to taking part in the hubbub and glamour that was a part of the theatre scene. She was attracted to the flashy images, the intellectual challenges, and a boyfriend who was a political agitator. All of those things took over her life and after a few years of schooling (or immersion) it started to become an obsession with her.

As a result, she ended up forsaking the good family values that she was raised with and becoming a part of the 'woke mob'. Why she chose that career path, I didn't know, but I didn't want to advise her not to do it lest she should see me as her enemy. In any case, I really did think that she paid too much attention to things that she shouldn't have paid attention to.

So what was she to do? Let her passion rule her life no matter what the consequences might be, or else she could find a more reliable profession that would give her a reliable income and more security in her life. It might also give her a good job that would cause her to become the best person that she could be, instead of being an actress who made a living pretending that she was somebody else?

THE RATIONAL GOSPEL

Perhaps the only alternative she could envision was that she should get a straight job, one that she might not like as much, but it would give her a chance to meet some real people and find some real challenges that suited both her needs and her abilities.

Her theatre work was good, but she entered into that world during the Covid pandemic and she did not get enough work to reach the heights and would fulfill her dramatic dreams of success. She was disappointed with the theatre world even though she did love it, but was she willing to take another gamble and strive to find a place where she could be relatively happy?

Somewhere along the way that young woman dedided that finding contentment in life should not be dependent on pleasing large crowds of strangers with your artistic talents. Her family and friends hoped that she would take a chance and explore the 'real world', but for a long time, she resisted that option.

Was that because she had an obsession? I don't know, but I do think that independent people will do what they want to do and hang the consequences. In any case, her friends and family all hoped that this fine young woman would find contentment by exploring the less risky path that her parents and those people who really loved her wanted her to explore.

To make a long story short, that young woman eventually decided to settle into a more simple life. She bought a house in a small city where she landed a decent job and where she was surrounded by people who respected her and respected her talents.

That small house that she bought had a nice fireplace and there was plenty of wood in her yard, so many times, she and her friends would gather there around the fireplace and tell stories and sing songs and have a few laughs. Basically, she was quite contented with the new life that she had found. She also was able to forget about the many disappointments that she encountered in the theatre world as a professional actress. Those disappointments, thankfully, became a part of her past.

Did she still have a spark of creativity in her? Yes, she did, but that creative spark was not enough to bring her worldwide praise and accolades, so she knew she should start to consider other options. Over time, she found that she began to enjoy her simple life more and more every day. That was enough to satisfy her basic needs and it was enough to bring many a smile to her still pretty face on many occasions.

I didn't know if my friend would ever come back to her old self, but as it happened she did come back to herself and she found a way to live a happy life and still maintain some creativity in the artistic life that she had such a passion for. I think that her guardian angel must have been smiling down on her. I will also say that she never played with fire again.

***

That brings us back to the issue of 'authority' and thus, authority can invite many legitimate questions into the equation. One question is, are all people able to find a perfect path for themselves by just having blind faith that God will provide? I would say 'no' to that, but I would also add that life is difficult for many people and often through no fault of their own.

That is just the way life is. It can be difficult, but a part of our mission is to gain the inner strength to overcome the difficulties in life and sustain the positive attitude that will allow for success or at least, satisfaction.

The key to maintaining that attitude is to be able to accept rejection of any kind and know that you are a child of God and that He loves you and know that, as long as you try your best, even though the odds are against you, you can still find happiness in ways that you do not yet even know about.

A theatre stage is basically a very small space. The world outside is a much bigger space. MUCH BIGGER. So just activate, or re-activate, your core beliefs that were given to you by people who thought things out on their own honest level. Then you decide to do the right things, find faith, or confidence, in a higher power, and things will work out for you.

Another question regarding revelations and divine guidance might be - "WHO DOES HAVE THE AUTHORITY TO SPEAK FOR GOD AND HOW WILL WE KNOW WHO THOSE PEOPLE ARE?

I will try to answer that question in this book, but for a moment, let me go back to the issue of the 'leap' that I was just talking about. That first leap might seem at first glance, to be easy, or even incidental, but no. That leap is much more than changing your strong opinions. It is changing the feelings of your heart and even changing the feelings and realistic expectations of your soul. Thus, everyone who wants to make that leap will

need to first ask themselves if they are prepared to do that.

If you are prepared and willing and humble, you may connect with divinity and that, in tandem with with the grace of God, will enable you to receive that divine spark and make the leap, whatever that leap might consist of. That comfortable fire that burns in a 'contained fireplace' always begins with a little spark will light up your day and, in time, cause a warm fire that will warm your heart every day.

The flint that creates the spark that lights a good fire will never grow dull. That is because that flint and that spark are created by God and thus, they are eternal things. When the fire lights up one realm, it will move on to another realm and provide light and energy to that realm, and so on and so on.

I have discovered that it is possible for we human beings to have access to that strong flint and, thus, it will bring about that spark.

Do you have an access to that flint? If not, would you like to have that access? Are you capable of receiving that 'gift of access' or are you <u>afraid</u> to receive it because it might disturb your 'old bottles' that you are used to using.

But I say, do not fear because that flame is an eternal flame and through your acceptance of it, you will be obedient to the source of it and obedient to the laws that are active in the eternal kingdom. Those laws have been given to you for your protection.

Agreeing to those laws and making covenants to live by them will be enough to qualify you to become a part of that eternal world and a partner to the Holy one of Israel, who is none other than Jesus Christ. That would make you a very special participant in a very blessed cause. The Lord loves it when his children are loyal and active in a righteous cause and who make the most of their talents, whatever those talents may be.

In other words, you can become 'joint heirs with Christ' *(Roman's 8: 17)* and the benefits of that will be felt not only in the next world, but in today's world as well.

Getting back to the question I just asked, who does have the authority to speak for God? I will give the simplest answer that I know, but it may not be the easiest answer to explain to someone else. The simple answer is <u>'he, or she, who feels the spirit of truth by the power of the Holy Ghost is the person who can have the Gift of the Holy Ghost, and he, or she, will be the person who can</u>

speak with genuine authority on any important matter.

Chapter 8

SEDUCTION AND THE SHATTERING OF REALITIES (16P.)

Subtitles: A Good Shattering; Shattering by Deserting a Friend; The Only Solutions

(I started writing this essay when a friend of mine talked to me about a predicament that her twenty-year-old daughter was involved in. The daughter moved to a distant city with her boyfriend. She was under the impression that they would soon get married. As it turned out, after they had moved to the new city, her boyfriend 'dumped' her. The young woman was heartbroken and she moved back home alone because it seemed, in the mother's words 'that her reality that she had faith in, had been 'shattered'.

Her mother was very concerned and even distressed about her daughter's situation. Her mother described the young woman as 'inconsolable' and was very worried about her daughter's mental state. I met the mother one night at her place of employment and she expressed her serious concerns.

*She knew that I was a writer, and even a writer of religious books, and so I said that I would try to write something that **might** offer a solution for the daughter. She had told me that her daughter was not at all religious, but I explained that I could only write about the only things that I believed in and the things that actually might cause her to rethink her situation.*

To my way of thinking, learning about true spirituality, as

found in the Bible and the Book of Mormon and contemplating those things and writing about them are the best things there are to cause a person to change their perception of reality, and do so for the person's good. I can write about the benefits that come with the power of positive thinking, but to be honest about it, making a connection to God, and coming to know that He is real, is the best way to bring about a positive change of attitude in a person who really needs it.

The mother said that she would pass along my words to her daughter. I do hope that the daughter gets something good out if it. After much editing, this is what I wrote:

REALITY SHATTERING

When our reality breaks down completely, it doesn't rip or tear or get a hole in it. It shatters like glass. Thus, it simply ceases to exist. A man who seduces a woman and subjects her to his will, causes the woman's reality to shatter like a pane of glass when the relationship falls apart. The same thing can apply in reverse when a man gets his hopes and his reality shattered by a woman. Any form of subjecting a person to another person's will shatters their former reality and that void causes another reality to come in and take its place. Will that new reality be a good one or a bad one or just an empty one?

Some people are victims in matters like this and some people, on the other hand, don't care very much if their realities have been changed or shattered. As someone once said, "If you don't stand for something, you will fall for anything".

Thus, there must always be some kind of adjustment, or even repentance perhaps, that must take place. Continuing to make bitter accusations however, will not bring closure to the problem. Some people can handle that adjustment that is needed well and some people can't.

To be **unaware** of this principle of reality shattering, is to, sometimes set oneself up to be easily persuaded into entering into a lesser state of being. That is what evil people and evil entities are all about. Some of those people are not fully to blame. They just get caught up in their own false expectations. In any case the results of that are usually disturbing to say the least.

Sometimes, a person will press on in a failed relationship and say to themselves, "it is better to associate with the devil we know than the devil we don't know". That is not really a rational solution to the problem. These problems and their solutions need to be thought out thoroughly and rationally and realistically. Whether a new relationship is available or not, it will be of no use to any 'dumpee' if their heart feels bound to the trauma and disappointments of the past.

Thus, I say that these problems are more a matter of finding and using truthful principles, rather than dealing with 'hurt feelings' that are usually out of the victim's control. .

In some cases, if a person is happy with their reality they will not allow it to be shattered without a fight. If they are not happy with their personal reality they will usually allow it to go its way and in some cases, be overcome by another reality that has more immediate appeal, but that, in reality, might be substandard to the previous relationship.

Part of the adeptness of some persuaders is in portraying himself, or herself, falsely, even when they use a seemingly innocent image to do that. Only if a person is firm in their inner beliefs and values, will they will not be taken in by those false images.

There are many ways of shattering someone's reality, but it always begin with a lie. If one person can destroy another person's good sense of reality with their <u>acting</u> or theatrical abilities, then that is an act of deception.

That is what is so wonderful about marriage. It is the making of covenants. When you make a marriage covenant, especially invoking the name of a sacred being, then that is a sensible thing to do because it can, at least to some degree, prevent a person from exercising the too-common human practice of 'changing their mind'.

Logically, however, the shattering of another person's reality will be of an evil nature. Both parties should be aware of that principle because someday, one never knows if they will have to deal with that. Then the people involved become victims of evil influences and/or victims of their own bad choices. Either way, all parties become pawns in a serious and an often-cruel game.

Alternatively, instead of a person trying to use cheap thrills to find more quality in their life, they are always free to choose, or import, a new and better reality. That means that they can shatter their old bad reality in a good way by simply becoming more conscientious, more spiritual and sharing their 'higher ambitions' with a friend or a new partner or even the ex-partner, and hoping they will understand where they are coming from.

Thus, it doesn't matter too much who gets the blame for the split in the relationship, the situation can easily end up just not ending well because of a downward trajectory that has no redemptive quality and is incapable of regaining some kind of forward, or upward mobility.

People who run away from reality are deceiving themselves. They can run away from the wrongness of what happened to them, but where do they run to? They cannot run away to somewhere in the past because the past is gone. However, it is quite possible for them to run away to an exciting and intelligent 'place' when they have an exciting and intelligent captain at the helm of their ship.

In a 'healthy mind', reality is a place where lies and fear and false judgments cannot go. Ideally, it is a place where real and lasting love can be found. As well, a Godly Spirit abides there. You can get to that place, but <u>sometimes a person needs to wait</u> for it to happen. That proper time will be decided, partially by the good sense of the victim and partially by the will of our benevolent creator.

THE ONLY THING THAT WILL BE REQUIRED OF US IS TO RIGHTEOUSLY WAIT. RIGHTEOUS_WAITING_OR OBEDIENCE, IS THE KEY. OBEDIENCE TO WHAT? OBEDIENCE TO TRUE PRINCIPLES. THAT IS BECAUSE ULTIMATE TRUTH IS THE ONLY THING THAT LASTS. WHEN YOU ARE READY, THE KNOWLEDGE OF THIS WILL COME INTO YOUR MIND AND THEN YOU WILL BE FREE TO BECOME THE PERSON WHO YOU ALWAYS WANTED TO BE.

TO AVOID THE SHATTERING OF A GOOD REALITY WE MUST BE HAPPY WITH WHO WE ARE AND WHAT WE DO. THAT IS OUR MOST IMPORTANT REALITY AND WHEN THAT GOES, THAT IS WHEN OUR BIGGEST TROUBLES BEGIN. THUS, WE WILL NEED TO PREPARE OURSELVES TO GAIN INSIGHT TO SOMETHING CALLED 'PERSONAL SATISFACTION'. IN OTHER WORDS, WE MUST LEARN TO 'LIKE OURSELVES' AND TO BE SATISFIED WITH ACHIEVING OUR BASIC NEEDS.

It seems like the height of irony, but I guess that I am saying in a way that – "to be happy, we must first be happy". Well, yes and no, but we need to, at least, be open-minded and willing to learn what the nature of true happiness is, even if that has always been outside of our experiences

That sounds simple, but how many of us really are capable of grasping that knowledge? I think that we can all reach that contented state at some point in our lives, but the trick is to <u>maintain</u> that slightly higher state and make it a part of our character, not only on a mental level, but also on an emotional and a spiritual level.

Being happy in order to be happy seems to come down to the fact that - **OUR WORLDLY CIRCUMSTANCES SHOULD NOT DICTATE OUR DISPOSITION.**

'Consider smiling'. Realize that we always have a choice whether we smile or whether we do not smile. Experiment with both ways and see which one gives you the most satisfaction.

The moral belief system that we have hopefully built up

and nurtured should take care of that. Thus, it becomes a matter of character, which is important because good character is what wins wars and other struggles. Good character is simply the proper, righteous and constant exercise of our <u>freedom of choice.</u>

Thus, choose to be happy and do so with all of the virtues that are implicated in that, **or** choose to be <u>unhappy</u> with all of the regrets, self-pity, anger and ambivalence, etc. that are implicated in that. Once we decide to be happy, only need to focus on how the Spirit moves us.

> *"but seek ye first the kingdom of God, and his righteousness; and all these things shall be added unto you."*
> *- Matthew 6:33*

People must seek ultimate truth and wisdom first in their own way, and then, as promised, the important things that we need to know about will be taught to us somehow, and probably through spiritual means. Lust can be an extremely powerful thing in some people's lives. Lust can only be eliminated by genuine 'love'. That means that we should learn of God's ways and to live and love by the Spirit.

A GOOD SHATTERING

One person can 'persuade' another person to shatter or abandon their false realities, but if it is to be to a good end, that persuader must always be of a good and pure character. He, or she, must have a good heart and must be able to work with the guidance of the Holy Spirit. To do that, the person needs to know at least a little bit about the Holy Spirit and how He works.

A 'GOOD SPIRITUAL EXPERIENCE' CAN SHATTER SOMEONE'S OFF-BASED PRECONCEIVED NOTIONS AND CHANGE THEIR LIFE FOR THE BETTER. THIS WILL BE DEPENDANT UPON WHETHER OR NOT THEY WILL ALLOW THEMSELVES TO GET A GLIMPSE OF A BETTER REALITY, ONE THAT IS BASED UPON TRUTH AND GOOD PRINCIPLES AND A CLEANER WAY OF LOOKING AT LIFE.

OUTSIDE OF RARE CASES, A GOOD SHATTERING IS NOT USUALLY AN AGGRESSIVE SHATTERING. IT IS ALSO NOT A LOUD SHATTERING. IT IS USUALLY QUIET AND ORDERLY AND DIGNIFIED. IT IS NOT REALLY A COMPLICATED THING OR AN UNSOLVABLE MYSTERY.

***

Another '<u>good</u> shattering' of reality, for example, can happen with a bride and groom on their wedding night and should even include the covenants they make with each other and with their God. It is good because it is a sincere and organized shattering and, hopefully, it is a benevolent one. It is a part of a positive progression that shatters the old ways, ways that are no longer of use to anyone, and replaces those ways with new and righteous ways.

When a woman gives birth to her first child it presents another example of this. Motherhood opens the door to a new stage in a woman's life. New creation gives new hope and can shatter thoughts that contain no hope. It is all quite astounding how that can happen. It is a good shattering of a former reality and it allows the mother to enter into the next phase of her healthy progression.

A person can have a spiritual enlightenment and realize that there is a spiritual process at work that is outside their normal mindset. That also enables healthy progression to take place. That is the best kind of shattering. It happens when the Holy Spirit works within a person to bring them to a closer relationship with their creator.

SHATTERING BY DESERTING A FRIEND

Shattering another person's reality often involves the 'desertion of a loved one', or the desertion of a 'once loved' one.

If a woman is 'in love' with her husband and her husband likes to flirt with other woman, is he shattering her realities? I would not know the details of the situation, so right now I would not condemn anyone, but I would probably say that she was having her realities 'disturbed' at least. That is not a comfortable situation. I do not want to get into hypothetical situations though, so what say we just move to another topic?

The shattering of a reality can happen when one person's status dramatically changes in the eyes of their partner. An example of that is when someone tries to lure another person into drug use or heavy alcohol use, or trying to intimidate someone with physical violence, or a threat of violence. Even more common is the act of continual verbal abuse, which can shatter someone's reality on a continual basis.

Manipulation techniques, or gas lighting, can take away people's good realities. 'Gas lighting' is when you personally cause someone to feel bad about themselves, or make them doubt their intelligence or their value as a human being. Their good realities are then replaced with bad realities. This never leads to anything positive.

To be <u>unaware</u> of this principle of 'reality shattering' is to set ones self up to be easily persuaded into a lesser state of being. That is what the evil entities are all about. They use deceptive persuasion that leaves a victim no choice, but to accept those lesser states, states that consist of little or no freedom.

Why do those minions or evil entities choose to be wicked? They do it to please a bigger entity, who they refer to as their master. I am talking about the 'evil one' here. It is that devil who seeks to displace, or even destroy every being who does not bow down to him and acknowledge his supposed superiority. I imagine that when the devil was in his formative years, in whatever world that was, that he never grew out of throwing a fit when he didn't get his way.

Another goal if his was to subvert, or destroy, the Holy Father, and His Son, and the Holy Ghost, and all active Christian Disciples of Christ.

He seeks his own glory and that is not after the pattern of our great Creator who made us. That was, and is, an act of blatant rebellion. It is present in the world today and we should remember that, and never think that we are not vulnerable to that, because we are or can be, or can be, under certain diabolical circumstances.

The devil's 'loyal subjects', who have been enveloped by his words, his attitudes, and his rebellious ways, support the devil and say that they are willing to follow him wherever he may lead them. A word that might suit the mindset of those demons AND their victims might be the word 'brainwashed'.

Do spirits have 'spirit brains' that can be 'washed' or changed into brains that come to believe in false doctrines? Why not? Can the spirit brain that a spirit possesses ever become unwashed or released from the bondage of having false ideals? I doubt it.

I doubt it because both good ideas and bad ideas can get embedded in people's human brains and so the same might hold true for good ideas and wrong ideas becoming embedded in the 'souls' of both rebellious spirits and obedient spirits.

That depends upon three things basically, their degree of intelligence, their degree of righteousness, and their degree of loyalty.

We must be somewhat aware of how many spirits have formally dedicated their very souls to the majestic plan of our righteous God, and how many other souls have decided to go the other way and have dedicated their immortal souls to the slick words of Satan, who was a liar from the beginning and still is. Yes, it is the sad truth that good and evil have been fighting against each other for a very long time.

THE ONLY SOLUTIONS

The only solutions to that quarreling and fighting are twofold. They are:

1. the redemption, including God's forgiveness of us.
2. the resurrection, which will come about soon and which will make for the permanent separation of good spirits and bad spirits. That would include the permanent separation of good people and people who are 'not so good'. The doctrine of the three levels of glory, or the three levels of Heaven, explains this perfectly in the Bible in 1st Corinthians 15: 40-42. Check out the following declaration:

> *40: There are also celestial bodies and bodies terrestrial: but the glory of the celestial is one, and the glory of the terrestrial is another.*
>
> *41: There is one glory of the sun, and another glory of the moon, and another glory of the stars: for one star differeth from another star in glory.*
>
> *42: So also is the resurrection of the dead. It is sown in corruption; it is raised in incorruption.*

If a person is happy with their reality they will not allow it to be shattered. If they are not happy with their personal reality they will usually allow it to be overcome by another force, even an evil or malevolent force. Part of the adeptness of the persuader is portraying himself or herself falsely, even when using a seemingly innocent and a seemingly well-meaning image.

Thus, I say that it all comes back to how people, or spirits, choose to use their God given 'freedom of choice'. Will that freedom to choose be used to follow the righteous ways of Jesus, or will it be used to follow the rebellious ways of Satan? It is worth noting that I can see this very same situation being demonstrated in our modern world every day.

There are many ways of shattering people's realities, but they always begin with a lie. If one person can destroy another person's good sense of reality with their <u>acting abilities</u> (**lies**) then that is an act of deception. Logically then, that shattering will be of an evil nature. Both parties then become victims of that devilish plot (and of their own bad choices). In either case, all parties will become pawns in a vicious game.

***

Do we need to be free from evil perpetrators or what might be called 'sexual professionals', who hire themselves out for money to other people so that those other people can use those other bodies for the purpose of degrading them? Are the sexual professionals okay with that because they are getting paid to do what they are asked to do? They might curse that life, but when they are actually doing it, then the reality is that they are 'okay' with it. That is what they do and, basically, that is who they are.

Prostitutes and strip tease 'artists' and certain movie producers make a living by shattering men's realities every day. It is also a fact that many average men can enter into those situations willingly. That is because that experience produces a temporary hormonal or adrenal rush in them and even some kind of feeling of euphoria, which in their narrow mindedness, they see as the 'be all' and 'end all' of their desperate lives.

The immediate solution for this is to not let one's life become 'desperate'. The plain fact is that it is sheer fantasy and fantasy is, as I have said, a lie. It is also an attractive lie to a weak mind that lacks any semblance of honor. For me, this solution was summed up neatly in three words spoken by Jesus. Those three words are:

"Come, follow me."   *- Luke 18:22*

If the victims of that kind of 'set up' do not realize it, the shattering of their good reality leaves them with no reality at all, other than a reality of fantasy, which is still no reality at all. It becomes more difficult, or even impossible, as time goes on, for people without a sense of moral purpose to recover from those shattered realities.

Instead of a person trying to find more cheap thrills in their life, they are always free to seek a new and more productive direction. That means that they can shatter their own bad reality in a good way by becoming better people, people who are more conscientious and more spiritually minded.

THAT IS THE KEY. WHEN YOU ARE READY, THAT 'OPPORTUNITY' TO CHOOSE RIGHTEOUS OBEDIENCE WILL COME TO YOU AT SOME TIME AND THEN, BY YOUR OWN FREE CHOICE, YOU WILL BE FREE TO BECOME WHO YOU REALLY WANT TO BECOME AND LIVE ON A NEW AND IN A TRULY FREE WORLD THAT WILL BE PROTECTED BY OUR RIGHTEOUS, LOVING AND ALL POWERFUL CREATOR.

***

A good spiritual experience can shatter someone's bad reality and, as well, shatter any preconceived notions, or ill conceived notions, and change their whole life for the better. That can allow the person to get a glimpse of a

'better reality' that is based upon good and solid principles, and as well provide for a cleaner and a more positive way of looking at life. A good shattering is not an aggressive shattering. It is quiet and orderly. It is quite simple and not a mystery.

In any case, true love will prevail and all life, in its mortal state, will pass away someday. Personally, as long asit can still be used for our Father's purposes, I will not complain when it does pass. That will be when Jesus and the Holy Spirit will rule over the earth, which was, in the beginning, the original goal of both God and His children.

IT IS OUR PERSONAL SPIRITUAL PERCEPTIONS THAT MATTER MOST. BY THAT I MEAN THE 'WELL THOUGHT OUT' PERCEPTIONS. THOSE PERCEPTIONS, OR BELIEFS, CAN DETERMINE OUR INNERMOST THOUGHTS, OUR ATTITUDES, OUR VALUES, OUR RELATIONSHIPS AND OUR CHARACTER. THOSE PERCEPTIONS MUST BE OF AN HONEST NATURE AND CONSIST OF THE FOUNDATIONAL BELIEFS THAT MAKE US WHO WE ARE AND GIVE US THE STRENGTH TO KEEP ON CARRYING ON. AGAIN, THOSE ARE THE REALITIES THAT MATTER MOST.

IF A PERSON HAS A LEGITIMATE SPIRITUAL EXPERIENCE IN THEIR INNERMOST THOUGHTS OR VISIONS IT FOLLOWS THAT THEY SHOULD REALIZE THAT THE SPIRIT IS REAL AND THAT THERE IS A SPIRITUAL PROCESS AT WORK THAT IS OUTSIDE OF THEIR NORMAL MINDSET.

THAT IS THE BEST KIND OF SHATTERING. IT HAPPENS WHEN THE HOLY SPIRIT, (THE COMFORTER) WORKS WITHIN A PERSON TO BRING THEM TO A CLOSER ACQUAINTANCE WITH THEIR CREATOR. IT IS SOMETIMES CALLED CONVERSION AND IT IS A SHATTERING THAT SHOULD BE WELCOMED, BUT WE NEED TO REMEMBER THAT IT STILL WILL REQUIRE WISDOM AND COURAGE AND FAITH IN ORDER THAT WE CAN

REAP THE REWARDS THAT COME WITH THAT 'GOOD SHATTERING'.

CHAPTER 9

WHEN THE DEMONS COME AFTER YOU - REMEMBER (10p.)

Subtitle: Fight Back

Demons are wicked spirits who are aligned with the Devil, who is also called Satan or Beelzebub. Under normal circumstances, demons don't have the strength to control people who have strong and righteous personalities, but if a person allows the demons to have free reign over their minds, including their imaginations, they will come to know that person very well, and that gives the demons an increase in the potency of their influences. Those influences consist mainly of the words and images that they can project into the minds of the people who they wish to influence.

Such demonic influences, when people pay attention to them, can bring about a change in the person's value system, and a negative change at that. That does not give them control over the person, but if a person pays heed to those influences that person's mind can become persuaded to stray into some very unhealthy places in their daily life.

They will approach that 'host person' in small ways at first and do so by portraying themselves as harmless entities who only want to give you 'a few laughs' and cause you to be impressed by their be 'unique' ways of looking at the world.

Those things will probably not matter too much if the 'host person' is of a strong character and has a good spiritual foundation. A person like that will be a man or a woman who is independent and who will have their own unique strength that will enable them to fend off, or resist, any influences that will tempt them to follow an immoral path.

If a person does not have strong values and is bored with a 'normal' kind of life, then the field for the investigation of foreign or carnal ideas becomes wide open. Still that does not put the evil ones in control, but if the demon is constant in his, or her, desire to be of a strong influence, then serious problems can enter into the picture. I do not know specifically what those problems might be because every life is unique, but any problems that might happen will eventually reveal themselves.

THUS, THE BEST HOPE IS FOR THE PERSON TO GAIN, OR REGAIN, A GOOD AND RIGHTEOUS FOUNDATION SO THAT THEY WILL BE ABLE TO CREATE AND MAINTAIN HEALTHY FORMULAS FOR LIVING. THOSE FORMULAS SHOULD BE ABLE TO ENHANCE, UPLIFT, AND STRENGTHEN THE PERSON, AND ALLOW THEM TO GAIN THE EXPERIENCE OF LEARNING ABOUT THE MOST VALUABLE ATTRIBUTE OF LIFE. THAT

ATTRIBUTE IS COMMONLY KNOWN AS 'WISDOM'. A WISE PERSON COMES TO KNOW WHAT HUMAN JOY IS AND THEN KNOWS WHAT IT IS LIKE TO BECOME AN INTEGRAL PART OF THE 'JOYFUL FAMILY OF MANKIND'.

This is a good feeling, as opposed to the natural feelings that cause a person to become depressed or lethargic or bitter or confused, or feeling any other kind of discomfort or negative attitudes.

If we begin to think in this negative kind of mindset, that will eventually be revealed as the entrance way into a 'danger zone'. Any kind of mindset can become habitual when the initial natural pleasure seems to outweigh the risk of experiencing the inevitable displeasure of feeling guilt or anger or envy or whatever is able to throw off the healthy trajectory of a person's mind.

If a person finds themselves without a strong set of values and identifies with the negative attitudes that I just listed, Here are some things that they might remember, or contemplate, as they grow older.

1. Remember the beautiful life that you have been given. It might not be so beautiful anymore and there may not be near as much joy in it as there once was, and you may even feel will feel like you

are at 'the bottom of the barrel.' You may feel alone and without the great prospect of joy in your future, but remember that if life was once joyful, then <u>it can be that way again</u>. That might just mean you need to make some new priorities. That might take a lot of hard contemplation, and it might not, but people can change. It happens every day. Could you be one of those people?

My point is that I know it can be done and I know from experience that a person can easily find happiness in their life once again. Remember that there is always hope for the faithful.

2. **Remember your faithful family.** You may not be able to look at them the same anymore. Thus, you may not be able to love them as much at particular times, but remember that they began their lives with the same righteous ambitions that you had when you began your life, so be patient with them.

3. **Remember how you have been blessed in the counsel that you have received** when you looked at your life with gratitude and a humble and spiritual perspective. Write the good things down that you have learned, or created, and read them frequently. Read your journals and give yourself small rewards for your best entries, the ones that might show the world or anyone who reads your words that you really are, indeed, a good 'thinker'.

4. Remember, the members of your family of origin who have, like all of us, have had their problems. Also, search for the presence of a loving God who provides blessings for all of His children, especially the children who show regrets for the things they did wrong.

5. Remember that the demons will cause you to see people in a negative light. Men. Women. Children. Strangers. And it will not be a better light. This applies especially to people who present a false sense of authority.

THE DEMONS HAVE A REASON FOR DOING THIS. THEY DO IT BECAUSE THEY ARE SERVANTS OF SATAN, AND THUS, THEY HAVE MADE A DELIBERATE CHOICE TO BECOME EVIL ENTITIES AND WORK AGAINST ALL PEOPLE WHO CONSIDER THEMSELVES TO BE 'CHILDREN OF GOD', WHICH THEY ACTUALLY ARE.

THE DEMONS HAVE ALL MADE A COVENANT TO DO THAT. THAT IS THE TEAM THAT THEY PLAY ON AND WHETHER OR NOT THE OPPOSITION MIGHT HAS 'NICE PEOPLE' ON THEIR TEAM, THAT DOESN'T MATTER BECAUSE THE ONLY DESIRE OF THE DEMONS IS TO BEAT THE OPPOSITION AS SOUNDLY AS THEY CAN AND

SHOW NO MERCY, EVEN IF THEY HAVE TO BREAK THE RULES TO DO IT.

ALSO, IT WOULD NOT SURPRISE ME IF THAT DEMONIC TEAM HAS A THEME SONG WITH LOUD DRUMS AND A MONOTONE, REPETATIVE MELODY LINE, AND AGGRESSIVE/MINDLESS LYRICS THAT WENT SOMETHING LIKE "WE WILL, WE WILL, ROCK YOU!"

HEY! 'ROCK' IS SUCH A COOL WORD ISN'T IT? JUST SAY THE WORD WITH SOME LOUD AND SIMPLE MUSIC BEHIND IT AND 'PEOPLE' WILL LOVE YOU FOR IT. IN FACT, "ALL HELL WILL BREAK LOOSE."

6. Remember: It is the demons who will try to separate you from your God, at least temporarily. They will also cause the Holy Ghost to become absent in your realm. As Russell M. Nelson once said. "Without the Holy Ghost, we simply, will not be able to spiritually survive in today's world."

7. Remember: It is the demons who will 'spur you on' to believe in fantasy and sensual things and devilish things, but you still have a choice as to whether or not you will pay heed to their spurs. If you still believe that 'YOU ARE A CHILD OF GOD', then let those words be your team's theme song. It may not have the violent affect that, 'we will rock you' song has, but it is much more likely that

those words will actually touch another person's heart, a heart that craves love and peace to be a part of their lives.

Also know that when you recite those words of truth, then will probably know in your heart you have a much tougher skin than you might have thought that you had.

8. Remember, The demons will remind you of past indiscretions that you do not want to take with you into eternity. They will limit your capacity to think clearly and to cause you to lose your valuable sense of humor and might even take away the great ability you have to be able to correct yourself and even to forgive yourself.

They will also take away, or lessen your ability to love others, and can even take away the ability for others to love you. They can even take away your gratitude, which is your ability to enjoy God's gifts, be they simple or complicated.

They will chase away your simple, peaceful and happy feelings. They will take away your crowning glory, your spiritual mucilage, your goodness, your iron rod, your maps, your self-esteem, your higher self, and other things that mean a lot to you. They will replant into you memories of your old life's ways with all of the confusion, fears, loneliness and lack of direction that your old life had.

9. On the other hand, if you rebuke the demons, you will slowly see your rewards revealed to you as you become more self-aware and more aware of the great goodness that you can find in your life if you try.

FIGHT BACK

If you desire change in your life, it just may be that your higher self has undergone some damage. It will be time to call the SOUL REPAIR MAN. He is also known as 'THE LAMB OF GOD.' He is eager to help you, so He will not be that difficult to find, although I can guarantee you that the yellow pages will not have a listing for him.

I am quite certain though that His first piece of advice that the Soul Man will give you will be to replace your shattered-ness with a restoration of your higher self, or the goodness that is within you. That is the only answer.

In doing that you will find a new purpose, and a better purpose, in your life. Replace your part-time love of carnal things with a 'full time love' of the beauty that is found in life. That may not be easy on your first attempt, but I guarantee that you will find it if you are persistent and if you look in right places.

> *"Take my yoke upon you and learn if me; for I am meek and lowly in heart: and ye shall find rest unto your souls. For my yoke is easy and my burden is light". – Matthew 11: 29, 30*

Dismiss the demons that surround you and summon the angels. And when you summon the angels, don't forget about the Holy Ghost. He loves to abide with people who are in distress or feel unworthy, and give people comfort in His own special ways when they ask for it.

Read inspirational stories or listen to inspirational messages every day, and pray that you might feel the power of the stories that are told in the scriptures. The Holy Scriptures are divinely inspired, and if you are even partially inspired, you will recognize inspiration when it crosses your path. You will gain a desire to fight against any all kinds of lies, like fantasy and false doctrine and false images. Just don't lose your focus to fight back when you need to.

Those things can, quite literally, attack your mind. Yes, the Comforter will also cause you to see the ugliness in carnal things like pornography, even soft-core pornography.

That rearrangement of your values AND your standards of entertainment will automatically put righteous priorities at the top of your list And then, when you come to a full understanding of what went on, and what is still going on, you will then become a new person who will expose what is actually going on and will then find the strength to support the good things that are going on and find the strength to FIGHT BACK against the bad things that are subtly going on.

CHAPTER 10.

FLOWERS ARE MEANT TO GIVE AWAY (2p.)

(Here is a story song that I wrote and recorded about twelve years ago. I sang this sing at the weddings of two of my daughters. I remember singing the song at both weddings, and I had a problem singing it because of the personal emotions involved in it. To this day it is still an emotional song for me to sing.)

***

I remember your first day in this world,
The first time I held my baby girl.
Your eyes seemed to look far beyond me
As you gazed into Eternity

With your silken hair and your flannel suits
And you tender skin and your baby boots
And when I looked into your eyes I could clearly see
Your love and pure tranquility.

It seems like only yesterday
When you were a little child at play
With dress up clothes from rummage sales
And dolls with names from fairy tales.

With your bright colored parka and your winter boots
Or your baseball hats and your bathing suits,
But when I looked past all that energy
I could still see the love and tranquility.

And now it is your wedding day.
Fears and doubts are far away.

Another man takes your hand today
Cause flowers were meant to give away.

With your flowing hair and your wedding dress
And a love that words cannot express.
And when he looks into your eyes I hope he sees
Your love and pure tranquility.

And you'll have babies of your own one day
And your hair will take on shades of grey,
But time will never take away
The picture I have of you today

With your flowing hair and your wedding dress
And a love that words cannot express.
Another man takes your hand today
Cause Flowers were meant to give away.

CHAPTER 11

EVIL SPIRITS (11P.)

Subtitles: *The Timothy Maclean Story, The Power of the Holy Ghost*

Lets get something straight from the beginning. When I talk about demons or evil spirits having an influence on us, I do not mean that they will cause us to go out and kill someone, although I am sure that has happened in rare instances. I do believe however, that unseen evil spirits exist and by their ability to transmit thought images, both visual images and audio images, into the minds of certain people, regular people or irregular people, who are vulnerable to such things and who are open to receiving those images, then very bad things are going to happen.

The god of darkness, or the devil, does not usually **force** John Q. Citizen to commit a heinous sin. If he did that, it would not be a 'definitive sin', because, in a way, it would be a form of 'entrapment'. Instead, that evil spirit can promote an evil act by projecting ugly or violent images into a person's brain or mind. Thus, the devil, or the demons, could strongly influence a person to take those images seriously, and then go out into the world and cause serious problems. How could that happen?

The perpetrator in a sin or a crime or an evil act could be, at least in part, driven by of some kind of powerful and coercive force and thus, that person would not be 'fully' responsible for being a part of that sin or a violent act. In other words, the men or women who got 'used' may not have been 'fully' complicit in the sinful act, but might actually be 'somewhat' complicit' in the act to varying degrees. When a person is not 'fully' complicit in committing an evil act, that argument in a courtroom, will always be used by scheming lawyers to get criminals released from prison.

The devil wants his victim to be somewhat complicit in any evil act. That victim would then be seen as an accomplice and would be much easier for 'an accuser' to accuse him, or her, of wrongdoing. That would also cause the 'accomplice' to lessen their own opinion of themselves, which was part of the devilish plan from the beginning.

The devil knows that 'demoralizing a person' is a big part of the game and thus, his plan is to tempt John Q. Citizen into contributing to a sin, even if only in part, but <u>by his, or her, own volition</u>. He also wants his victims to spend their valuable time thinking up lies, or excuses, whereby he could convince people that he was not really guilty of any great sin.

Many people will accept those excuses while not realizing that they are forfeiting their basic honesty by doing so. When a person forfeits their basic honesty, they are changing all the rules of the game. The game itself then becomes a dishonorable game and the perceived winners and losers of the game also become irrelevant, and in reality, and because of their irrelevancy do not exist anymore in a world that has meaning, which is the only kind of world that actually matters.

The winners of the game, in many cases, are not the lawyers who can express principles of truth better than anyone else, but the financial winners are often the lawyers who can tell the biggest lies.

People who have evil inclinations will rationalize things in their own biased ways and accept the lies and excuses that are presented to them. But the Lord is the final judge of our affairs and He is aware of all the things that are going on.

Thus, John Q. Citizen would become an accomplice or a co-conspirator in it all, knowingly or unknowingly, and they would probably feel the pain that comes with the subsequent guilt and regrets, but could have a twisted form of mercy given to them by a judge or a jury who mistakenly holds there is 'tolerance' to be one of the highest virtues there is.

This is often the case in an earthly court of law where the sentence of justice can become watered down and a violent assailant can be <u>excused</u> for committing a heinous act, even a heinous act of murder, by following the orders of an evil spirit who seeks only for the degradation, or the even the destruction of John Q. Citizen.

Freedom can be granted to criminals if the defendant's lawyer can manipulate the evidence and prove that the perpetrator was, at least partly, manipulated by some unseen, but power wielding invisible force that was beyond their control. In other words, <u>they can be excused from an act of murder by 'reason of 'insanity'</u>.

This has happened in many courtrooms around the world, mainly courtrooms that are controlled by liberal judges. That means that, when such a thing happens, the person (or 'the accused sinner or perpetrator' might be <u>declared by a judge to be not totally responsible for a heinous act</u> That person could, in a short time, be free to walk the streets without anyone knowing where they are or what they are doing.

When this does happen, it can set a dangerous precedent. Well paid lawyers lawyers will make demands to the judge or jury for leniency on the part of that judge or jury. That strategy can work and when it does work, true justice will not happen. The entrapment that an evil spirit sets up will be evil of course, but let us remember that a person who allows themselves to be entrapped will do so firstly by their own consent.

Those judgments can cause all kinds of harm and even disasters, in innocent people's lives. Regarding the original act of violence, when those evil spirits present images in people's minds, the hormones in John Q. Citizen's body 'kick in' and that can cause further problems and illusions, and even create an evil psychological momentum to form.

This can greatly multiply the problem even more because the affect can lead to further harmful images, and subsequently, to more harmful actions from either the perpetrator or from outside of the perpetrators mind (IE: provocation of some kind). This 'outside provocation' can be triggered by pornography or other wicked portrayals of the world or of people in general.

What follows after that initial stimulation is an acceleration of the sexual urge or the urge to commit a crime. This would include more images and more adrenalin flowing through the assailant's brain. It can even increase the level of abandonment of any morality, respect, or decency in the criminal mind.

Thus, it becomes possible, and maybe even probable, that sin, or wickedness itself, will come into full bloom. People should be forced to be accountable for any crime that they decide to take part in. And so the cycle continues and may continue in ways that the people involved never even dreamed about.

THERE ARE SPIRIT ENTITIES THAT EXIST WHO HAVE THEIR OWN <u>IDENTITY,</u> AND IF THAT IDENTITY SHOULD BECOME VOID OF CONSCIENCE, IT WILL THEN BECOME LITERALLY EVIL, AND THEN THAT PERSON'S MIND WILL THEN BECOME THE MIND OF A PSYCHOPATH. IT WILL FOLLOW A NATURAL, BUT EVIL PATH, THAT WILL PROBABLY LEAD TO UNRESTRAINED CHAOS AND EVEN TRAGEDY.

***

Good spirits influence us in positive ways, and bad spirits influence us in negative ways. This evil case that I will talk about is a 'worst case scenario' and lawmakers must decide how to deal with that problem. That is for the sake of the human dignity and for the sake of establishing virtual peace and order for all human beings in society.

As I write this, I cannot help but recall a case that took place in Winnipeg, Canada back in 2002 that was very disturbing.

THE TIMOTHY MACLEAN STORY

This story involved a murder that took place on a greyhound bus outside of Winnipeg, Manitoba where an innocent young victim named Timothy Maclean was brutally murdered in cold blood and the murderer was subsequently found 'not guilty' by reason of insanity.

The murderer in that case is now free to walk anywhere in the world that he wants to walk, and does so as a free man according to the twisted laws of the Canadian justice system. Canada is a country that is usually perceived by most people as a 'civilized country'. Such a view is erroneous to say the least. In any case, here are some newspaper accounts of the incident :

NEWS CLIPPINGS:

> *"The driver and passengers fled the bus but watched in horror as VINCE Li decapitated the 22-year-old Winnipeg man and mutilated and cannibalized his body."*
> *- Winnipeg Free Press 2008*

> *"In 2011, two of the bus passengers filed a lawsuit against Vince Li, Greyhound, the RCMP and the government of Canada asking for $3 million to compensate them for "witnessing the defendant Li stabbing Mr. McLean Jr. to death, mutilating his body and performing acts of cannibalism."*
> *- Winnipeg Free Press*

The name of the murderer, at that time ,was Vince Li. He was 52 years old. His name has since been changed.

> *"Nothing changed for everybody else. The traffic still went. The sun still shone. And it was so maddening to me that the whole world didn't just stop. Mine did. It stopped, and it took a long time to really want to get up every day."*
> *- quote from Carol de Delley, mother of Timothy McLean*

As horrifying as it might be, this is a true story. I do honestly believe however that the blood of people who die like this will cry out from the earth for justice. Someday, and in some way, I believe that our just God will graciously provide for that justice to take place.

I don't remember the name of the judge who let Vince Li off the hook, but let it be known that I think his action, or inaction, was a criminal offence and If I had the authority, I would see that he was brought up on trial himself as an accessory to murder.

THE POWER OF THE HOLY GHOST

In this story, Vince Li said that he received a message from God to kill Tim Maclean in the Greyhound bus that they were both passengers on. Li had some knives in his possession that would get that job done, and they did get the job starting when Tim was asleep. It was a horrible crime that took one innocent man's life and damaged many other lives. That included Mr. MacLean's family and witnesses of the horrible act that happened on that bus..

Anybody who knows religion knows that a God of any kind would never command a person to do such a thing. Thus, Mr. Li's excuse of God's influence (IE: a mysterious voice that Lt said he heard, in the murder is totally invalid.

I might be convinced that Mr. Li was getting a message from a spiritual realm, but <u>it certainly was not from a God of any kind</u>. Only a complete fool, or a Liberal Social worker, would believe something like that. A message might have been given by the devil or a demon or something like that, but that is not for me to say except to repeat a verse in the Bible that reads:

> *"abound in hope through the power of the Holy Ghost"*
>
> *– Romans 15:13*

A few years after that incident there was another story in the news that disturbed me. It was about two young women from Scandinavia who went on a camping trip in the Middle East. I don't remember the country, but I remember that it was in the middle of Muslim territory. Their friends said later that the young women wanted to prove to the world that Islam was really a religion of peace. It did not work out however, and the two women were brutally murdered at their campsite.

I feel like I should relate to you some other stories about the benefits of caution and prudence, but to tell you the truth, I find stories like these are difficult to talk about. I find them very disturbing to talk about them or write about them.

Nevertheless, some of the stories should be told so that naïve young people do not go out into the world thinking that nothing bad is going to happen to them.

Why do they do that? I would guess that someone told them once that all people are basically good and that no person people would intentionally not harm another person. I say that such a parent who would tell a child something like that does not deserve to be a parent.

In my Christian church we believe in the power of the Holy

Ghost that was promised in the scriptures. He works positively and works for the good of all and He communicates with people when danger is present in their lives, even though He does not have a body and would be unable to stop it once the act is underway. He is at one with God's purposes and is sent from God and Jesus to influence us when we invite him to do so, and even warn us to beware when we are open to receive that message.

Thus, I would say that all people, young or old, men or women, should always seek out the Holy Spirit of God so that He might counsel them and let them know when there might be trouble ahead, especially when they dare to go to places where they might be at risk. The Holy Ghost dies not have a body, so He cannot protect us physically, but He does have infallible insight and is able to dwell IN us at certain times to let us know when there might be trouble ahead.

The Holy Ghost, firstly, testifies of Christ. We must gain a certain amount of knowledge of the workings of God the Father and Christ and we must come to know gospel principles, as they apply to us as individuals, and as they apply to us as parts of mankind in general.

This is necessary if we are to come to a solid understanding of what the Holy Ghost is actually testifying of, and indeed, know what the good purpose of our life really is about. I think that we are assured by personal revelations that the Holy Ghost actually has the ability to dwell within each of us and warn us of trouble when the time to do that is right.

"That good thing which was committed unto thee

> **keep by the <u>Holy Ghost which dwelleth in us</u>".**
> **- *2 Timothy 1: 14*** *(emphasis added)*

Another name for the Holy Ghost is the name, 'THE COMFORTER. I was reading through the topical guide in the bible recently and I noticed that the Holy Ghost is actually identified by the name , **'the Comforter'** more times than He is called 'The Holy Ghost. I found that interesting.

Space is infinitely large and infinitely small. No matter how big something is one can always double it. No matter how small something is one can always cut it in half. Thus, I say, never discount an enemy because you think it is too small to cause you any damage, and never think that because an enemy is invisible, it cannot harm you.

I would also advise everyone to steer clear of the supernatural. Don't even dabble in it. It is a journey that can cross unknown borders. Those borders might be 'partially' known to some people, but that will only encourage certain other people in their recklessness.

Those people are usually desperate enough to ignore warnings and proceed in listening to an evil spirit with a sense of false security that tells them that nothing bad could happen to them, or that, if that did happen, then they could handle it. Nevertheless, not everyone is faulty in their Judgments. Timothy Maclean was an innocent young man who just fell asleep on a Greyhound bus when he was murdered. How could anyone let an act like that go unpunished. I don't know, but I still believe that justice will, SOMEHOW, be served in the end.

That is what human pride can do to some people. Most of us know there will be a price to pay down the line for the flagrant misuse of truth. Some desperate people, however, find that true principle easy to ignore.

This problem of the desperation that leads to fantasy, and even hallucinations, is very real and especially in weak people. This can be alleviated, but not by indulgence, or further searching in all the wrong places. In realty, it can only be alleviated by making a commitment to serve the Prince of Peace, who is Jesus Christ.

If you spend some time, even years, coming to know the Holy Spirit, you will begin to realize that the previous years you spent living <u>without</u> the Holy Spirit were really of little or no use to you. That realization may involve making some other difficult decisions in your life. In any case, those difficult decisions will always be worth the effort to think them through. They could very well be life-saving decisions.

CHAPTER 12

MY SECRET LOVE (9P.)

Subtitle: My Secret Love – the song

(This is the title of a popular song that was written sometime around 1953 by Sammy Fain and Paul Webster. At that time it was a big hit for the singer/movie star Doris Day.)

One of my favorite renditions of this song is a version released a few decades after Doris Day released it. This version is by the Mexican/American singer Freddie Fender. The song is a poignant one and I have always thought that it could easily have a have a gospel interpretation to it, if an editor wanted to change a few of the lyrics. One might wonder what this song has to do with the gospel. I will now proceed to tell you.

It is my belief that, throughout history, most of mankind has had a missing element in their worldly lives. That missing element is a desire to have a firm connection with their Creator, who is an Eternal Being with an eternal status, and who also happens to be the receiver of heart felt and eternal love by millions of people.

Yes, the true and our invisible God is the 'secret' love that many men and woman have sought for in the past and even seek for now. That is the love of our creator who invites us to help Him fulfill the righteous purposes that we had in the past and that we have now in the present. Learning about how this love works is not usually an easy process. Therefore, when we came to Earth and gained bodies it was similar to an entry level apprenticeship where we had a lot to learn.

As it happens the Heavenly status of the Holy Father (and Holy Mother), dictates that there must be a 'growth period' whereby God's children can learn the necessary steps to reach the same level that their heavenly parents are at.

These steps usually come into the light as we undergo a variety of life's experiences. That includes the good things that we do in the world as well as the various mistakes that many of us have made in the past, and may be destined to make in the future.

In any case, it should be essential that we mortals should have instruction from our Maker as to how we should live our lives in the most righteous way that we can that we be successful in this great and eternal quest. We will also need this intelligent instruction to be promoted by chosen men and women who are not only very knowledgeable about the issues, but who are also righteous people, perhaps not perfect, but righteous people.

What those steps will consist of may vary from person to person, but I do believe that there will be many commonalities in the processes, both in the experiencing of them and on the learning that can take place when we 'repent' of those mistakes, or in other words, 'rethink' those mistakes. Also, it seems in our case, that there was a need that there was to be some kind of outstanding sacrifice that was needed to be made by our God, in order that He can prove to us that we can trust Him. Thus, it would need to be an ultimate sacrifice and thus, an <u>eternal</u> sacrifice.

Hence, in our case, that would be the coming of a Holy Messiah who was promised to us in the beginning. This is a vital part of the 'learning processes' and our Heavenly Father knew that. That is why he gave us scriptures so that we could learn about His plan and learn from the Messiah personally, who was His only begotten Son, and so we could learn from His very painful sacrifice, how we can properly live in this world and live in harmony with our fellow human beings. Personally, that is the only way that I could consider my mortal life a success.

It is worth noting now, however that some people will learn from those mistakes quickly and make behavioral changes, and some people will do that slowly, and some other people might not do any learning at all.

What then might we learn? One important thing that we must learn is that bad decisions lead to bad actions and bad habits, and thus, bad consequences. Some people, if they can learn wisdom will be able to avoid bad habits and bad attitudes more easily. When they do that and endure to the end, then they can partake of the great Celestial glory that is a part of our Heavenly Parents plan.

***

The following is our Heavenly Father's first counsel. It is the first of the Ten Commandments.

> *"And thou shalt love the Lord thy God with all thy heart, and with all thy soul, and with all thy mind, and with all thy strength: this is the first commandment."*   *– Mark 12:30*

Righteous judgments will be made someday concerning certain people who choose to break righteous laws. That includes people who seek to fill their minds with an 'intellectual void'. This is because that neglectful practice allows those people to feel that they are unaccountable for their sinful actions, but the Heavenly plan just doesn't work that way.

It is still true that some people will actually 'choose' to become intellectual simpletons. Those people, as it turns out, will also be people who have little respect for other people, people who have chosen to live by higher moral laws.

Nevertheless, I maintain that in the deepest regions of most people's hearts, there is a seed of love that was once planted in all of us and it will continue to grow in strength if people have the necessary faith and are determined to assist our righteous Heavenly Father as He tries to build up his Kingdom on the earth.

Do not mistakenly think that our mission as human beings has gone away, just because the visual evidence of it is absent. It is absent mostly because of our lack of faith, but it is still active in the minds of people who are faithful and, in the end, that faith will be active for all to see.

If our faith should dwindle, it is still possible that it will return one day in its fullness. That will happen on that great day when human beings, en masse, finally learn what they were sent here to learn.

MY SECRET LOVE (The song)

1st verse
In my version of this song I rewrote the third line of the chorus because it aims directly at the affection that the singer has for the secret love of his life who is none other that our Creator who is God, the 'author of life', and who most people do not know much about for reasons that I will explain in other essays.

Like many of us, the singer of the song does not know a lot about this invisible God and who is potentially and ultimately the driving force in the life of all human beings.

In certain lyrics that I added to this song I felt strongly that this 'God' is alive and cares very much for all of the children who He has created. Otherwise, the idea of a God, like any 'good parent, who was not directly involved in the creation and the teaching of His children, would simply not make any sense.

This next couplet is an important line:

"And now I shout it from the highest hill,
And if God wants me to testify of Him, I will.
And now, my heart is an open door
And my secret love is no secret anymore."

***

The human Spirit, with the assistance of the <u>Holy</u> Spirit is quite capable of naming life's problems, big and small, and addressing those problems, and finding solutions for those problems in the clearest of terms when some assistance from God is asked for.

As children of our God, we can use our faith and our intelligence and our gratitude to work as a strong and cohesive unit, through which we can all reach a state of happiness or satisfaction in all of our righteous quests.

I speak here not only of personal quests, but quests concerning the mass healing of millions of families and individuals who had once decided to sincerely commit themselves to follow the laws of our Heavenly Parents. This is for the mutual benefit of all concerned. In their secular environments however, people who 'heard the word' were often tempted by Satan's minions to 'water down' those righteous ambitions.

***

Let me be clear that my personal life has <u>not</u> been totally exemplary and it would be would be a mistake for me to just assume that I, and my wife, would be given high positions in the celestial kingdom of God after our mortal lives are over.

I do, however, have faith in the wisdom of God and I will hereby resolve to sustain His judgments on all matters. In other words, my personal dreams of grandeur consist of not much more than standing in, or outside of, a clean and beautiful chapel or temple, and promising to give service to my Endless God. I might add that it would be my great pleasure to do so with some of our beautiful smiling children standing at our side, possibly even with the addition of some grandchildren.

Differences in opinions between my wife and myself have become more common in the last few years. I realize that I am not perfect and that neither is she. (This is another vital principle that we all must learn.)

I am glad that I learned this though because it has made me aware that even good relationships of the flesh are not a guarantee of establishing an eternal bond that I once thought would be given freely by God to all of us romantic types. I have had cause to reconsider this notion, but I still believe my ambitions are still basically honorable and simple and good.

Thus, the principle still stands that a righteous man, and a righteous woman, who live together with a love for the truth can partake of a Holy state that may endure throughout the Eternities.

> *"But seek ye first the kingdom of God, and his righteousness; and all these things shall be added unto you."* - *Matthew 6:33*

Still, we must all exercise caution. This is for the reason that the devil still walks upon the earth and still seeks to devour those people who would be foolish enough to be tempted by his deceit.

In this life we all will need protection from the 'entanglements' that will beset our minds through substances like alcohol or drugs (prescription or non-prescription), and we will even need protection from idle distractions and especially the kind of idle distractions that will misinform us about how we should look upon the world and on people and on God and on our basic perceptions on the goodness of life.

The sheer audacity of evil entities can actually damage an innocent person's brain, including their imaginations, leaving their brains to be subjected to evil entities from the spirit world who do nothing but try to make mischief and cause harm for all men and women who have totally different ideals.

Thus, I say that all men and women, old and young, can never afford to give up the fight. We all have some vital principles that we should valiantly defend no matter how old we may be. The noble human Spirit, whose power can at times be severely 'watered down' by the enemy, will hopefully still persevere until the end, will do so with assistance from our God. Amen.

> *"But where there's hope inside, true love will reside, and where mortals fail, true love will prevail."*
> *- from the song: "True Love will Prevail" by Bob King*

At the beginning of this essay, I said that my secret love was my Heavenly Father who has always been active in giving be personal instruction in one way or another. The heavenly version of 'love' is different from the mortal version of love. The Heavenly version of love has nothing to do with sensuality. Sensuality, in a matrimonial sense, will be dealt with when the time is right.

Firstly though, we must work towards establishing a Heavenly love that deals with more important things. Some of those more important things are: honor, kindness, loyalty, knowledge, courage, faith, honesty, friendship, joy, charity, and other things too.

Now I have told my story and expressed some of my inner feelings. I hope you have benefitted by my words. And I say again that we should have faith in the love that we have for our Creator and know that that love will eventually become evident and people like you and me will know about it and celebrated it.

Then the greatness of the blessings that follow will be much greater than we can imagine. Then, in reality and truth, our secret love will be no secret anymore. And that will be another example of 'the truth setting us free'. There will be no more secrets.

CHAPTER 13

THE SIX REALMS OF TIME   (10P.)

Subtitles: How can I make A Bad past Become Good? The Two things that Matter the Most in Life.

I mentioned the importance of having a good spirit accompany us in our daily lives; namely the Holy Ghost (The Comforter). It is commonly said that there are three basic realms of time - the past, the present and the future.

I would divide time into three additional realms however. Chronologically speaking, the differences in time are obvious – past, present and future. Spiritually speaking however, I have divided each of the three realms into two parts each according to the spirit that abides with us in each realm. Thus, there is good past and a bad past; a good present and a bad present; a good future and a bad future.

The thing that makes them different is the spirit, or the feeling, that is present within us as we live in each realm. Is it good or bad? Is it trustworthy or not? This makes each realm different from the others. The three good realms have a good spirit about them, even, on occasion, the Holy Spirit. The three bad realms do not have a good spirit about them. A good realm and a bad realm are not incidental things. They are the difference between a happy life and a life of mediocrity or even a life of misery.

The kind of spirit that is with us, in whatever time realm that we are in, makes a huge difference in our lives, even a difference comparable to the difference between night and day. That is why I say there are six separate realms. Which realm do you mostly identify with the most as you consider your life experiences?

1. Good past – having a clear conscience and a clear vision of the past, feeling forgiveness for past errors
2. Bad past – feeling remorse or guilt from bad memories
3. Good present – feeling contented or joyful or blissful, having a glimpse, and an anticipation, of eternity.
4. Bad present – feeling anxiety, worried, bored, or angry
5. Good future – feelings of hope and anticipation, feeling the reality of infinite possibilities.
6. Bad future – feelings of worry or anxiety or despair, feeling fears of self-imposed limitations.

Because of the different feelings for each realm all of them are distinctly different. All of us are capable of feeling the effects of each of these six realms. My personal aim is to live in the good realms <u>only</u>. We should try to do this automatically, and even unconsciously, but in times when we seriously contemplate our lives, we should do it consciously as well.

I can understand if someone should ask – "My past was not a good one. It was filled with turmoil and confusion. I cannot change the past, so how can you say that I can make my bad past a good one?"

That would be a good question and my answer is that we can make our past good, or at least acceptable, by coming to a clear understanding of it first, and then <u>accepting it as something that was beyond our control</u>. It may have even been necessary however, for some of us to experience a difficult past in order for us to become the person who we are today. Even though you might not be aware of it that just might be a good thing.

WHEN THE SCOPE AND GREATNESS OF OUR RESURRECTION IS REALIZED IN THE NEXT LIFE, I BELIEVE THAT WE WILL THEN KNOW THAT IT WILL FAR OUTWEIGH ANY SUFFERING WE UNDERWENT IN THIS MORTAL LIFE, A LIFE THAT IS OFTEN UNFAIR AND CRUEL. WE SHALL RISE ABOVE THAT AND LEARN FROM IT AND BE BETTER PEOPLE (SOULS) FOR IT.

HOW CAN I MAKE A BAD PAST BECOME GOOD?

I am a writer. I not only write books, I write my own life, and so do you. Whoever you may be, you are a writer too. Like it or not, your life is like a book. You are the writer of it and <u>you are also the editor of it</u>.

It is the job of the editor to make corrections to the original script. This takes intelligence, discernment, vision, faith and many other things. Editing is a long process and it is often the most important process. As a writer, I am editing all the time.

To edit does not mean that you are in denial about what you first wrote. Our lives are works in progress. Over time, you should have accepted the mistakes that you found in your earlier and sloppier writing, and have, hopefully, corrected them or improved your narrative.

You have then, in a creative sense and in a self-improvement sense, 'repented' of your earlier mistakes. You are now more creative and a better writer, one who is worthy of some praise because of your improved skill.

Your creator, I assume, has forgiven you for the mistakes that you made in your life. I assume that because that is just the kind of righteous Being that He is. He asks us to forgive others, so surely, He would do the same thing Himself.

When you expressed a desire to become a better person and to become better at the often complicated task of living productively, God was on your side. That was because He knew that you were still in a learning phase. Some of us are fast learners and some of us are slower learners. God understands this and will righteously wait for you if you need more time to study it out more thoroughly.

You are not necessarily 'in denial' when you choose to ignore the past. You could actually be involved in an act of correction, or even an act of dismissal. It is legitimate to say that you have chosen to dismiss the sloppy events of the past, including your own lack of initiative, or your lack of understanding of the growth process.

At the present time though, you have chosen to accept the corrected and edited version of your life. That corrected version is the version that you now wish to present to the world. None of us are 'who we were' in the past. We are now 'who we are', or even 'who we are becoming', or even 'who we would like to be in our hearts'.

The past is irretrievably gone. The key word there is 'irretrievably'. You cannot be who you physically were, but you can <u>still</u> be, spiritually, the kind of person you once wanted to become. That is a much better path to set foot on because it is a spiritual path and a spiritual path is a permanent path.

Acceptance is a positive thing. That holds true even when you 'accept' your own 'dismissal' of the past. It is a very positive thing when you fully <u>accept</u> 'the new you'. That is a 'you' that you now deem to be much more valuable and more presentable than the 'old you'.

Why would you want to present to the world an earlier and more flawed version of yourself? You are 'now' more than what you 'were' because, hopefully, time has moved on and the <u>vital process of maturity</u> will, hopefully be in the picture now.

You can, and should, admit your earlier mistakes, but never dwell on that embarrassing unedited version of yourself. You are better than that now, since you have made your corrections, or edits, and it would be foolish of you to present to the world that earlier and sloppier version that you once presented a long time ago. Right?

When you have the approval from God, who was our creator, and who, at much sacrifice, gave us the opportunity for Eternal life, you will be much better off than you were before. On the other hand, <u>you and I, and everyone else, are basically nothing without God</u>. We are nothing but beggars in this precarious existence. We will ask, and even beg, God to fill our lives with good things and much happiness. That is because the alternative is a frightening one.

The biggest part of God's approval comes because of the intercession of God's Son who gave his life for us. His Son, who was the prophesied Messiah, stands as a mediator between the Father and us. A full account of this narrative is found in Jacob 5 in the book of Mormon. In chapter five, the author explains it fully in plain language and for many people, myself included, how the story of the redemption and the parable of the vineyard, now makes sense.

Jesus approved of us, despite our obvious faults, and explained why he advocated our forgiveness in the presence of the Father. Jesus also asked the Father to approve of us in the Biblical accounts of the crucifixion. His final words at His crucifixion contained the sentence:

> "Father, forgive them for they know not what they do".
> - Luke 23: 34)

Once we come to that realization, and we realize what a great opportunity we have been given. We should be able to see that even our suffering can be for our good in the end. Suffering will always happen in a fallen world. The important thing, though, is not that it happened, but it is how we deal with it when, and if, we can understand its significance.

If we were victims of evil in the past, or are victims or perpetrators of evil in the present, this story can allow us to come to a better understanding of what is truly good. Sometimes, coming to understand ultimate sacrifice is the only way to find that truth or knowledge that we seek for. That will allow us to actually become stronger people. As the Bible says, **'ye shall know the truth and the truth shall make you free'**. (John 8: 32)

Most of us will have some regrets in our lives and most of us will suffer in some way, be it in a large way or in a small way. This suffering will certainly be the case for anyone who seeks for righteousness, justice and knowledge in this life. They might even be persecuted for that. Suffering will usually be short lived though. Freedom and redemption, however, can last forever.

If the knowledge of truth is asked for with sincerity, we are told in scriptures that it shall be given to us. Thus, I interpret that as saying that as we receive the gift of being able to re-edit our lives on earth. We will even receive the gift of being able to re-live our lives, perhaps in a different setting, after the promised resurrection.

On our parts, there should be much gratitude shown for those gifts. That means that there should be something 'reciprocal' about it all. It should be seen as a two-sided deal in order to be to be complete. <u>Merely giving thanks to the giver of the gift seems like a small price to pay, but still, the scriptures say that it qualifies</u>. A truly grateful and humble person will be recognized as someone who is contributing to the whole process of grace through their <u>sincere gratitude</u>.

I find this idea quite amazing. Gratitude is such a small thing to ask. It shows that the Lord is not as demanding as some people make him out to be. All he asks from you is <u>gratitude</u> for the giving of the truths that he has revealed to us, and for the wisdom, love and strength that he will also give to us at the right time.

Showing gratitude is a small price to pay, but the gifts we get from it are not small. They are the most important gifts you and I will ever receive because they contain a true knowledge of the past, present and the future. Let this premise of gratitude help us to appreciate the <u>goodness</u> that can be found in our lives.

THE TWO THINGS THAT MATTER MOST IN LIFE ARE:

1. JOY.
2. PERMANENCE.

Without permanence, joy is useless. Without joy, permanence is useless. Joy is a good thing, but when joy is passing and not permanent, it will probably only set you up for disappointment at some point down the road.

Therefore, if you have joy, but are a stranger to permanence, you will have some catching up to do in your overall understanding of this sometimes complicated life. If your faith causes you to expect permanence in the life after this one, but you have no joy in your daily life, then you will have fallen behind in your understanding again, but this time in a different way. Thus, a new and important quest begins.

SO FIRSTLY, I SAY TO YOU THAT YOU MUST LEARN ABOUT PERMANENCE AND GAIN THE FAITH TO REALIZE THAT PERMANENCE THAT WAS PROMISED TO THE WORLD THROUGH THE SCRIPTURES, APPLIES SPECIFICALLY TO YOU.

THUS, IT BECOMES OBVIOUS AND PROBABLY EVEN NECESSARY, THAT YOU GET CONNECTED TO A HIGHER BEING WHO KNOWS WHAT IT WILL TAKE FOR A MERE TEMPORAL MORTAL BEING TO INHERIT AN ETERNAL STATE OF PERMANENCE.

ONE OBVIOUS THING ABOUT THAT IS THAT IT WOULD BE FOOLISH TO EVEN WANT TO BE ENSHRINED INTO A PERMANENT STATE IF YOU CARRY INTO THAT STATE BAD MEMORIES OF A SINFUL OR SELFISH PAST. SUCH BAD MEMORIES FROM THOSE PAST ERAS WILL NEVER SERVE YOU WELL IN THE PRESENT OR FUTURE, NOT EVEN IF YOU SHOULD, FOR WHATEVER REASON, MANAGE TO MAKE IT INTO SOME LEVEL OF HEAVEN. THAT IS ONE REASON WHY THE BIBLE TEACHES US THE ABSOLUTE IMPORTANCE OF FORGIVENESS.

SECONDLY, YOU MUST LEARN HOW TO CREATE JOY, OR GENERATE FEELINGS OF JOY BOTH IN YOURSELF AND IN OTHERS. THEN, AFTER YOU HAVE A GOOD IDEA ABOUT HOW TO DO THAT, YOU MUST IMBED THAT KNOWLEDGE INTO YOUR CHARACTER, SO THAT YOU CAN BRING IT FORWARD ANYTIME YOU WHAT TO.

THUS, JOY WILL COME TO YOU THROUGH THREE MAIN THINGS – WISDOM, LOVE AND GRATITUDE. PERMANENCE ALSO COMES THROUGH THREE THINGS – ONE IS TAKING THE <u>INITIATIVE</u> TO BECOME HAPPY. TWO IS TO <u>MAINTAIN</u> THAT HAPPINESS THROUGH PERSEVERENCE, AND THREE, YOU SHOULD CONSCIOUSLY <u>LOVE AND BE THANKFUL FOR THAT WONDERFUL, AND PARTLY SELF-GENERATED STATE OF HAPPINESS THAT YOU HAVE DISCOVERED.</u>

MAKE A CONNECTION WITH A HIGHER BEING WHO IS PERMANENT, AND AS WELL, ONE WHO HAS PROVEN TO BE HOPEFUL, JOYFUL, RIGHTEOUS, PURE, INDESTRUCTIBLE, HUMBLE AND LOVING.

Chapter 14

AN OLD FRIEND (16P.)

Subtitles: The Balm of Gilead

I spent many years teaching music in elementary schools and in particular teaching kids how to write songs. One of the favorite topics to write about was 'friends'. The general consensus among my students was that friends are very good things to have. it is important for young people to keep in mind though to never compromise your morality for the sake of making friends. If you kids don't know what 'compromising your morality' means you can ask one of your parents later.

I was pondering in a sacrament meeting recently about friends and in particular, old friends. It seems that old friends can either be special, or they can be taken for granted. We can take them for granted because they have always been there, or else we can treasure them for that same reason – that they have always been there.

Today I choose to treasure old friends, especially an old friend whose name is Jesus Christ. Personally, I picture Jesus as an 'old friend'. After all he did say to his disciples in The Doctrine & Covenants book:

"I will call you friends, for you are my friends."
- Doctrine and Covenants 93: 45

I always take Jesus at his word.

I have been a member of the Church of Jesus Christ of Latter Day Saints for thirty-two years now and Jesus has guided me through some difficult situations, mainly because of His wisdom and because of His beautiful nature. He is still with me today and I am thankful that he is still my friend even though I am sorry to say that, because of my imperfections, I did not always paid strict heed to his counsel.

I treasure Jesus especially on the Sabbath day, which is a day that has been set-aside specifically for people like me so that I can rest and contemplate my blessings, including the blessings of His friendship.

I will treasure his friendship as I go to my church classes today and learn of him. I will treasure his friendship as I walk down the halls in my church building. I will treasure his friendship as I walk across the parking lot later to my car, and also as I get into my car and drive home. I will treasure his friendship when I arrive home and lie down for my afternoon nap, as we older people like to do. I will treasure his friendship tomorrow when I go out into the work-a-day world, and as I try to be kind to his other spiritual offspring, who I will meet as I go about my business.

When I was in my youth I intuitively thought that the idea of Jesus as the Son of God made some sense, but because Jesus could not be seen, I did not really understand the magnitude of our friendship. Nevertheless, i made a vague commitment that I would allow him to tag along with me as I went through my life.

As I grew older though, I began to understand that it was really me who needed to ask Him if I could tag

along with Him in his life, instead of Him tagging along with me.

That is because his life is an eternal life and it is mostly spent in the presence of the Father, who is absolute purity. Having faith in the things that go on in my mortal life outside of God is, as it says in the book of Ecclesiastics, <u>vanity</u>.

So eventually, I became committed to learning about Jesus and I asked him to let me tag along with Him whenever that was possible

"come and follow me." - Luke 18:22

As I learned of Him, I came to understand that the rewards that I would receive for following Him would be greater than anything else in my life. In my life I know that there are times when I feel strong and times when I do not feel so strong. When I need to feel more strength than I usually feel, I know that I can borrow personal strength from Him even just by simply being associated with Him.

I also receive strength by the encouragement of righteous friends. That is why I seek friends who are of good character. Such friends can be like a cool drink of water in a desert. Even when they are not with me, the good memories of those friends can still have a good influence on me.

The strength of Jesus Christ is the ultimate strength. He proved that in the garden of Gethsemane, where he was tormented and faced destruction. Consequently, He bled 'great drops of blood from every pore'. His great strength was there, and a short time later, it was also there when he was nailed to the cross and left to die. Those times were when he had the strength to take

upon himself the sins of every person in the whole world.

After he made that painful atonement in gethsemane and in the cross, which was the ultimate sacrifice one might ask anyone to make, was he rewarded for his sacrifice for the sake of mankind?

NO. HE WAS BEATEN, MOCKED, TORTURED AND MURDERED ON THE CROSS. STILL, BEFORE HE DIED, HE HAD THE INNER STRENGTH TO ASK THE FATHER TO FORGIVE THE PEOPLE WHO KILLED HIM.

That kind of strength is quite unfathomable to most of us, if not all of us. Could I, personally, ever do something like that? I have my doubts. I fear that I just do not have it in me. It is certain though that Jesus does have it in Him.

Thus, he really is my greatest example. I have learned of him though and I know that his desire to have me as a friend is an honest and heart-felt <u>invitation</u>. I will not hesitate to ask him to lend me some of his strength when I need some, as well as to borrow some of his wisdom through the influence of the Holy Ghost. I am gratefulnthat He gives that to me and I also think that He is grateful that Ishould ask Him for it.

If I use that strength for His purposes, then He will actually <u>give</u> some of that strength and wisdom to me to use, even if He is not physically there. I don't know how he does it, but I can attest that He does it. That is why I treasure His friendship every day, and especially on the Sabbath when we are asked to remember our old friend and even to take His name upon us.

THE RATIONAL GOSPEL

JESUS IS MORE THAN MY FRIEND HOWEVER. IN FACT, HE IS MY REDEEMER. HE IS MY REDEEMER BECAUSE, AS HE IS MY GOD, HE HAS THE POWER TO FORGIVE ME FROM EVERY MISTAKE THAT I EVER MADE IN MY LIFE. HE IS ALSO THE ONLY ONE WHO CAN GIVE ME COMFORT WHEN I AM IN MY DARKEST HOURS, EVEN IF I SHOULD ENTER INTO THE VALLEY OF THE SHADOW OF DEATH. (PSALMS 23)

I KNOW THIS NOT ONLY BECAUSE I READ IT IN THE SCRIPTURES OR BECAUSE I HEARD A PROPHET SAY IT. I KNOW IT FROM MY PERSONAL EXPERIENCE. IT IS A PART OF MY TESTIMONY.

THE GREAT ATONEMENT WAS THE MOST IMPORTANT EVENT TO EVER HAPPEN IN THE HISTORY OF THE WORLD. IT IS ABOVE ALL ELSE IN IMPORTANCE, NO MATTER WHAT RELIGION YOU ARE OR WHAT YOUR PERSONAL SITUATION MAY BE, THE ATONEMENT WILL FILL YOUR LIFE IN THE PRESENT WITH GOODNESS AND WILL DO SO IN THE FUTURE. HE WILL ALSO DISPLACE ANY BAD MEMORIES THAT CAN HAUNT YOU.

NO MATTER WHAT YOU ACCOMPLISH IN LIFE IN BUSINESS OR ACADEMICALLY, OR PROFESSIONALLY OR ROMANTICALLY OR SOCIALLY, THOSE THINGS WILL BE WORTH ABSOLUTELY NOTHING IF A PERSON DOES NOT ACKNOWLEDGE THAT ATONING SACRIFICE THAT WAS MADE TWO THOUSAND YEARS AGO.

THE BALM OF GILEAD

Historically, the Balm of Gilead is made from a spice mentioned in the Old Testament. It was an ointment and a healing balm that was known as a 'universal cure.' The balm soon became synonymous with the gospel of Jesus Christ, which is the real universal cure.

There was a talk given in 1987 by one of our apostles named Boyd K. Packer in which he said:

"There is a balm in Gilead,
To make the wounded whole,
There is a balm in Gilead,
To heal the sin sick soul."

He also said, "if the burden is guilt, then repentance is the balm of Gilead. Some, however, seek to cure guilt with self-justification, a quack medicine which only covers the symptoms; it will never cure the cause. Self-justification leads one to blame another for his mistakes."

The balm is also referred to in one of our hymns,

"Ere you left your room this morning,
Did you think to pray? …
When your soul was full of sorrow,
Balm of Gilead did you borrow
At the gates of day?
Oh, how praying rests the weary!
Prayer will change the night to day.
So, when life gets dark and dreary,
Don't forget to pray"

Prayer is a necessary part of the balm, but I think there is more to it than that. To pray effectively we should have some knowledge of who we are praying to. I have a scripture here that backs that up.

> *"According as his divine power hath given unto us all things that pertain unto life and Godliness, through the knowledge of him that hath called us to glory and virtue."*   *- 2 Peter 1:3*

According to this quote, a major part of the Balm of Gilead is to gain knowledge about why Jesus told us to 'learn of him'. As we learn of Him we will learn about the things He did.

The main thing that he did was to perform the great atonement by laying down his life so that we might become clean through him and be able to live once again in the presence of the Father.

The church is often the main place where we learn of him and receive the balm. It is the place where we pray together and where we can receive sacred ordinances that will be of great aid to us because it helps us to further connect with Him.

How do we receive a solid understanding of the Atonement? it says in the Bible in in the Book of Isaiah that we need to offer up 'a broken heart and a contrite spirit'. A broken heart can be a dreadful thing. It can even kill a person. But by the same token we can sometimes learn valuable information about life itself, information that we can learn by no other way.

So it might seem that, perhaps a broken heart may not necessarily be a bad thing. Why? Because a broken heart can be the currency by which we are allowed to participate in sacred things, like the 'healing of our souls'.

We all have bloodlines that, at times, can hold our families together, and it is good that families should be together, but we also have spiritual lines. The Spiritual lines are the most important things because those lines are eternal in nature.

Bloodlines are not as important as spiritual lines. In the end, bloodlines don't really matter because when you die your body will be taken to the morgue and your blood will be drained from your body and then washed down the sewer. That might sound ugly, but it is the truth. Your Spiritual lines, however, will last forever. That is why we need to strengthen those spiritual lines in this life.

Fortunately, we do not need to fully experience a broken heart ourselves. That is because if we are connected with Jesus then we will be able to feel a part of the intense sorrow that Jesus had, even in a vicarious way. He has been through all that. He has taken our place when He allowed himself to be lifted up on the cross.

That understanding of the Atonement, combined with the faith that comes with prayer, has a healing spirit about it that has seen me, personally, survive through much trouble and disappointment. it can do the same for you if you wish to use it as it was meant to be used.

Because the Atonement came as a result of God's love for us, that means that love is an active ingredient in the Balm of Gilead. Coming to know Jesus is coming to know love. Thus, that is also when we will come to know what a true friend is.

The world is not really our friend. All of the people in the world are not our friends. It seems like it is a righteous thing to say that we want to be friends to the world, but it is not wise. It says in the book of James:

> *"Know ye not that friendship of the world is enmity with God? Whosoever therefore, will be a friend of the world is the enemy of God."*
> *- James 4: 4*

The Atonement of Christ was the ultimate act of love. It can comfort you and give you strength in various ways. From my experience, real love is the only thing that can do that. It forms a kind of invisible cocoon around you that protects you from evil thoughts and feelings of despair or of hopelessness.

> *"A testimony of the gospel of Jesus Christ is a 'pearl of great price' and if a person knew the worth of it they would sell everything they own in order to own one."*
> *- Matthew 13: 46*

We are not born with a strong testimony. None of us are. We will need to earn it and we earn it by studying it and with gaining confidence and trust in it as we study it. We also get 'true learning' by exercising self-control and by 'experimenting on the word'. It is also a matter of 'eternal vigilance', to use Thomas Jefferson's words.

The gospel of Jesus Christ is about freedom, or as it says in the book of James, it is 'the law of perfect liberty'.

> *"But whoso looketh into 'the perfect law of liberty', and continueth therein, he being not a forgetful hearer, but a doer of the work, this man shall be blessed in his deed."*
> *- James 1:25*

In short, once you study what you need to learn, your choices will be narrowed down to two options. You must either follow satan's ways or you try to do God's will. Again, you alone will be held responsible for whatever decision you make. It is not God who will be held responsible for your decision and it is not the devil. It is you alone.

> *"and he said unto me: Behold, there are two churches only; the one is the church of the Lamb of God, and the other is the church of the devil."*
> *- 1 Nephi 14: 10*

Nowadays it seems that there is a lot of anti-Christian talk in the media. Atheist groups, the ACLU, entertainers and Hollywood personalities are out to get publicity for themselves. Other organizations or individuals will either mock religion or over exaggerate the harm that has come from it throughout history. Yes, some people seek to promote the good word of Christ, but others who are troublemakers and apostates prefer to tarnish His reputation and promote a negative perception of Christ. For some odd reason, they see that as being a benefit for themselves. For such people, complete skepticism is a virtue.

Many of the things that these critics say about Christianity may be partly true, but those are only half-truths used for purposes of deception. The history of any religion is not perfect, but to me, their arguments against Christianity always fall apart when it comes down to two basic and pivotal points that are at the center of the church. Those two central points are:

1. THE ATONEMENT OF JESUS CHRIST (ALSO KNOWN AS 'THE REDEMPTION)

2. THE ENSUING RESURRECTION THAT WILL HAPPEN FOR EVERYONE WHO FULLY ACCEPTS IT.

WHEN CRITICS OF CHRISTIANITY ATTACK THOSE TWO EVENTS, THEY WILL BE LEFT WITHOUT ANY SOLID GROUND TO STAND ON. THE ATONEMENT IS SACRIFICIAL ACT THAT WAS PROPHESIED TO HAPPEN FROM THE BEGINNING, AND IT HAS GREAT POWER ATTACHED TO IT. THAT POWER IS THAT IT CAN, POTENTIALLY, GIVE US ETERNAL LIFE IN THE PROTECTIVE PRESENCE OF OUR HEAVENLY FATHER.

THE PRINCIPLE OF THE ATONEMENT OR (*AT-ONE-MENT*) IS AT THE VERY CORE OF OUR HUMAN EXISTENCE. FOR BOTH CHRISTIAN AND NON-CHRISTIAN ALIKE, IT IS THE ONLY WAY TO RETURN TO THE PRESENCE OF GOD FROM OUR VARIOUS PLACES IN THIS FALLEN WORLD. AND YET, MILLIONS OF PEOPLE IGNORE IT.

WITHOUT THE SACRED ATONEMENT AND THE PROMISED RESURRECTION, THE CRITICS WOULD HAVE A POINT. THE RITUALS AND ORDINANCES OF ANY CHURCH WOULD BE BASICALLY IRRELEVANT IF THAT ULTIMATE SACRIFICE DID NOT HAPPEN.

BUT THERE WAS A GREAT SACRIFICE MADE THAT DID HAPPEN AND IT HAPPENED BY THE WORD OF GOD AND THROUGH THE SACRIFICE OF HIS SON.

IT IS THE GREATEST BLESSING TO ALL MEN AND WOMEN THAT THEY WERE INVITED TO BE A PART OF AN ETERNAL KINGDOM AND PART OF A SPIRITUAL FAMILY WHERE PEOPLE ARE REUNITED FOREVER WITHOUT ANY DISHONESTY OR GUILE OR PHYSICAL FLAWS?

THAT ATONEMENT WAS PROPHESIED FROM THE BEGINNING, NOT ONLY IN SCRIPTURE, BUT THROUGH THE SYMBOLIC RITUALS OF THE JEWS WHEN THEY REGULARLY SACRIFICED THE FINEST LAMB FROM THEIR FLOCKS ON AN ALTER AS A SYMBOLIC GESTURE OF WHAT WAS TO COME.

The great atonement happened in the Garden of Gethsemane two thousand years ago and on a cross at Calvary hill outside Jerusalem. That was when the only sinless person who ever lived did what no other person could do and took upon himself the transgressions of all mankind and in so doing, was forced to bear unfathomable and excruciating pain that caused him to tremble and to bleed great drops of blood from every pore.

> *"And his sweat was as it were great drops of blood falling to the ground'. - Luke 22: 44*

THE LONG TERM REWARDS CAME LATER FOR JESUS. HE HAD CONQUERED DEATH AND WAS GLORIFIED BY THE ANGELS FOR IT. HE ALSO MADE IT POSSIBLE FOR ALL MORTAL MEN AND WOMEN WHO HAD MADE COVENANTS WITH HIM TO DO THE SAME.

NOW HE SITS AT THE RIGHT HAND OF GOD AND INVITES ALL PEOPLE WHO WANT TO PARTAKE OF HIS TRIUMPH TO DO SO AND LIVE ALONGSIDE HIM IN AN ETERNAL STATE OF PEACE. HE DOES THAT BECAUSE HE LOVES US WITH A LOVE THAT IS TRUE, AND EVEN, PERHAPS IN SOME WAYS, A LOVE THAT COULD BE BEYOND OUR UNDERSTANDING.

THUS, BECAUSE OF THE PRINCIPLES OF THE ATONEMENT AND OF THE RESURRECTION OF JESUS CHRIST FROM THE DEAD, RITUALS LIKE PARTAKING OF THE BREAD AND WATER, WHICH IS DEEMED SILLY BY SOME PEOPLE, SUDDENLY, BECOME ULTIMATE ORDINANCES THAT ARE OF GOD AND ARE UNDERSTANDABLE AND CRITICAL TO THE HAPPINESS OF ALL MEN AND WOMEN.

LET ME OFFER UP SOME OTHER THINGS THAT I THINK A KNOWLEDGE OF THE ATONEMENT CAN DO.

ON GAINING A KNOWLEDGE OF THE ATONEMENT SAD PEOPLE CAN BECOME HAPPY PEOPLE. ON GAINING A KNOWLEDGE OF THE ATONEMENT, BAD PEOPLE CAN BECOME GOOD PEOPLE. THESE THINGS CAN HAPPEN SLOWLY OR THEY CAN HAPPEN IN AN INSTANT.

ALSO, PRIDEFUL PEOPLE CAN ACTUALLY BECOME HUMBLE PEOPLE. HUMBLE PEOPLE WHOSE LIVES MAY BE SEEN AS TRIVIAL OR MEANINGLESS, CAN BECOME GLORIFIED ETERNAL BEINGS.

I AM LITERALLY TALKING ABOUT MIRACLES HERE. MIRACLES HAPPEN. THEY HAPPEN EVERY DAY. THE GREATEST MIRACLE OF ALL TO ME IS TO SEE SOMETHING BAD CHANGE INTO SOMETHING GOOD.

BY THE POWER OF THE ATONEMENT, COVENANTS THAT ONCE MIGHT HAVE BEEN CONSTRUED BY SOME PEOPLE TO BE MEANINGLESS WORDS, SUDDENLY BECOME LIFE-GIVING UTTERANCES AND SUPPLY US WITH ENERGY THAT QUICKENS OUR SPIRITS AND CONNECTS US TO OUR ALMIGHTY GOD, EVEN IN AN INSTANT.

BECAUSE OF THE ATONEMENT OF JESUS CHRIST, WIDE EYED YOUNG MISSIONARIES, FRESH OUT OF HIGH SCHOOL, ONCE THEY HAVE BEEN TRAINED AND SET APART, BECOME <u>MESSENGERS FROM GOD</u>, EVEN IN AN INSTANT.

BECAUSE OF THE ATONEMENT OF JESUS CHRIST, LONG FORGOTTEN ANCESTORS WHO ARE NOW DUSTY CARCASSES, OR A SPECK OF DNA IN SOME FORGOTTEN PLACE BECOME QUICKENED SPIRITS PEERING INTO THE PRESENT TIME FROM THEIR ANCIENT PERCHES TRYING TO CATCH A GLIMPSE OF HOW THEIR PROGENY ARE FARING AND TO INQUIRE AS TO WHEN THEIR REDEEMING ORDINANCES MIGHT BE PERFORMED FOR THEM SOON IN A HOLY TEMPLE.

ALL OF THESE CHANGES HAPPEN BECAUSE OF THAT EVENT THAT IS CALLED THE ATONEMENT. A SUNDAY SCHOOL TEACHER ONCE TOLD ME THAT THE WORD 'ATONEMENT' OF JESUS CHRIST APPEARS ONCE IN THE BIBLE. IN THE BOOK OF MORMON THE WORD APPEARS 55 TIMES. THAT WAS SOMETHING THAT INCREASED MY PERSONAL TESTIMONY OF THE TRUTH OF THE BOOK OF MORMON.

ATTEMPTS BY CRITICS TO ATTACK THE IDEA OF THE ATONEMENT WILL ALWAYS BE FEEBLE ATTEMPTS. I SUSPECT SUCH CRITICS MIGHT EVEN SUFFER THE SAME INEVITABLE CONSEQUENCES OF ANGUISH AND GUILT THAT THE ORIGINAL CRUCIFIERS SUFFERED.

In short, it doesn't really matter how much money a person makes. nor does it matter how many friends a person has. nor does it matter how often they get their picture in the newspaper or on facebook. and it doesn't really matter who will win the super bowl this year, etc.

At the end of the day, these two things, the redeeming Atonement of the Son of God and the resurrection of all mankind, are the two things that really matter to us in time and space. We should always keep this in mind.

i am speaking here about the need for a sound and rational religion, one that presents a true story about ultimate love.

Thus, we have got to bear each other's burdens and watch each other's backs. We also need to be unafraid to celebrate together the great gift of this gospel that we have all been given.

This was the blessing that 'my old friend' gave to me. this is also the same blessing that your old friend can give to you. Even though you two may have never officially met, when you come to the point where you feel you can trust Him, He has the power to extend his influence over to you.

When his glory is combined with your trust in him, miracles can happen and it so happens that our God is a God of Miracles.

CHAPTER 15

IT'S ALL ABOUT OBSESSIONS (22p.)

(SUBTITLES: Negative issues and faulty perceptions, Self-censorship; Swatting Mosquitoes and God's Job; Repentance is a Gift; Sex and Obsessions; Transgenderism; Saddle Soap?; What Have WE Learned?)

NEGATIVE ISSUES

Familiarity, it has been said, breeds contempt. That may, or may not, be true, but I think in some cases, that it just might be true. When we get too familiar with some things we might find out, regrettably, that it could end up being an uncomfortable situation and it might be difficult for a person to get away from that situation, especially when they develop a fascination for that negative thing, or that negative person, or that negative ideal.

That is a negative issue and a person who dwells on negative issues is treading on some dangerous ground. That dangerous ground might be called an addiction but in my opinion in can resemble something even worse. It can resemble something called an OBSESSION, which is something that allows giving certain pre-occupations total control in a person's mind and thus, total control of their attitude or behavior.

An addiction can cause a person to succumb to the powerful notion that certain issues have the ability to set the general direction of someone's life, but an obsession has the power to actually take complete control over a person's life. It is difficult to dissuade someone to give up that notion because it may have become an extreme passion. It is powerful because that is based upon human pride, or in other words, the human ego.

To some people their ego is what drives them to do what they do and to think what they think. It has nothing to do with reason or rationality or common sense. The driving force is ego and anyone who argues with an obsessive person will be automatically dismissed as a person with mental problems. People with obsessions are also <u>accusers</u> towards anyone who thinks differently. By the way 'the accuser' is one the names that Satan is referred to in Revelations 12: 10. That is the way that such people think.

People who are obsessive are always adamant about their faulty opinions, whether they are misinformed or uninformed. The first priority of such people is to always put their very precious ego at the helm of their ship. That ego, they have decided, can never be wrong.

Anyone who disagrees with someone who has an obsession will just have to deal with them. That is because they fully believe that they are correct in their opinions. They see themselves as unassailable, and as a result of that they see themselves as 'PERENNIAL VICTIMS' and they never look at any of the contexts that influence their perceptions of an issue, and as well, never look at the contexts in which they should see THEMSELVES, and see the egocentricity of their driving influences.

Why that happens I don't generally know, but is a 'new reality'. Ironically, that new reality is based upon an 'old and false reality'. Does that even matter to a person with

THE RATIONAL GOSPEL

the obsessive personality? No it doesn't. That just seems to be the nature of the beast.

That doesn't happen casually. It is something that has fermented over time and results in the person who has the obsessive attitudes becoming totally devoted to their faulty opinions and to their perennial victimhood. To describe the reasoning of people who have obsessive attitudes would be very complicated. It would also take a long time to explain, more time than I have to spend on it today, or this year.

Basically I think it happens exclusively for the reason that 'faulty perceptions are mainly the cause of obsessive behavior. I am talking about a person who could have a faulty perception of reality, a faulty perception of right and wrong, a faulty perception of decency, a faulty sense of empathy, a faulty sense of sin, a faulty sense of privilege, and on and on and on. All of these factors will combine to bring about much disharmony and even self-destruction.

Self destruction happens when an ideal that is based upon fantasy and self-aggrandizement becomes a person's ultimate authority and the people who hold those attitudes will defend themselves from their perceived enemies at all costs, although the person who has the obsession is usually too comatose or too drunk to figure out what is actually happening to them. Incidentally, from my observations, alcohol could be the main fuel that a person uses to ignite his, or her, obsession.

Thus, perhaps it might be more better and easier to discuss a few of the ISSUES that obsessive people will

argue about and certain prideful attitudes that will, in the end, lead to some kind of self-destruction

An obsessional attitude is a trap that a person can fall into because it might stem from hostilities that have been brewing for a very long time. That trap, or the desire to get away from that trap, could lead to lead to a serious obsession, or even a more fervent desire for a person to prove themselves to be totally, without error.

On the other hand, when we take on an attitude of humility, we can bypass that trap. That is because we can bypass the notion that we feel inadequate because we are humble and we know that we are really not that wise, or maybe even in some cases, not really that smart.

Some traps that can be confusing and can <u>entangle a person's mind</u>. A trap can even cause a person to question an established value system. Also, it can make a person try **desperately** to escape from their negative obsession. Thus, they let it become a habitual worry in their mind. That can make a person try 'desperately' to escape from it. **DESPERATION** is a sign that a person is not in control of their life. Thus, It is probably a good thing for that person to work at gaining control back, whatever that takes.

SELF CENSORSHIP

Many young people do not know <u>how</u> to self- censor their viewing habits , or know <u>when</u> to self-censor them. Perhaps they will learn in time how and when to do that. But perhaps they will not learn that. Theoretically, that is why those particular people need smart and caring adults to watch over them.

Are smart adults easy to find? Not necessarily, but I do believe that there are many smart adults out there. Young people will need to use their powers of discernment and seek them out. And they should be taught how and when to use that power. Everyone is the captain of their own soul and souls are what we are dealing with here. Healing is needed when sick people are trying to manage pain or discomfort. We have to be able to suppress that pain and we do that by "pounding our bad inclinations into submission", as my old friend Hobby Hobson would say.

To prevail over the sorry state that a trap can bring into a person's mind we will need superior weaponry. I am talking about superior 'spiritual weaponry'. That means that we will need to summon our faith, be confident, be smart, and pray for the comfort that only the Comforter, or the Holy Ghost, can provide. In my books, I often suggest spiritual solutions to people's problems. In the matter of becoming obsessed with some bad issues, my advise would be no different.

NEGATIVE ISSUES, SWATTING MOSQUITOS, AND GOD'S JOB

A negative issue can slowly, but constantly gnaw away at a person, and that is where the pain, or the itch, comes from and we definitely need to try to correct that. You may need to continuously swat it away like you would a mosquito. Thus, you must put yourself into a 'swatting mode'.

What is the best way to do that? First of all, you need to know that you do not need to fear that. You may not be a mighty person, but I am confident that you are mightier than a mosquito. Thus, exercise your mastery over the mosquitos and other pests in the world. Coming across a swarm of mosquitoes is like coming across a thousand tiny and winged Justin Trudeaus floating through the air buzzing around and looking for a place that they can stick their noses into, so that they can suck your blood out of you, even on a constant basis. .

Look at it this way. Mosquitos are pests. They do no good in the world. It actually feels good to see their crumpled up brainless bodies lying lifeless on your skin. Then you can know that you are actually making the world a better place for all humans.

SET YOUR MIND ON HIGHER PRINCIPLES AND WELCOME THOSE HIGHER PRINCIPLES INTO YOUR WORLD. HIGHER PRINCIPLES COME FROM TRUTH AND THAT MEANS THEY COME FROM GOD. GIVEN THAT YOU SHOULD ALSO KNOW, BY DEFINITION, THAT GOD CAN HEAL. THAT IS GOD'S MAIN JOB ACCORDING TO THE PROMISE THAT HE MADE WHEN HE SAID THAT HE WOULD ALWAYS BE WITH US. HAVING NEGATIVE OBSESSIONS IS ONE THING THAT GOD CAN ACTUALLY HELP US OVERCOME, MAINLY BY TEACHING US CORRECT PERCEPTIONS RATHER THAN FAULTY PERCEPTIONS.

THE SECOND PART OF GOD'S JOB IS TO KNOW WHEN THE TIME IS RIGHT FOR A PERSON TO BEGIN TO HEAL. A PERSION SHOULD BE AWARE WHEN IT IS TIME FOR THEM TO HEAL THEY WILL NEED TO PREPARE FOR THAT. THAT IS BECAUSE THEY

SHOULD ALSO KNOW THAT THEY WILL BE COMPLICIT IN THE HEALING PROCESS AS I WILL EXPLAIN.

A person can prepare for healing by studying the holy Scriptures. That is because the scriptures try to encapsulate wisdom and explain to everyone why ultimate truth is important for all people to learn. It is also important for helping ordinary people to realize who they are and what he, or she, is capable of doing.

THEN THOSE PEOPLE WHO NEED HEALING AND FREEDOM FROM OBSESSIONS CAN TAKE THAT DIVINE COUNSEL TO HEART AND THEN THEY CAN SEND OUT RIGHTEOUS SIGNALS TO EVERYONE TO LET THEM KNOW THAT THEY ARE READY TO BE HEALED.

THE THIRD PART OF GOD'S JOB IS TO ASSIST THE PERSON BEING HEALED TO ARTICULATE HIS, OR HER, FEELINGS IN THE BEST POSSIBLE WAY. ENCOURAGE PEOPLE TO WRITE DOWN THE IMPORTANT THINGS IN THEIR LIVES AND HOW THEY SHOULD DEAL WITH THEM. THAT IS HOW A LEGACY IS CREATED.

THAT IS A VERY HEALTHY PRACTICE. IT MIGHT SOUND TOO SIMPLE, BUT IF YOU WANT TO MAKE A DIFFERENCE IN THE STATE OF THE WORLD, THE FIST THING YOU WILL NEED TO DO IS TO LEAVE A POSITIVE WRITTEN LEGACY BEHIND TO LET PEOPLE KNOW ABOUT YOUR OWN LIFE AND WHAT YOU THOUGHT ABOUT YOUR MORTAL EXPERIENCE, BOTH GOOD AND BAD THINGS. IT IS VERY THERAPUETIC FOR THE PERSON THEMSELVES TO THINK AND WRITE ABOUT HEALING MATTERS AND WRITE THEM WITH

CLARITY SO THAT EVERYONE CAN UNDERSAND THEMTHAT COMES WHEN YOU COME TO AN HONEST CONCLUSION ABOUT THE SOURCE OF YOUR PROBLEMS.

The best expression of our inner feelings needs to come when we forsake non-effective tools and use simple tools. <u>Those simple tools would include things like feelings of joy and love.</u> Again, if you are trying to help someone change remember that sometimes people need more than good advice. In other words, <u>people won't care how much you know until they know how much you care.</u>

Again, having strong core values and having trustworthy people around you is the best way to maintain your resilience. Also, we should remember that Satan is evil, but he is not stupid. He has been dealing with people like you and me for centuries and he has been successful in the past at 'pulling the wool' over many people's eyes. He knows all the tricks. Thus, you must be 'wise as a serpent'

> ***"Therefore, be ye as wise as serpents and yet without sin; and I will order all things for your good, as fast as ye are able to receive them."***
> ***- Doctrine and Covenants: 111:11***

I was quite a dreamer in my younger days and I did not realize the value of the strength that would be available to me when I had a 'rock solid value system' that held up a red flag whenever the presence of sin was very near. Thankfully, I think that I have now, years later, come to see the wisdom in that principle.

In my youth, I did not consider the possibility that it might be a time in my life when the devil's chickens were coming home to roost. Most chickens 'cluck' when they roost, but the devil's chickens don't cluck. They are very, very quiet. You will probably not even notice they are around when they come home and roost.

There were many times when, before I could 'come to myself' and use the good sense that was a part of my higher self. I admit that I indulged in certain traps and they subtly turned my head around and encouraged me with silent promises of sensual gratification. Those traps turned out to be harmful to me because they put me off of the worthy and well-meaning course that I had mapped out for my life many years ago.

I came to learn that it was possible for sin to put on a disguise and quietly enter in to my life. Many red flags were on the scene, but there was just too many other distractions for those red flags to grab my attention. Thus, I came to know that it was possible for me to pay a very dear price for allowing myself to get involved in any temptations and especially, to get involved with any obsessions.

So, these days, I am resolved to stay away from those lower things. That is something that I think may be the best thing for me, no matter how appealing they might be to my lower self.

Because there is much joy and happiness and kindness in life and all people need to focus on those things if they want to get the most out of their lives. Look for signs that show that those good things exist. Look for beauty in a sunrise and look for the leaves dancing on the trees on a cool spring day. Look for anything that

has some life to it. Look for the decency in all people and value it when you see it.

REPENTACE IS A GIFT

Sometimes things on life can get complicated. Complications are not things that a person should fool around with. Obsessions might seem like simple, strait forward answers on the surface, but below the surface they are often very complicated, so complicated that we will not even want to deal with them. That is when **the attitude of 'denial'** can set in. Certainty though, if you look for solutions for your anguish or your anxiety and you think intensely about it, a desire for 'self-correction', will hopefully and by the grace of God will come into the picture. That self-correction is also called **'repentance'**.

Repentance is not a trial or an ordeal. It is a gift. And it is a great gift. It will always bring forth good results. That is because when you are dealing with self-correction, you are dealing with repentance. Repentance is one of the main principles behind God's beautiful gospel, as it says in this verse from the Book of Mormon:

> *"O that I were an angel, and could have the wish of mine heart, that I might go forth and speak with the trump of God, with a voice to shake the earth, and cry repentance to every people!"*   *- Alma 29:1*

That is an endorsement that is definitely worth seriously thinking about. It has a lot to do with being certain about something that was once problematic, and then

organizing your affairs so that certainty, or truth, will be uppermost in your mind.

From my experiences, certainty, or truth, can bring peace and freedom like nothing else can. How will you know when you gave been given the truth? There is only one answer too that. You must ask for it and inquire about the details of it. If you should come upon principles of truth, you must follow up on it, and love it with all of your heart, might, mind, and strength. Does that sound familiar to you?

SEX AND OBSESSIONS

Did a person who you highly respected ever tell you that it is <u>not</u> a good thing to have unnatural sex with another person? Someone who I greatly respected once said something like that to me and I have not forgotten it.

In today's world a large part of the average citizen's unpleasant work consists of dealing with other people's aberrant behavior, or obsessive behavior, or criminal behavior, or in some cases, dealing with our own aberrant behavior.

At some point in their lives, most young adults have some desire to explore the world. That includes the world of sexual relationships.

A PERSON WHO IS WITHOUT A STRONG MORAL VALUES CAN BECOME ADDICTED TO SEX OF ANY

KIND, BE IT AN ADDICTION TO HETEROSEXUAL SEX, OR HOMOSEXUAL SEX, OR TRANS-GENDER SEX, OR AUTO - EROTICISM, OR ANY NUMBER OF DIFFERENT KINDS OF SEX.

HAVING A STRONG MORAL VALUE SYSTEM IS REALLY THE ONLY DETERRENT I KNOW OF FOR THINGS THAT CAN BRING A PERSON TO RESIST ANY WICKED TEMPTATIONS.

THAT IS SOMETHING THAT I THINK EVERYONE SHOULD HEAR AT LEAST ONCE IN HIS, OR HER, LIFE. CONTINUING TO CRAVE RANDOM SEX OR ANY ADDICTIVE HABIT ALWAYS COMES DOWN TO THE SAME THING. <u>IT COULD EASILY SOON BECOME AN OBSESSION.</u>

WHEN CRAVINGS BECOME TOO STRONG FOR THE PERSON TO CONTROL THEY BECOME OBSESSIONS. THE HORMONES THAT YOU ACTIVATE IN YOUR BRAIN, INCLUDING ADRENALIN, WILL BE THE THINGS CAN THEN ACTUALLY DRIVE YOUR LIFE IN A WICKED DIRECTION IF YOU SHOULD BECOME OBSESSED BY THEM. THAT IS, IF YOU ARE THE KIND OF PERSON WHO FINDS NOTHING WRONG WITH CRAVING CARNAL WAYS OF THINKING AND BEHAVING.

HENCE, IF THAT IS THE WAY YOU ARE, THEN REALIZE THAT IT IS TIME FOR A CHANGE, NOT ONLY FOR YOURSELF, BUT, IDEALLY, FOR ANYBODY WHO IS IN YOUR CIRCLE OF INFLUENCE.

HOW CAN YOU TRY TO MAKE A PLAN THAT WILL SHOW YOUR SON OR DAUGHTER HOW TO LEAD A SENSIBLE AND RIGHTEOUS LIFE? FIRSTLY, YOU

SHOULD PRACTICE SELF-CONTROL YOURSELF. THAT IS FOR THE PURPOSE OF ESTABLISHING A BETTER WAY OF LIVING AND A BETTER WAY OF LOVING FOR YOURSELF FIRSTLY, AND THEN FOR OTHER PEOPLE WHO YOU ARE CONCERNED ABOUT.

YOU SHOULD ALSO PRACTICE HONEST SELF-ANALYSIS REGULARLY. THAT JUST MIGHT INCLUDE RECALLING SOME UNPLEASANT DETAILS OF YOUR PAST, AND DOING THAT WITHOUT TAKING IT ALL TOO PERSONALLY.

If you are tempted to believe what critics of abstinence say, (IE: that abstinence is not a good thing) then you should try to square off the balance sheet at some point and take part in some righteous activities. (IE: perform acts of service, go to a <u>good</u> church and partake of the sacrament, read the scriptures and even study them intensely. If the things you read do not make sense at first, read them again and even use a good and informative study guide. One simple thing you can do every day is to try to lift the spirits of a person who needs that 'lift' in their life.

There are many good things that you could do for other people, and many good things you can do for yourself, that is, unless you have come to believe that you are already perfect and do not need any kind of counsel from anyone. (RED FLAG, MISTAKE, OFF COURSE.)

When I first joined my church, I was given a calling by my bishop to be a Sunday school teacher. Plus, I also had five young children who I needed to help raise and needed to teach them about righteous principles. One day, I heard some words from my bishop that rang a bell with me and I have remembered them to this day. My bishop always believed that good words were excellent, but they were not often not enough. There was something else that was more important than good advice. The saying that he quoted went something like this:

> "A child won't <u>care</u> how much you <u>know</u>, until the child <u>knows</u> how much you <u>care</u>".

***

A sex obsession of any kind starts out as a curiosity. Then eventually, the young person's imagination steps in and fantasy enters into the picture. It can all 'sneak up on a person'.

In the past, fantasy has been promoted as being a positive thing in the media. IE: As the old Steppenwolf pop song, Magic Carpet ride says:

"Why don't you tell your dreams to me? Fantasy will set you free."

Falling for lines like that is a mistake.

***

TRANSGENDERISM

As an example of an obsession, take the example of an innocent young child who might find it interesting to contemplate what it would be like to have the surgery that would make her, or him, into the opposite sex of what he, or she, she biologically is. Is that child old

enough to realize what she is actually doing? No. I submit that he, or she, is just not mature enough to know what the consequences of such a decision will be, and it doesn't even matter what a social worker or a doctor or what a so-called 'qualified psychologist' might recommend.

The surgery, plain and simple, goes against human nature. It demeans person. It turns them into a guinea pig. It is just another example of how humanity itself has gone over the edge in this twenty first century. As Dr. Jordan Peterson once said about those surgeons who performed gender changing surgery, "They are nothing but liars and butchers".

So why would that young person go ahead with the surgery when there is a very good chance that the change of gender could turn out to be an utter disaster. I believe the innocent child's decision could be because the child got caught up in an OBSESSION. It is an obsession that has actually been promoted by the media and by the education system, and by many governments, be they left wing or right wing.

An obsession can be a powerful thing to a young person and sometimes, even to an older person. Thus, I say that it is not worth the risk. If a person has anything of worth to lose by doing that, they will probably lose that thing, whatever it may be.

Mature people, including some friends and some family, who respect both gender and respect human dignity, will probably just ignore such people who fall for that kind of risky 'OBSESSION. Most parents will need to consider ethical principles before they decide to give their consent to their child expressing a desire for their child to order a surgeon to go ahead and permanently change their sacred bodies with the surgery. In some places, state legislators have said that a parent's consent for their child's surgery is not even necessary. In any case I will quote from 1st Corinthians.

> ***"Ye are the temple of God."***
> ***- 1st Corinthians 3:16***

Fantasy is something that some people consider harmless, but it is not harmless. It can be a deadly thing because in in most cases, there can be no turning back. Without any consideration for prudence or self-control, the imagination will expand the picture until the picture until it becomes a bizarre adventure to those who lack any true meaning in their life. That might be exciting in the beginning, and there will be much propaganda to accept it unconditionally. The truth of the matter though is that those thoughts are from an evil source and the consequences that happen when they are acted upon will never end well.

Bizarre adventures can cause the picture to expand even more until it triggers the adrenalin glands. Wild and prideful emotions can then take control and it will end up as a single minded desire to perform any kind of sexual act and bring on a craving to bring one's physical desires to a climax AT ANY COST.

To someone with an obsessive personality, those last three words are the definitive words that will define a strong addiction or an obsession. That means it is a strong desire to act out physical desires at any cost. Doing that is a denial of true and unchanging principles like like examples of 'cause and effect'. On such cases,

something tiny may be gained, but something huge can easily be lost.

That is why self-discipline, self-control and prudence are vital characteristics that we should always keep in mind and practice. If you can do that, it will be a noble accomplishment on your part. So congratulate yourself, and know that God approves of your sensibility. Then a person can move on to a more dignified and more fulfilling and a more rational part of this 'wonderful life' that we have been given.

SADDLE SOAP?

Any unusual desires that a person thinks needs fulfilling do not even have to be sexual. A strong desire can sometimes be simply A DESIRE TO **SIN,** even if it is just for its own sake. A desire to sin is also a desire to rebel. That means to rebel against any authority that demands obedience, whether they have been called to obey the will of a parent or a teacher or to anyone who has the persuasive ability to try to convince another person that they actually have a right to control that person's life, even if it is only for a few minutes.

Thus, I say that sin can be tempting, but it does not need to be about sex. As an example of that, let me tell you about a young man whom I met when I was younger. Around the time I was about nineteen years old, I met a man one day who was about two years younger than me. He made it clear that he felt great satisfaction when he stole items from a large local department store. As I got to know him it became obvious that that young man had an obsession about stealing, and maybe just an obsession with the simple act of sinning. Part of that obsession was the pleasure that he got from 'getting away with it'.

The boy showed me a bar of saddle soap that he stole from the local Hudson's Bay store. This young man was not a cowboy. He didn't have a horse. He didn't have a saddle. It seems that he just liked to steal and found satisfaction when he actually got away with it.

Having been raised by parents who had integrity, I, personally, found this young man's thinking highly unusual, and I didn't understand it at all. I still don't. That kind of thinking was very foreign to me, and it came from this friendly young man who seemed quite normal to me in all other ways. It was a complete mystery to me. I wasn't close to that young man and I lost contact with him and now, occasionally, I find myself wondering whatever happened to him. Did that young man have an obsession with saddle soap? No, but I think that he did have an obsession with **SIN**.

What is my point here? My point is that that young man in question had a very stupid obsession that would probably hold him back from accomplishing anything worthwhile in his whole life. He was a kleptomaniac and he seemed to think that there was nothing wrong with that. Maybe he changed. I don't know. Maybe he thought he was born that way, I don't know, but maybe he simply had a compulsion to steal and to take away something that rightfully belonged to someone else.

I didn't know his reasoning, and I didn't what to know what his reasoning was. That was because I just knew that his reasoning was wrong, and that his values were

values that I wanted nothing to do with. In other words, I had no sympathy.

The young man's crowning reward, or so he thought, was that that 'he actually got away with something that was wrong' and was quite proud of that. His rebellion was complete and, in his eyes, successful.

So what does a sex addict get away with when he, or she, uses someone else's body for sexual gratification and gets away with it? Again, I don't honestly know, but I do know that it is wrong and that is where it ends for now.

So what can I do about the kleptomaniac? Should I become a social worker and coddle him and try to politely convince him that his values were mistaken, and those values were probably from an evil source. Or maybe I should I become a 'right winger' and preach law and order and insist that that man should be put in jail? That might be the only thing that might convince the man to change his ways of thinking, but not necessarily. In any case, neither of those options appealed to me, so what should I do about it? What would you do about it?

I say in some of my other essays I have written that a man or a woman who is living in their senior years has a responsibility to state their best opinions about how people should live their lives according to what they have actually learned in their life. I think that now, maybe, it is my turn.

***

WHAT HAVE WE LEARNED?

Thus, I will explain that I, personally, like to borrow some of the ideas that I have learned from reading the scriptures. When a person sees all sinful things from a perspective of truth, then they can see those things from one big 'whole', instead of from a bunch of tiny parts, and wicked parts at that. Thus, I would do my best to teach high moral values to my children, something that I feel everyone needs. Is there anything wrong with trying to be the best person we can be?

Thus, I would say that it is my first ambition would be to lead a Christ-like life and forgive people who have wronged me whenever the Spirit prompts me to do so.

I WOULD ALSO LIKE TO BE FIRM WITH MY OWN CHILDREN AND TELL THEM THAT IT IS A TRUE AND A UNIVERSAL PRINCIPLE THAT BAD THOUGHTS AND BAD ACTIONS WILL ALWAYS LEAD TO BAD CONSEQUENCES, AND THOSE CONSEQUENCES CAN SHOW UP IN MANY DIFFERENT WAYS. SO BE SURE TO 'POLICE YOURSELF' ACCORDINGLY.

ALSO, I WOULD TELL MY CHILDREN TO WATCH OUT FOR 'OBSESSIVE BEHAVIOR' BECAUSE IT CAN SNEAK UP ON A PERSON, AND ESPECIALLY AN INNOCENT PERSON WHO DOESN'T SEEM TO HAVE A DIRECTION TO GO IN THEIR LIFE THAT THEY FIND FULFILLING.

***

I think that when we get too familiar with some questionable activities, then we might find out, regrettably, that those could very well be traps. A trap, or the desire to get away from a trap, could lead to lead to an obsession, which could lead to either misery or tragedy.

The biggest problem with obsessions in my opinion is that it is a 'one – off, or an 'experiment'. After that 'one – off' is over that relatively innocent person can get captivated by the intrigue and the adventure of the experience, and start thinking that maybe it is not a one-off. Maybe it is an 'all-off'.

Maybe that is just the way that person really is. Maybe they can start thinking that the gender that they received at birth was a mistake. If that idea takes seed and grows over time, then a myriad of other considerations come into the picture and the idea might very well become an 'all-off'.

Over time, that will be the new way that they will perceive themselves, and in their minds they will see that as a non-negotiable truth. Thus, they may never go back to the idea that it was a one-off or an experiment.

It could become 'their new life' then. And they could just choose to ignore any suggestions by loving parents or friends that undermines their 'new way of thinking'. All thoughts of going back to the old way they were will get dismissed, partly because of guilt and partly because of the 'new friends' that they have made, but mostly because they are unable to put their one-off sexual experience into a one-off category and because of the guilt they feel when they think they have betrayed their family heritage, they will instead put it into put it into an 'all-off' category and will proceed down that path, hoping that the people who love them will understand and continue to love them. Those people usually will still love them, but there can be many complications in that regard.

Those complications will come about not because their parents don't love their children, but their hesitations come because the things that are happening to them are very new to them, and they actually do not understand them at all. Thus, an obsession can become a matter of self-deception.

Yes, the answers will be there, but God will give them to you "line upon line, precept upon precept, here a little, and there a little." (Isaiah 28: 10) He does it that way because it seems that that is the best way to learn things and to see how some pieces of truth can confirm many other pieces of truth.

The truth is more than hearing one piece of truth. It is about compounding dozens, or hundreds of pieces of truth, so that they all come together in the end as one great whole. And after that happens, the Lord will then say in the end, that - "IT IS FINISHED".

Why does God do things that you can learn from? There are three reasons why He does it. One reason is because He knows you. The second reason He does it is because He loves you. The third reason is that He does it is because He is good. Because of those three things, It will become obvious when you view those things with your spiritual eyes, THEN YOU WILL KNOW THAT YOU CAN TRUST HIM.

***

Chapter 16

Bob's Obbs #1 (observations) (9p.)

Have you got good words on your mind? Write them down. If they ring true and make sense, keep them and expand on them. If they do not ring true or make good sense, dump them.

"Go", said the brain. Nothing happened. "Go", said the body. Nothing happened. "Go", said the Spirit. Nothing happened. Unfortunately, they were all out of fuel. They all forgot to fill their tanks the night before. Thankfully, the Spirit had been built with a reserve tank in the back. It had enough fuel in it to drive itself and the other two vehicles to the nearest prayer station where they are all able to fill their tank. Everything will go well after that."

Can I receive a revelation or a prompting from God even if I do not deserve it? Yes, but I can receive it only if I have chosen to seek out His Word on a regular basis. If you choose to stand in Holy places, God appreciates that and rewards you by giving you other revelations that you will need in order to progress

There is a difference between 'harder' and 'stronger'. A denial of the truth can make me hard of heart, but an affirmation of the truth, with its softness, can make me 'stronger' in heart. Soft things can facilitate strong things when wisdom is there. 'Hardness' is tough, but it is not much fun. Strength has a certain amount of softness, which makes it more enjoyable and worth fighting for.

There are some good people in all churches, Christian or not. There are also some hypocrites in all churches, Christian or not. Thus, it is a matter of the 'abundance' of good. The question is, 'which church has the most intelligence in their doctrine, and the most kindness in their members and the most inspiring spiritual promptings that a person might experience when attending that church?' If that is true, then religious traditions alone are not always of ultimate relevance.

March 16, 2023. I had a feeling of NOTHINGNESS this morning. Is there ever comfort in feeling nothingness? No. If there is comfort there, it is not nothingness. It is comfort. Appreciate it. And know that comfort can only come when you ask for it and when your mind is free from doubts and guilt.

Many people will balk at the mention of the mere name of Jesus Christ. That is they're choice. If they will refuse to acknowledge Him or even talk about Him, they may do that for any number of reasons, but when people balk at the mere mention of His name, or balk at certain words like 'repentance' or 'faith', they unknowingly reveal something about themselves and not in a complimentary way.

Sometimes we must draw moral 'lines in the sand' and not allow ourselves, or others, to cross those lines. Sometimes it can be tempting for people to ignore those lines and cross them anyways, or allow them to be crossed. The more righteous among us however will not back down. They will have the courage to speak the truth no matter what.

Regarding evil - The devil is real and like an expert fisherman, he knows what lures to use. Also, he does not play 'catch and release'. Once he gets his grasp on you he will proceed to squeeze every bit of pain and trouble out of you that he can, <u>right up until the day you die</u>. The only solution to that is to trust in God and fill your days with righteous endeavors.

I think that the ultimate question that awaits us all after this life might be – "Aside from trying to impose your own prideful opinions upon others about how they should live their lives, ask yourself what have you done to make the world the place that you think it should be?"

When I was young, I assumed that civics and even civility would never be displaced in this society. How wrong I was. Nowadays disrespect, narcissism, and people who believe in their own moral superiority are very common. How naive I was back then.

Have you and your spouse agreed on something recently that benefits you both and makes you feel good? Good. When those moments happen, appreciate them. Even if it's a small thing acknowledge it, then give your spouse a big smile and a HIGH FIVE.

We cannot find a higher realm of existence if we never choose to look in a higher direction. Heaven is right in front of us, but Hell is right in front of us too. Neither of these realms are visible. Heaven is hidden by the harsh reality of this world and Hell is hidden by it's own disguises.

There are two kinds of evil. One is stupid/evil and the other is evil/evil. When left without care or correction, the former will follow a natural path downwards and evolve into the latter.

Ignorant people who are well intentioned are still ignorant people. So don't be too trusting about them.

There are some people whose integrity I trust, but not their intelligence. Nevertheless, I try to be kind because God works with all of us in our own spheres and in His own time.

Quote from Peter 2:19 - "While they promise themselves liberty, they themselves are the servants of corruption: for of whom a man is overcome, of the same is he brought in bondage".
Some people interpret this as saying that a person who is brought into bondage by their thinking can be persuaded by a self-interest group that that group has a better way of thinking that can make them more free. In such a case, the person in bondage can feel better temporarily, but he or she, may actually be in a different kind of bondage. What say you?"

As we get older I feel it is incumbent on all of us, and for the sake of future generations, to be able to declare near the end of it all what the main purpose of it is for people in general. In a sentence or two, what is your purpose? If you are _not_ able to give a good answer to that question, does that mean that you have literally _failed_ in fulfilling your mission here on earth, that being to gain knowledge? I suspect that this is so.

Artists and musicians - If you have been blessed with talent you will probably receive a certain amount of notoriety. If you do not use that notoriety well and do something stupid like proclaim your moral superiority to the world, it will not end well. Ego-driven mental habits are always born out of pride as opposed to being grateful for the creative gifts that you have been given.

I know there are some comparatively good people in the world who do not go to church. Perhaps they don't need to go to church and partake of the sacrament every week, I don't know. I only know that I do need to go there. It is not a weakness. It is a physical medicine for me. It is an intelligent and effective antidote (99% of the time) that can create healing for me."

The Holy Spirit is like a radio wave with a delicate frequency. I have a hard time tuning it in when my radio receptor (my capacitor) is either stuck or else over greased.

Spiritual people are usually called to live their lives at an accelerated pace, but that will also include some slower things like caution and patience. It is also good to seek out, and fellowship, with others who have been called to work at that same pace. In some cases, it is an individual effort. In other cases it may be a relay race. It can be a good thing when you pass your baton to another person.

Forgiveness is a process where self-cleansing can take place. Forgiveness will always make my life easier, because evil spirits will not be effective when they try to 'stir things up'. They will withdraw because they do not know how to fight against the 'forgiveness strategy'.

It is true that Jesus can wash away our sins, but the question is: 'what will be left over after the bath?

Statistics show that life is always more enjoyable for people who have a spiritual side to them and who know how to access that spiritual side. They are just happier people. If you have that opportunity to gain access to that spiritual side, use it regularly and do not let the pagans of the world take it away from you, even if your beliefs are not yet fully developed.

On inspiration: When making decisions we should think things out as much as we can and then make our decision based upon correct principles and reasoning, and then seek the Holy Ghost, who I sometimes call the great under-liner, or the great highlighter, to confirm the correctness of those conclusions.

There is much evil in the world. Aside from having a connection to the Powers of heaven, the best way to fight it is through STRONG families. 'Strong' is the operative word here. Weak families, feeble-minded families, divided families, and even families who are fierce, but lack understanding, will be of no good use to anyone.

Having a strong family means having a collective wisdom, love, and the courage to protect each other. Families also need a spirit of gratitude, and a set structure for learning. Good spirits will attend you when your family commits to those things.

If you are not familiar with creative writing and using words well, I would highly recommend that you spend some time working on it and get better at it. Keep a journal and I guarantee that it will work to your advantage and to your children's advantage too. Once you have harnessed your words, then you can work on harnessing your imagination and your actions.

Just like there are stages in sleep, there are stages in wakefulness. Paradoxically, human beings do not usually recognize this. That is because they cannot recognize the lower and higher stages of wakefulness. Why not? It is because they are not really 'awake' enough to do so.

When we connect with good things we create a bond that is invaluable. That bond, however, can be broken under pressure. The pressure may be a result of outside forces or inside forces, but nevertheless, the bond will always broken with our consent.

Some people may be well intentioned, but they may be too naive to see where real evil lurks. Such well-intentioned people can do more damage than good when they try to save the world.

Observe a beautiful sunset. The elements of that sunset might be randomly placed in the atmosphere, but for those elements to even exist together in the first place, and in such a way that provides such reoccurring beauty, must surely be a sign of a great Creator and a true artist.

For God to have newness, it is required that that newness be aligned somehow with His nature, otherwise it would be foreign to him. <u>We human beings</u>, in our present state, are that newness. At the same time, we are not new or foreign to Him. That is because we are His children.

I was parked in the parking lot of a strip mall today and I saw some fellow walk into a store that sold marijuana. I had a thought come into my mind. The thought was – **'Oh well, there goes another wasted life'.** The remarkable thing about that thought was that I did not take the time to consider any opposite aspects of it. Plus, I had no desire to investigate the effects of the drug through the internet. It was just a no-brainer. It came to mind simply because I had personally 'been there and done that' when I was younger and it was not the slightest bit productive. That was all I knew, and all I needed to know. End of story.

I fully believe that God can speak to us today. The heavens are not closed. He would not abandon us in these most confusing of times. We just need to activate our spiritual radio and tune in to the right channel.

If sensible religion is of great importance, as I believe it is, then we can bet that <u>all</u> efforts will be made by evil forces to pervert it and discredit it. Given the fallen state of mankind today, these efforts will often be successful with some people. God and His prophets, however, <u>by the power of the priesthood</u>, still have the power to sanctify and protect the true church.

People should be free to believe what they want to believe, but it is impossible to really accept all doctrines? Some doctrines will contradict each other. Thus, it is not a sin to be critical of another religion if it's doctrine does not make sense. It is a sin to accept false religion or no religion in the name of tolerance. People will often do that though. Why? I think it is because, I think, they just do it because they do not have a strong enough passion for the truth.

17. FAITH, HOPE AND CHARITY (13P.)

Subtitle – The only kind of 'wokeness' that matters

At certain times in my life, I feel that do not have a lot of hope for the future, and I begin to wonder if there is some different kind of hope that would lift my spirits if I was able to 'latch on' to it.

I am smart enough to know that the grass is NOT always greener in the next pasture and I do not intend to abandon a woman who has been a good companion for me for many years, but still I wonder if I can recapture some of the hope that I had in my younger years. I wonder if somebody is calling for me from a vague far away place saying,"Yes. You can do it Bob."

Is there really such a thing as a 'call of the wild' calling for me to seek a new and exciting adventure? Even though I am happy with my present wife and my present children and my present life, I sometimes wonder if I am missing out on something that I have never experienced before. Is that just idle thinking in my part? I know from my past experiences that a new hope can lift my spirits if I decide to pursue it, but I also know that something old is always lost when something new is gained. Is it worth it? Right now, I don't think so.

Maybe I should start my day tomorrow with a new hope for that day. Maybe I start my life tomorrow with a new hope for my life? Perhaps I should be more realistic and think about something more practical, like "Maybe I should start my life tomorrow by trying something new, like forgetting about my fantasies and **'growing up'**." Hmmm, food for thought.

We all have hopes naturally, but they are not always by substantiated by truth or even by reality. That is why I am of the opinion that all if the different kinds of hopes that we have **should always be based upon reality**. We can try basing our hopes in fantasy, but once time has played it's hand that the evidence will be in that such fantasy thinking, like the fantasy itself, is a lie.

I think that religious people who believe in a just and merciful and loving God all have basically the same hopes. We all hope that we will find happiness and we also hope that our God will play a large part in causing that happiness to come about. Even our ultimate hopes, which are the Resurrection and the Redemption. We also hope that those desired hopes of all people will apply specifically to us.

Is that selfish? No. It is a simple wish for the sake of our self-preservation. It is the same as hoping we will get enough food eat or having enough water to drink. There is nothing selfish about that.

So what are the ultimate things that religious people hope for? I think that outside of our own prosperity and the safety of our loved ones, there are two things that religious people hope for ultimately, aside from just hoping that our beliefs are true. Ultimately though, there are two things that are promised us in the scriptures that keep all of my hopes alive. Those two things are:

#1. THE RESURRECTION. That means continuing to live our lives in a resurrected body that has many of the same physical qualities as the person we were before our mortal bodies died.

#2. THE REDEMPTION. That means starting our new life with a clean slate. That means:

#1. having received forgiveness for our past sins and mistakes and;

#2. gaining meaningful knowledge of how a good life should be lived. In other words coming to know, with all certainty, <u>the many truths that we should come to fully understand</u>. After we accomplish that we must decide to embrace those truths and make them a part if our very being. That meaningful knowledge is something that we must <u>LEARN</u> and the only sure way to learn something for certain it is to be taught it by the best possible teacher, or (plural) teachers.

So who should we try to get to teach us the best possible way for us to live and to prepare us for the coming resurrection and the coming redemption?

I am talking about healing here on an ultimate level. That includes in a physical way, a mental way, an emotional way AND IN A SPIRITUAL WAY. Keep in mind that we are not talking about a normal disease here, so the doctors we use in our hospital visits <u>will probably not be useful healers in spiritual matters.</u>

We are talking about the future for our spiritual selves, so the healers we will need must be spiritual healers with an exact knowledge of heavenly principles. We may be talking about angels here, angels who teach truth or even very special and inspired beings who have themselves been taught exactly how to teach the gospel by the Spirit. Also, the very presence of inspired teachers alone who have been ordained to teach us will cause our faith and our confidence in our Lord to be strengthened greatly.

True faith, or a strong testimony of a loving Creator, is the most important thing for me because it gives me personal strength. I have that strength in my life at this time now because I have gained confidence in Jesus Christ and in his teachings'. That 'confidence' or 'assurance' can also be called our 'faith'. That faith should be witnessed by our own personal testimony.

Thus, ultimate happiness will come from God and the correct teachings of the revealed word. That is when the good things, even the best things, will happen for us.

God knows what good things will become the BEST things in our lives and His teachings will go forward in that direction. He knows that stuff much better than what we know about those things. That is why the qualities of obedience and trust are of such great value to us as students of the Divine Beings.

The quality of charity, or love, comes after hope and faith because it is essential that we give back to the giver of life, who is also the giver of all good things. He deserves deserves to be praised for His goodness and His kindness, and we should also watch out for His beloved children, all of them. That is very important to Him and so we should strive to do that. .

Plus, being charitable will actually give us a better understanding of <u>empathy</u>. Empathy means knowing with more surety, just what suffering people have to go through in their lives. That will cause us to be more effective healers for the people who really need legitimate healing. When we help another person in their struggle, we literally become a part of the wonderful and heavenly process that we refer to as 'healing'.

Thus, we will need to be active in our charitable work. We must resemble the good Samaritan man who stopped to help a stranger who was beaten and robbed as he was travelling on a deserted country road. It would have been sinful for any man to just look the other way and do nothing to bring about health and healing to that stranger.

According to the story, doing nothing was what other passerby's did when they saw the man covered in blood. That was what happened according to the story that Jesus told when he told us 'the parable of the good Samaritan'. (Luke 10: 25-37)

Those three things, which are faith, hope and charity, make up the first phase of the plan for a successful life according to the gospel. Thus, it would appear that our righteous hopes and our faith and our charity should be our prime concerns.

> "And now abideth faith, hope, charity, these three; but the greatest of these is charity."
> - 1st Corinthians 13

After we accept faith, hope and charity, as prime virtues, I suspect that another thing to consider is that we must be 'doers of the word' and not just pay lip service to the doing of charitable deeds. We will need to DO the work that is needed to be able to say that we were good and faithful servants.

I must know <u>exactly</u> what to do once I have, in reality, truly woken up and I am not walking around in a mental fog or not just followed the trendy thinking of the 'woke mob'.

That is why a church should have, and be thankful for, good teachers who can explain all the aspects of the gospel with exactness. To be able to teach with exactness is the best quality that a good teacher can have along with knowing exactly what all of his, or her, students should be learning according to their needs. That includes knowing how powerful and truthful gospel principles should be able to touch a student's heart and affect a person's life for the good.

THE ONLY KIND OF 'WOKENESS' THAT MATTERS

Being 'woke', as some people call it, is a way of thinking that I never really took to heart in the past. That was because there wereere are too much trendiness to it and too many bad connotations to it. IE: being politically correct on most issues that are on the world stage.

Being politically correct means showing allegiance to the people in power. That might not be the wisest thing to do when we consider all of the contributing factors. On our side of the world the people in power usually work for governments and those governments are usually left wing, or 'left leaning' because they desire to give the signal that they are more conscientious and virtuous than the rest of us. What is lost in this quest that they have really no basis for claiming that they are morally superior to the rest of us?

In one word, FREEDOM is lost. In other words, they want to promote their values of diversity and absolute equality at any cost. Also, as an offshoot of that, they put their children's futures into the hands of University professors and government bureaucrats to bring to pass their twisted views of justice. Those views ignore good and realistic values like merit, ingenuity and hard work.

Personally, I have surpassed the 'illusion' now that power hungry governments know best how to govern ordinary people. Now I realize that being 'woke' to the reality and the righteous mission of Jesus the Christ (the anointed one) is the only 'woke-ness' that really matters, both in this life and in the life beyond.

***

Recently, I awoke from my sleep one morning in a tirade, and cursing the fact that a certain aspect of my business might be failing. I was engulfed in a realm of bitterness. According to my sacred beliefs I knew that I would need to **detach** myself from that secular realm for that reason alone. I hoped that it was not too late for me to detach from that pervading and selfish mindset.

It has been prophesied in scriptures that, at the end of times, the entire world will burn and be engulfed in flames. Then, I would think that all of the possessions of righteous people may be taken away, maybe even to a distant planet, but I don't know anything about the details of that. I just know that nothing lasts forever, except that is, for the Father, Son, and Holy Ghost. and the Holy kingdom where they dwell, alongside their suppirters.

In essence though, I gather that when the earth is destroyed, every possession of every human being on earth will be burned and will exist no more. Hence, there will be no need for anyone to seek to possess the things of this world, no matter what those things are. That will be because we are all going somewhere else.

That does not matter too much though because those things have all been, at least partly tainted. That is because of the wickedness that has existed on the earth in the past, and in some cases, still exists upon the earth.

For anyone to make the claim that those former possessions will have ultimate value will be very questionable. Those possessions will be worth nothing except for using them for vanity purposes. As well, nobody should worship or emulate the soul of any human being, unless that person, male or female, is 'pure and undefiled'.

It is true that people who live in earthly worlds can expect some impurity, but in Heavenly world's people are under a covenant that they will live by higher standards, and that is non-negotiable. That is because our God is at the head of our new world and God has stated that He seeks as much perfection as possible.

> ***"No unclean thing can dwell with God."***
> ***- 1 Nephi 10: 21***

Would you have it any other way?

In the end, there will be a 'clean slate' created by the Lord for all people who desire it. People who wish to live by the old ways and the old rules and their own uncleanliness will have their wishes granted to them as well.

I don't think that that is a wise wish, but still we all have our free choice. Today though, powerful administrators in today's mortal world will try to dissuade us from promoting righteous behavior in any form. They do that mainly through through propaganda and censorship of free speech, despite the fact that freedom of expression and freedom of the press are part of our country's written and legal constitution. In any case, I do believe our new world, under God's guidance will be free from all that corruption.

In our new world under God, righteous ideas will never be used for purposes of virtue signaling. (IE: I am more virtuous than you are). Righteous principles will be preserved and activated by courageous human beings, so that those principles will be put into practice among all the people who have decided to follow them. That will allow us to be able to make the best use of that clean slate that I spoke about earlier. It will make our new realm a righteous living space where peace and love and harmony will be present and active.

I think that it is true that if there is a political environment when the lawmakers of a country decide to institute laws that will actually promote creativity, intelligence, individuality and quality workmanship that the biggest guiding factor in those laws would be the word **'freedom'**.

There are some sinners who will use the word 'freedom' to justify selfish behavior. This is not good according to the laws given to us in the scriptures. The following scripture from Jesus says that we should indeed be wise as serpents, but harmless as doves.

> ***"be ye therefore wise as serpents and harmless as doves.   - Matthew 10:16***

The phrase 'be harmless as doves' is a qualifying phrase according to my understanding. It is saying that in using the thoughts of a serpent, we should make sure that we are not doing anybody any harm. But is that clear enough? In the book of Doctrine and Covenants there is a similar phrase. It says:

> ***"Therefore, be ye as wise as serpents, and yet without sin."   - Doctrine and Covenants 111:11***

If the first quote that I offered up, it could be seen by some lawyer as unclear and arguable. That might have some validity in the eyes of some people, but I think that the second quote is clearer.

It basically infers that it is possible that the words 'be harmless as doves' might not be used to be used to promote God'd purposes, whereas the words, "be without sin" are not as open to interpretation and are more exact.

I, personally, will try to detach myself from all things, including certain words that could be interpreted as being vain or virtue signaling. I will be more than satisfied with the new Heavenly kingdom that comes.

The proper words must come directly from the influence of reliable gospel teachings. Otherwise the laws could be seen as faulty, and thus, things would not work to perfection. That Heavenly kingdom will be a world where our righteous King reigns and where righteous Saints will be incorruptible, like God Himself is.

THE RATIONAL GOSPEL

The Father, Son and Holy Ghost will be the only beings who are fully worthy of our worship. That will be because of the sacrifices that they made for all of the men and women who lived on the earth and for all the work they did in the building up of the Kingdom of Heaven.

That is what we had in the beginning and it is what we will have again. The only difference is that the new realm will come after the resurrection when we have gained a much deeper understanding of the difference between good and evil. When that time comes and we start to understand things even better, we will finally be able to live without obstacles like false doctrines and live our lives with a fullness of love in our hearts. In other words, we will need to <u>use</u> the knowledge that we have gained or else it will all go for nothing.

That is why it is so important to have a common consensus about the truth of the gospel amongst the congregations. Associating with like minded people always promotes unity and a singularity of purpose among the righteous followers of Christ.

The righteous laws that promote goodness and justice and charity, will not be changed. Even God will not be able to change them. That is because it is a literal message from our Heaven and states truths that saints have lived by for many millenniums. The people who love goodness will have had righteous attitudes grafted, or embedded, into their hearts Those people will be courageous people and will not be afraid to fight for the establishment of righteous laws that have been inspired by our living God. In other words, WE WILL BE UNITED AS ONE.

The laws I am speaking about here are Eternal laws. In some cases, they might need to be fully explained to souls who may be sincere, but they might lack understanding. Thus, there might be some legitimate questions put forward. The answers to those questions will be given to us by legitimate prophets, and by real angels, and by the good people of God who have the knowledge and also have the authority to explain those things. In many cases <u>some of those answers we seek could be answered by Jesus Christ Himself.</u>

Hence, in my case, I will watch what I do and watch what I say and be careful as to who I will choose to keep company with. I will also watch out for the people who my children keep company with. This is because I now know that, if I am worthy, both as a human being and as a parent, then I may become a part of a magnificent and mighty kingdom that will be available to all of us by the grace of our Creator.

This charter that I choose to live by can be seen as complicated or it can be seen as simple. A person can gain a simple perspective of it by reading one line from one of my favorite hymns entitled:

'I KNOW THAT MY REDEEMER LIVES'.

Some of the lyrics go thusly:

**I know that my redeemer lives.
What comfort this sweet sentence gives.
He lives, He lives who once was dead.
He lives, my ever living head.**

**He lives and grants me daily breath
<u>HE LIVES AND I SHALL CONQUER DEATH.</u>"**

THE RATIONAL GOSPEL

What simple and beautiful words. Jesus, who was the Son of God conquered death, and as for us, if we have a bond with Jesus, then He will make a way whereby we, too can conquer death and continue living, but living in a much better world, one where peace and love and joy and good health will reign over all.

Our loving Father in Heaven will make all of this happen. As well, there will be no more wars and no more hunger and no more suffering. <u>Still, we will all have a part to play in this great plan.</u>

The main thing about our part is to be simply grateful, even Eternally grateful. Gratitude will become an integral part of our being. I would even suspect that we might make our contributions to the building of the Kingdom according to the talents that we have all been given.

> **"and the work of righteousness shall be peace; and the effect of righteousness quietness and assurance for ever"**
> **- Isaiah 32: 17**

May God bless you all. I say this in the name of Jesus Christ. Amen.

Chapter 18.

IN APPRECIATION OF TRUE ARTISTRY (20p.)

(Subtitles: Let Us Appreciate Good Art, Good core values and Freedom, Encourage Good young Artists, Serious Sex and Novelty Sex, Standards of Entertainment, Evil Spirits and Pornography)

I think that it is a good thing for people, both artists and audiences, to bring the 'standards of entertainment' that they hold into line with what their moral values are. Those moral values are values that we fully believe to be true even if they are only spoken in a theatre. Those basic values will need to be embedded in us for them to become an intrinsic part of our freedom on earth and in Heaven.

Those core values might be taken from the Bible, or they might not be, but this decision must be made one way or the other in everyone's mind, and it should come into our mind after we carefully measure THE QUALITY of the words we hear and the images that we see and the morality of the characters that are presented in the performance of an artistic work. The people who create and produce those products will be asking us to totally accept those products no matter how stupid or obscene they are. That is a part of their job.

***

GOOD CORE VALUES AND FREEDOM

As I edited this essay, it occurred to me that I left out an important aspect in the 'discouraging kinds of thinking' that goes on in the arts world. I was thinking here about political censorship and specifically about government officials censoring social media by taking away certain tools that help writers to expand their creative abilities while they are working on their craft. Aside from censoring commentaries from right wing thinkers, which is obviously happening, I am thinking about the censorship of things that are less obvious. Those tools that I mentioned are important in utilizing 'literacy' in the arts.

As I write about good 'art' including good writing, I also write about good 'literacy'. I think that good literacy is the main component of creative writing and thus, of good 'art'. Here is a good example of that.

I was editing an essay in this book this morning. In the past I have used a literary tiils from the internet like 'a thesaurus, or 'a dictionary' and I always found them useful. I was looking for a synonym for a word this morning so I looked up the words 'thesaurus' and even 'dictionary'. I could not find anything. Those sites have been censored. The sites were declared to be 'unsafe' or 'not private'. The following statement is a facebook page that I posted today.

> "Justin Trudeau has sunk so low that he is actually censoring 'literacy'. I tried to look up the word 'thesaurus' and also tried to find the word 'dictionary' on Google, but nothing came up. I was told that the sites I was seeking were not 'safe' or 'not private'. And it told me to 'go back to safety".

Has it come to this? Is the dumbing down of the general public now complete? Does the moron of the western world,

Mr. Trudeau, now have the power to censor tools designed to promote literacy? Is there anyone out there who will dare to stand up for literacy?

***

AS I WRITE ABOUT ENCOURAGING GOOD ART, I HAVE TO ASK THE QUESTION, 'WHAT IS AT STAKE HERE'? WHAT IS AT STAKE IS OUR GENERAL LOVE FOR FREEDOM ITSELF IN THIS WESTERN WORLD. THAT DOES NOT MEAN THE FREEDOM TO BE OBSCENE. IT INVOLVES THE FREEDOM TO BE BASICALLY CLEVER AND SUCCINCT IN OUR WRITING AND MAINLY, TO BE ABLE TO HOLD ON TO THE TRUTH AND TO BE ABLE TO EXPRESS THAT TRUTH WITH CLEVERNESS AND EXACTNESS WITHOUT BEING IGNORED OR 'DEPLATFORMED'.

WE SHOULD HAVE A RESPONSIBILITY TO STAND UP IN FAVOR OF EXERCISING GOOD MORALS IN THE STORIES THAT WE PERFORM. IF WE DO NOT DO THAT BECAUSE WE ARE AFRAID OF BEING SHAMED (IE: BEING CALLED A PRUDE OR A RELIGIOUS FANATIC, THEN THE FINAL RESULT WILL BE THAT FREEDOM ITSELF WILL EVENTUALLY PERISH AND OUR QUALITY OF LIFE WILL BE SEVERELY DIMINISHED.

Thus, I think that it would be a good thing if everyone tried to build up an appreciation for the 'arts' in the media and in the conversations that we have with friends. By the word 'arts' I also include literary writing and performances of all kinds. I am mostly talking about the <u>legitimate</u> arts, not the commercial or sensationalist art forms.

Thus, we should learn to appreciate good writing skills and character development, and good storylines or plots, and clever dialogue, and 'all the things that make good art good'.

The ultimate purpose of 'art', ideally, is to make the world a better place for everybody to live. This would not include creating things like cheap thrills, gratuitous sex and watching any kind of immoral behavior taking place. That would only be a bad influence upon the more innocent people among us.

Like I just mentioned, it is the good writing skills, good storylines, good humor and clever dialogue, etc. that make good art good and not just being accessible to left wing fascists who now, according to them, own the definition of the phrase 'community standards'.

Making a change in our standards of entertainment or 'art' and deciding to watch, and/or create, good quality material rather than watching the usual pablum that is loaded with cheap sex, violence and profanity, etc. is a smart decision. When you choose to watch or listen to, or read high quality art, that is a decision that will cause people to respect you more on a highly personal level and cause YOU to respect yourself more.

All people, I think, have an inner respect for artists who make good art, but those artists probably try to avoid shocking or titillating an audience with sensationalist content. Even though the people without core values who don't see much value in such art will 'make the leap' and try to find some meaning in portrayals of unusual and risky behavior that have never been proven to be beneficial for anybody.

Thus, people's questions become questions like 'who defines what community standards are?' or 'how much attention should we pay to principles that have never been proven to be good?'

When a person creates 'quality art' it is a sign that they ARE NOT casting aside their moral and intellectual core values that give people a respect for 'clean living' and even a respect for life in general. Possessing a respect for clean living is never advertised in the promotion of a movie or a play, but those unspoken values are there nonetheless, for good or for bad.

For an audience to become aware of the good values that are focused on in a presentation always gives the viewers a feeing that 'the world is not a bad place after all' and they will appreciate being given a good message that they can take home with them.

OUR CORE VALUES ARE THE MOST IMPORTANT POSSESSIONS THAT WE HAVE. BUT WHEN WE CAST THOSE VALUES ASIDE SO THAT WE MIGHT GET A CHEAP THRILL OF ONE KIND OR ANOTHER, FROM SOME OTHER KIND OF VISUAL STIMULATION IS THAT NOT JUST ANOTHER 'SELL OUT'?

So please, don't play games with your core moral values or you might lose them. They are probably the most important part of who you are, and if you lose sight of them, whether you know it or not, you may never get them back again.

To establish a HIGHER appreciation of this life that we have been given, a conscientious person needs to begin to think about HIGHER principles of character more often than they normally do.

WHEN THOSE GOOD PRINCIPLES GET ENTRENCHED IN PEOPLE'S THINKING, THEY WILL FIND THAT THEY JUST ENJOY ENTERTAINMENT MORE THAN BEFORE, AND THEY PROBABLY EVEN ENJOY LIFE MORE THAN BEFORE.

THAT IS BECAUSE THEY HAVE MORE CONFIDENCE IN THEIR INNER BEING, OR THEIR 'HIGHER SELF'. THEY KNOW THAT THEY DON'T HAVE TO FEEL EMBARRASSED OR ASHAMED ABOUT ANYTHING THEY WATCH OR PARTICIPATE IN. THUS, AS A WONDERFUL BONUS, THEY WILL HAVE GAINED SOME FREEDOM OF EXPRESSION IN THEIR LIVES.

We will need to be our own censors in these matters. Think of that kind of censorship as a noble pastime reserved for people of conscience. If you should discover a movie or a play that has a good moral to it and good characters and an exciting storyline, and witty dialogue then watch that production, even more than once, and appreciate it.

A person who enjoys life is not an elite person, but he, or she, is just a person of GOOD TASTE, rather than a person of bad taste, or mediocre taste, or of no taste at all. Is that elitist? EVEN IF IT IS, SO WHAT? Life itself, as well as being a forum for art, is an elitist adventure. Life, and art, will offer us portrayals of high quality stories or low quality stories. What kind of stories would you prefer to watch or to listen to?

LET US APPRECIATE GOOD YOUNG ARTISTS

On one hand, young artists can be susceptible to wild ideas where ethics are abandoned. On the other hand, our Heavenly Father desires artist, musicians and writers, to create works that will be enduring and uplift people's spirits. That is also when an artist, if he, or she, is gifted, can be a better influence to younger audiences and support them in their growth and in their quest to find happiness. Young artists need encouragement and good examples to follow so they will not feel constrained in choosing the better path, one that will preserve their honor and not cause the reputation of the arts itself to be tainted or permanently stained.

Young artists can even invent new forms of art. William Shakespeare, for example, had an amazing mind and a love for language. He was also a very hard worker. He was an example of one man in history who managed to accomplish an amazing body of work that changed the course of literature in our world.

So let me be clear to any aspiring artists out there that there is a definite responsibility on their part to familiarize themselves with the finer aspects of the arts and gain a good overall perception about life itself. This knowledge will be more available to a young artist when they pay heed to the proven artists who have created meaningful creations and were able to ignore the 'bottom feeders' who will do anything to get people to like them.

Specifically, an artist should learn about whatever mediums they are the most interested in. Those will usually be the genres that they will excel at.

A young artist must learn things from acknowledged masters and even learn other things from other beginning artists, musicians, actors, writers, etc. They should gather information from other talented artists and perform for random audiences whenever they get the chance. Their experiences, when channeled properly, will come to some kind of fruition in time.

If that fruition doesn't happen, a person can always drive a bus. Driving a bus might not be as exciting as working in the arts, but in the end, that doesn't matter. A bus driver's life can be simpler and can often provide a 'safer 'way of making a living.

A person, who thinks at a higher level, will be, by definition, a 'smarter person'. So what? I know lots of smart people who are smart in the eyes of the world, but at their core, they are not happy people. So ask yourself what is more important, being smart or being happy.

Personally, I would choose the latter option. I would do that because being happy IS being smart. After all, as I said earlier in a quote, "**men are that they might have joy**".

In any case, aspiring artists will lead a very busy life. They will learn some valuable things in increments of time and they will gradually accomplish good things if they are able to present their best values in the most articulate and in an interesting way. On the other hand, if they always go for the cheap laughs, smart people will see them as 'only in it for a buck'.

There is an additional factor in that declaration however. That additional factor is that the serious artist should not lose sight of their original, unique and conscientious core values. If they do lose those things, they will have, basically nothing left that will be worth expounding on.

QUALITY SEX AND NOVELTY SEX

Many people will go to a movie with the hope of seeing some naked bodies. So a person might then ask, 'do our 'lower sexual perceptions' fit in with our 'supposedly higher artistic views'?

Sexual activity is a natural impulse in adults. Sometimes it can work for our good and sometimes not. A strong desire for sexual activity should never be considered a small matter or a whimsical matter because it just might set the direction that we choose to take for the rest of our lives. As well, that direction might end up being not subjected to change, which is not a good thing.

To my artist friend who likes to cry in his beer because he doesn't feel that the world is being fair to him then I could say:
"If your personal direction in life turns out to be not a good thing, it probably makes little difference. That is because there may be nothing you can do to correct that. That is because life itself doesn't really care. Life has more important things to do that to be a wet nurse for you. God cares, but life doesn't care. So you had better get used to it. The ball you are playing with will be in your court. It is not in life's court. Again, God cares, but life doesn't care.

To be discriminating in this matter, we must **always** be cautious, or even prudent, in our sexual activities. This is for our own benefit as well as for the benefit of all people. It is also a factor in maintaining a healthy PDM, which is our

Personal Default Mode. Our PDM is, basically what we are thinking about when there is nothing else to think about.

Our thoughts will always originate in our minds. Those thoughts can also include thoughts in our imagination. An imagination can be a wonderful thing, but it is also a two edged sword. Imaginations can be deceptive in some cases. Can this be a problem? Definitely. It can be a problem when a person's core values are transgressed. It can be a problem when a person over-reaches <u>the bounds of reality. Our 'realty' includes our 'real values' or our 'morality'</u>.

The 'bounds of morality' are the bounds of one's conscience. Will a person's conscience let the person know if they are going off track? That depends. A person's conscience can be a powerful thing, but then, a person's ability to <u>justify</u> their actions and let their passions rule is also a powerful thing.

You might feel comfortable if you should decide to use, or exploit, another person sexually for the sake of your selfish desires. Does that mean that you have forsaken your conscience when that happens? Figure it out. Having a conscience has been called 'having the Spirit of Christ'.

Having a conscience means that you know that there is a higher moral law available to us. Having a conscience implies that a person has a responsibility to portray the good things that his, or her, conscience, or their 'higher self', tells them to portray.

When a married couple has sex it is for three basic reasons. The first reason is that it is for pleasure. The second reason is for reasons of intimacy, including the showing of love in an intimate way. The third reason is for purposes of procreation. All three of these reasons are legitimate reasons. Any one of these reasons should be enough to allow the man and the woman to go ahead and fulfill their needs to their satisfaction.

If there is another reason that is NOT legitimate the couple may not even realize it. But the best gauge to find that missing legitimacy is to check with your conscience, in all honesty of course. That gives a person a good feeling when they know that there are no secrets being kept.

There is a psychological term for people who live their lives without a conscience. In the world of psychology, a person without a conscience is also known by the word **'PSYCHOPATH'**.

If your imagination is running the show, then I say that it is important that you do not explore the lower realms of your imagination. That includes the realm of 'novelty'. Novelty includes desires that are 'novel' or new, or have no proven worth in the grand scheme of things.

There should be TRUE EMOTIONS expressed in the sex act, not phony emotions or a desire for novelty. That kind of lesser behavior will always drag a person down emotionally, mentally, spiritually and even permanently. Having sex for reasons of novelty, like having sex with a stranger, has nothing to do with 'love' in a matrimonial sense, or in a long term sense or in the sense of two people finding heart-felt pleasure by making a physical and an emotionally commitment to each other. Novelty usually comes from trying to satisfy one's physical needs alone. Is that a smart thing to do? Figure it out. Will that set a precedent in determining who a person really is?

THE RATIONAL GOSPEL

Has a scantily dressed, good-looking woman ever tempted me? The answer to that is a definite '**yes**'. Does that mean that I **might** consent to take part in some kind of 'novelty sex? That is another '**yes**', although the word 'might' is a key word and is not an indication of certainty. Another question is, 'does physical gratification alone make the sex act legitimate?' The answer to that question is **'no'**. Those are the times when indulgence trumps self-control and intelligence. That is not the way things should be in a meaningful relationship. Confusion and disharmony will always be the end result in that case.

Also, the provocative sexual images that 'pop' into a person's mind when sex is happening does not come from a person's heart, but they come from either a person's attraction to things of novelty or else comes from an evil spirit who is trying to tempt us by flinging evil images into our mind. If that is the case, it might be a good thing to just stop the game, and deal the cards again, only this time using a real deck and not a stacked deck or a fantasy deck.

Thus, it comes down to a major choice as to how much we should let our moral standards determine what our behavior will be. That will be when we have a moral choice to make, like it or not. That will also be when we will need to examine our own mind set and **DECIDE** once and for all, just how far we are willing to go in the exercise of our morality. We will also need to ask ourselves how many minutes in a day should we should spend fantasizing or imagining any kind of erotic scenario.

That will be a time when we will need to make another strongly felt DECISION as to whether to indulge ourselves sexually or whether to make a blanket policy in our minds to just leave all that stuff behind us and

look towards living a clean life in the future. That decision will need to be made one way or the other, and it will, and should, affect the way you will choose to behave for the rest of your life.

It is that important.

'Happiness', which is, theoretically, the ultimate goal for all human beings, will be absolutely unattainable for the seekers who look out only for novelty. 'Novelty' actually works to dilute our core values. It is a counterfeit perception of happiness. Thus, seekers of novelty will be separated from the seekers of truth and basically, live in a world of darkness instead of a world of light.

Most of these thrill seekers of novelty may be cognizant of the immorality that they practice and they probably realize that novelty sex doesn't lead to anything significant, but still many of those people will make the 'leap' to that place for the sake of their physical satisfaction, or even for the sake of their misplaced allegiance to their obsessions, or in other words, to their addiction.

The problem is that once a person makes the leap to indulge themselves, they cannot 'unmake' the leap. Thus, one way or another, certain consequences will ensue even though we may not know what those consequences will be they will still be there and our conscience will probably give us a pretty strong hint that it will not be a good consequence. A consequence might happen in our mind (IE: make a change in our values) or it might happen in real life (IE: the forming of an obsession or an addiction).

STANDARDS OF ENTERTAINMENT

(Evil Spirits and pornography)

As I have said, I think that it is a good thing for people to bring their 'standards of entertainment' into line with what their moral values are. Besides that, those moral values will need to be embedded in us. The decision to embed certain images in our mind will be made one way or the other, If the **weight** of that decision doesn't sound good to you, it might be best just to leave all that stuff alone and then, find some lighter kind of weight that you can carry around with you.

Whatever our decision is, it would still be good to know where sexually explicit images come from in our minds, at a time when we had absolutely no desire to bring those images into our minds. The source of those images is not always of our own making. Many times, those images just seem to come 'out of the blue'. This is especially true of people who make a habit of watching pornography including pornographic videos, movies, pictures, etc.

Sometimes those erotic images can be projected onto the walls of your mind by a nearby evil spirit. Evil spirits exist and have cognition. They can also be creative. Plus, they probably know you well and know what your weaknesses are. Never forget though that nothing canenter into ypour mind longer than one second without your conernt. If such an image should ever into your mind, please dump it. Go and to something else. Even write a story about how you chased a demon away. This is called 'RESILIENCE' and it is a gift that you can use at any time. I have used it many times myself and I have never regretted using resilience.

The sexual urge can be triggered by real life situations or imaginary situations. Just remember that it is quality that really counts, not quantity. It is also true feelings that count and not novelty.

There is a class of people who do not commit to living a moral lifestyle and those people will usually live a very 'risky' sex life, and in the end, a disappointing existence in general.

Being constantly aware of those lies may be seeing certain things in reality, but when the truth enters into the picture then those situations will be seen a truthful way of seeing things. "that way is, in a word - an UGLY WAY. Never be 'content' with ugly. Never get excited by 'ugly'. Avoid ugly like the plague. Watching pornography and acts of degradation is an ugly way to spend your time. Also, it is totally non-productive. Those lies when a person partakes of them will definitely shrink a person's spirit. Will that person actually become less of a person? 'YES'.

Will that person be able to redeem himself, or herself, and become a different person, or become somebody else? I say, 'NO'. Will God or Jesus be able to redeem that person and teach them how to become someone else? I say, YES AND NO.

The answer to that question will depend totally upon the person's willingness to co-operate with the divine will. Thus, our own allegiance to goodness and truth, at the expense of forsaking all worldly values, will be the deciding factor in every person's destiny.

Getting involved with pornography is not only filthy, but it is also stupid. That is a fact. You can rail against it. but it is still going to be there. The consequence of disobeying the truth is to be denied the truth in all situations.

When you are denied the truth, you will be denied certainty. When you are denied certainty, what do you have left? You have uncertainty. You will also have the companions of uncertainty as well. Those companions are confusion and ignorance. Good luck with those.

When you disobey the truth permanently, you will be denied the blessings of the truth permanently. Thus, because there will be no permanence there, there may not be any redemption there either. That is a very unpleasant thought

Watching porn is too distasteful for people who have a certain amount of 'class' in them. Plus, there is another problem there. It is possible is that when people watch pornography, many of those people can actually get 'hooked on it'. It is an addictive thing because it activates brain drugs in a person's mind.

A 'hook' can be a deadly thing for a fish, but it can also be a deadly thing for a human being as well. There are different kinds of hooks, but they all lead to the same place - captivity.

We can be led into captivity by the devil, but the more likely scenario is that we will be led into captivity by our own foolish choices. Either way it amounts to the same thing.

So I ask the question, 'can we over-rule that carnal part of our nature and make our entertainment habits less foolish and take on a smarter and healthier and a more respectful mindset'? I am not fooling around here. Our actual destiny could be hanging in the balance depending in what your decision is.

I say, yes, we can change our entertainment habits and make them better and even have them contain more intelligence, but there is only one way that we can do that. That is to build our viewing habits around good taste in the programs that we choose to watch and then maintain those habits.

If a person does not see the very real danger in watching pornography, which is addictive, then i am afraid that that person will end up as nothing more than a 'sitting duck'.

***

Those 'things' that artists learn about their craft may seem like little things in the beginning, but a creative writer will soon learn how to expand their ideas in a good way, and by doings so, make their ideas work better with an audience. Being creative, aside from receiving inspiration, is a cumulative thing. You never know how you can use certain experiences, or a certain combination of experiences to 'touch' other people and even larger audiences.

The most difficult part of that is organizing those events into an intelligent storyline that 'flows easily'. It also needs to flow with humor and with some kind of likeable qualities in the characters. The skill that makes that happen is essential in performance art, and it is not always an easy thing to do for anybody. It takes hard work and a special 'personality'.

That personality can be developed over time, but one needs to ask if it is worth sacrificing the opportunities for having a more normal kind of life.

I, personally, would refrain from giving any advice, one way or the other, to a young man or a young woman, who is thinking about going into the arts as a profession. I will say, however that those people who can master the skills involved in that line of work, and can still maintain their righteous core values, deserve all of the accolades that I would give them. If they cannot maintain those values, I say that the only honest emotion that i can feel for them is PITY.

***

There is no set formula for success in the arts. Sometimes you just need to follow the muse. Sometimes you need to just do a ton of writing and do it from unique angles. Then you filter out the bad stuff, or the mediocre stuff, and go with the stuff that you know 'with reasonable certainty', what will actually work. That can come partly by instinct, but it is possible for that to grow bigger over time, as long as the 'muse' knows that you are being true to your core values.

In the old days, I performed with a friend of mine for many years. My friend took a lot of risks when he interacted with his audiences. The thing was, that he always came out smelling like a rose. The only way that I could explain it was just to say, 'he had a definite knack for it'. It wasn't something that he learned in a theatre school. He just had a knack for it.

What would be my advise to a young person who wanted to perform comedy. I would say, "try to develop your knack. If you can't find one, then do something else for a living. Just don't forget to enjoy your life."

Still, I believe in having a good time in my life, even if hard times might come my way. My love of art and music allows me to find a lot of pleasure as I work with various concepts that I find interesting and talented people, whose company I always enjoy. That also implies the assumption that I can avoid all the egotism and the 'games' that go along with 'show business'.

Writing songs and books and acting has given me the opportunity to experience creativity first hand, I have learned a lot and like other kinds of 'learning' that is not something that you can easily write down for some student to follow, no matter how eager they are. The best comedians and performers are successful in my opinion, because they have developed a special 'knack' for it.

It has to do with one's natural personality, but other than that, there is no way that you can establish a formula that will work every time. Developing that knack to perfection is not guaranteed, but I say that it is possible. Just stick to your core values and acknowledge your supreme being whenever it is appropriate. One of the funniest comedians of the 1990's was Phil Hartman. I once heard Phil say that he never starts a show without saying the Lord's Prayer first.

Even great comedians like Richard Pryor have fallen down on his faces once in awhile. That happens at times when the material is old and there is just no 'spark' on it anymore. The knack that a good comedian once had can just go away and it won't be there anymore.

Discovering an artistic talent, if only as an admirer, is like finding a gold nugget in a watery stream full of ordinary rocks. Good citizens should encourage artists who they feel are gifted and tell other people about them. If that is important to you then you can feel confident that you are actually contributing to, what I call, the good taste of the world at large.

Chapter 19

ANATOMY OF A SMILE (16 p.)

Subtitles: Smile generators; Give them an opportunity to remember something good; Remember the Shining moments; Yippee, A Good Thought has Arrived; Nurse Jen.

SMILE GENERATORS

An appropriate title that I might use for this essay is: **'Could you become a 'smile generator'**? (an S.G.) Ask yourself, 'does your spouse, or a friend, or someone dear to you, have a beautiful smile?' Then ask yourself, 'Do they give out that smile freely or do they hold it back or keep it hidden?' If they keep it hidden, or if they too often seem morose or uninterested in anything, ask yourself, 'could **you** be an 'agent of change' in that matter?' Or **'COULD YOU ACTUALLY BECOME A 'SMILE GENERATOR'?**

Your answer to that question can take time to think about, but that is okay, because a good answer can make a big difference both in your day and in someone else's day. If you can somehow inspire another person to smile more often and more freely, then you could become involved in an honorable quest of **actually improving their life,** and things like that always count for something good.

It is quite unlikely that you can force someone to smile by saying to them something like, 'Why don't you smile more often?' Too often that just doesn't work. I think that it usually goes against human nature to expect someone to 'smile on command'.

Yet, if you are successful in your 'Smile Generating Quest', you can make a difference in someone's life and even in your own life too. You might even, 'make their day'.

If you desire to be a smile generator, here is something that I suggest you think about. Visualize the person you wish to see smile. See them in your mind as they might actually smile a healthy and sincere smile when they are in your presence. That should be a pleasant undertaking. Also remember that a phony smile will just not do the job.

SO WHAT ELSE CAN YOU DO? ANSWER – THINK OF A PLEASANT THOUGHT FIRST. IF YOUR LIFE HAS ANY VALUE YOU MUST BE ABLE TO THINK OF AT LEAST ONE PLEASANT THOUGHT THAT CAN CAUSE YOUR OWN LIPS TO CURL UPWARDS EVEN SLIGHTLY. THEN LET THAT PLEASANT THOUGHT SET YOUR MOOD AND THEN USE IT TO IT'S FULL POTENTIAL BY TALKING ABOUT A SIMILAR SITUATION THAT BRINGS A SMILE TO YOUR OWN FACE AND THEN LET YOUR POWER OF INFLUENCE DO ITS THING. THAT SHOULD CAUSE OTHER PEOPLE AROUND YOU TO SMILE TOO.

Contemplate this for a few moments and then decide on another scenario or a memory that might make you want to smile again. Take your time if you want. The point here is that <u>you will first be making yourself smile</u> instead of making someone else smile. That's the way it works - 'YOU SMILE FIRST, THEN LET THEM SMILE.' Smiles are contagious things. Do it and see what happens.

If it works and the person smiles in response to your smile, take note and be prepared to repeat the experiment again when you feel prompted to. It may take more than one try.

A warm smile is not something cheap. It is simply a non-verbal way of expressing yourself. That non-verbal way of expressing yourself can often be more effective than a 'verbal way 'of expressing yourself. Thus, you should put a lot of value on a simple smile.

Good values are transferable and you can start to generate it without using words. If you can generate a good and meaningful smile in someone else and repeat the process again as needed, then you will be a man ,or a woman, who has a special talent. Do not ignore a talent like that. It is a special knack that you can have or that you can develop. You can actually become 'a smile generator'

Furthermore, ask yourself if a friend who frowns a lot likes to carry on an interesting conversation. I mean a 'pleasant conversation', as opposed to a soliloquy that is filled with complaints. If you think your friend 'might' be willing to crack a smile, then it is time to begin to 'generate' that valuable form of self - expression.

Why do 'smilers' smile so much? You could always just ask them. Do they know something that you don't know? Maybe they do and maybe they don't, but there is only one way to find out. Ask them what their secret is. If they give you a good answer, pull out a pen and write down their answer.

Then compliment them on it. Even if they don't have a good answer, make it clear that a smile always reflects a positive attitude. They will probably catch on to that and give you, at least, a little grin. That would mean that something good is starting to happen.

A smile comes from having a good attitude and a good attitude comes from having the ability to recall a good event from the past and elaborate on that event or a similar event. If you talk about such events with a friend, good things can then happen as a result of your combined ideas. In a way you will be choosing to direct the conversation in a positive manner. That is a good start.

That is because, often times, the old axiom that 'two heads are better than one' can be a true axiom. While you are at it, start to talk about good things that are happening in your own life. Smile about those things and try to let that smile be of a contagious nature'.

The 'generation' of a smile can be the same thing as the 'expansion' of a smile. That is how you can actually give a smile to other people. It is just a matter of 'spreading a good thing around'. Thus, having a good sense of humor is a big help. It is not that complicated. It can be simple, and can also be fun.

A SMILE IS A SIGN THAT SHOWS YOU ARE 'AT EASE'. A FROWN IS A SIGN THAT YOU ARE 'NOT AT EASE'. THEY ARE TWO OPPOSITE THINGS. IF A SMILE IS THE OPPOSITE OF A FROWN THEN IT COULD BE SAID THAT A FROWN IS A DIS-EASE, OR A 'DISEASE,' AND THAT A SMILE IS A 'CURE' FOR THE DISEASE. IT IS A MAGICAL CURE THAT IS ALSO VERY SIMPLE.

I CALL IT THE 'BOB KING CURE'. I DON'T EXPECT TO GET ANY ROYALTIES FOR IT FROM BIG PHARMA COMPANIES, BUT, HEY, I AM JUST HAPPY TO BE OF SERVICE TO DEPRESSED PEOPLE OR TO THE CYNICAL PEOPLE OF THE WORLD.

WHATEVER WORKS. AS LONG AS A PERSON'S SMILE IS NOT BEING GENERATED FROM OTHER THINGS LIKE A WHISKEY BOTTLE OR FROM SOME KIND OF PILL BOTTLE, IT WILL BE A GOOD THING.

If the person you want to make smile can think of a good event that happened in the past, ask for details and, if they have fond feelings for that particular event, I will guarantee you that their face will take on a pleasant glow, and even the beginning of a healthy smile.

Everybody wants people to think they are funny or witty and there is nothing wrong with that. Also, i would say that the more you practice 'good humor', the better you will become at it. Get a friend to say something interesting or funny, then watch their face closely. Then show interest when you see their face begin to develop a glow when they get involved in a good topic of conversation.

View their contribution to that conversation as something valuable, and if your friend should say something smart, point it out to them as a compliment. Everybody wants to be appreciated for their willingness to contribute something good to a conversation and most people have some good opinions on life that they seldom get a chance to express, so they tend to just forget them. In cases like that, many people will actually know the cure, but too many of those people have short memories and they will often just forget that cure.

***

GIVE THEM THE CHANCE TO REMEMBER SOMETHING GOOD.

Share with your friend your appreciation of people who have the courage to smile in a situation when smiling might not be an easy thing for them to do. That could be a sign that YOU know how to make the best of a bad situation. SO SMILE. IT'S A MIRACLE CURE AND IT DOESN'T COST A PENNY.

Even if your smile is not totally sincere, that is okay because you can still give people a 'rehearsed smile'. That is not necessarily something that is phony or a pretense. Look on it as a good conditioning exercise for your delightful face.

Such a smile can cause your face muscles to loosen up. Then, when something <u>joyful</u> actually happens, your face muscles will then be ready and they will be up to the task of regaining the joyful smile that could then be transferred to someone else. you might even dazzle onlookers with your smile and then everyone will benefit. <u>This is one of the benefits you can get when you play a part in generating a good conversation.</u>

***

REMEMBERING THE SHINING MOMENTS

There are some moments in my life that I fondly remember and i sometimes try to recall them if I need an emotional lift of sorts.. You probably have some of those moments too. Make use of one of those moments. I don't want to forget them and neither should you. If you have erased them from your memory, they might as well never have happened. What a waste of a good memory that would be.

The memory of a good moment might not last very long, perhaps only a few seconds, but if it is a good memory, then it is a valuable thing. We should sustain our good memories for as long as we can and even share one or two of those memories with another person, assuming it would be of interest to them.

You may consider it to be a performance, but that is okay. Our social life is often full of performances. What happens in those performances doesn't really matter, but what we feel or learn from those performances does matter. Also, a good learning experience It might come in very handy one day to tell people about a time in our youth when we actually did something exciting.

I may be talking about reliving good past experiences, but we should <u>not</u> live in the past. Occasionally, though it is good to remenber the shining moments'. Those shining moments should be strong enough to make you smile, or even laugh. That is good, and it may be the first sign that you are 'on to something'.

THE RATIONAL GOSPEL

When I remember my good memories, I find that other good memories will more often creep into my mind. i don't know exactly where those good memories come from, perhaps it is the law that says, 'like attracts like', or 'one good memory will attract other good memories'.

I only know that good memories can multiply and reveal themselves more than once. Maybe they have a life of their own, and they can wait in a line while you wait for your 'higher self' to recall them, and then summon them back into your mind so they can make you smile again. Summon them to that kingdom that you call your mind, where a memory can get spurred on and come back to life again.

***

I don't know where those good thoughts come from and I don't really care. I just know that I appreciate them when they show up and I smile when they do show up. Such is a worthy activity for me, as long as the spirit of good humor and the fellowship with my friends is there.

Good memories can also be recalled by remembering beautifully produced movies or shows. Many years ago, In a production by Walt Disney, I remember thinking that the cartoon character Johnny Appleseed was a very cool guy. He once sang these words and in a joyful voice:

"OH THE LORD IS GOOD TO ME AND SO I THANK THE LORD.
FOR GIVING ME THE THINGS I NEED,
THE SUN AND THE RAIN AND THE APPLE TREES
OH, THE LORD IS GOOD TO ME."

I concur with Johnny's thinking when I think about the good times, I realize that they were mostly simple times in my life. They were also many other good times too, even if I no longer remember how good those times actually were.

***

KAY KAY

Many years ago I developed a friendship with a couple of families who I vaguely knew. One of the people in one family was a woman who I knew named Laura. I knew her from high school, and she later became a single mother. She had a daughter who everyone called KK. KK was handicapped physically and mentally. She had a cassette that I recorded and gave to her. She loved to listen to my music on her stereo. Most of my music back then was geared for children and she was a big fan of mine.

One day we decided that KK should join a bunch of us for a party on her birthday. For a present, I brought her another cassette that I recorded in my basement on a cheap little recorder that I had. Some of the songs on that cassette were recorded from other recordings that I had previously made professionally. But that one song that I recorded in my basement was called KK's Birthday song. I don't remember the whole song, but one verse that I do remember that went like this:

"So lets sing a song for KK
Because it is her birthday
She's older than her brother

**She's older than her mother
And she"ll live to be a thousand I am told."**

We played the cassette at the party table and when the birthday song came up, KK squealed with delight and she was amazed that I would write a song especially for her.

I am not saying that I would try to immortalize myself because of a kind gesture that I once made, but as I get older and look back on my life, I can slightly recall some simple moments that actually meant a lot to me.

That moment when KK heard the song that i wrote for her was one of those shining moments. I will always remember the look on her face when she heard the song and she realized that it was made for her. That memory can always bring forth a little smile on my face and thus, i will classify that memory as one of my 'shining moments'.

Even today, I get a good feeling when I witness something meaningful, or intelligent, that can make me smile. I might hear a faint whisper of a word like 'YIPPEE' or 'AWESOME' or 'BEAUTIFUL', or some other word. That word, or image, might rever in my mind. Why? Because I know it is a confirmation that something good once happened to me. '.

Shining moments tell me that I am on the verge of 'paying my own way'. 'Paying my own way' to me, means accepting and giving credence to a good idea and making that idea and the feeling that goes along with it a part of my being. When I accept that 'shining moment, that special word, like 'YIPPEE' or something similar, will grow louder in my mind over time. Soon, It can become more like a shout, either a soft shout or a large shout, but it is one that will resonate between God and me. In other words, it is good to create such moments and it is good to share them with others.

***

YIPPEE! **A GOOD THOUGHT HAS ARRIVED**

(This is an excerpt from the play 'A GOOD THOUGHT" which features a man named Uncle Bob talking to his niece Cindy. Uncle Bob uses words 'Yippee' or 'Yahoo' Today a person might use the word 'AWESOME' or 'BEAUTIFUL'.)

.
Uncle Bob:

YIPPIE! I feel good Cindy. I don't know why. I just do. AWESOMME!

(Cindy looks at him with a puzzled expression. Uncle Bob sees her look and stares at her.)

Cindy:
Why do you feel so good?

Uncle Bob:
Do I need to tell you why I feel good? My feelings are who I am. They make me smile. Some days I might feel not feel so good. Then, a few weeks later perhaps, I might remember those good feelings again, and I will smile again. It's a hit and miss game I guess, but today, it's a hit with me. Tomorrow, though my 'hit' might be forgotten about. So would you like to celebrate my 'hit' with me today?

Cindy:
But I don't feel like I've got a 'hit' in **me** right now. Aren't you kind of presumptuous expecting me to latch on to the good things that you say you are feeling?

Uncle Bob:
No. I am just giving you an invitation, Cindy. You can take it or leave it.

Cindy:
I'll leave it, thanks.

Uncle Bob:
Suit yourself.

Cindy: (pause)
I don't understand how you can expect me to feel what you are feeling when you can't even tell me what you are feeling or why you are feeling those 'happy' feelings.

Uncle Bob
I call them 'YIPPEE' feelings' Cindy, or even 'BEAUTIFUL' feelings. They are a part of something called 'life'. I think you are familiar with that concept called LIFE, but I think that you will better understand the concept of 'Yippie feelings' when you get older.

Cindy:
Oh, so now you are saying that I am Immature?

Uncle Bob:
I didn't say that. I prefer to think of it this way. Life is a waiting game and **we all need to pick our times when we**

should 'decide to blossom'. When will your time to blossom come Cindy? Next week? Next year?

Cindy:
But I think that I, personally speaking, need a reason to yell 'Yippee'. Do you think that is a stupid way of thinking?

Uncle Bob:
No. But like I said, I am just offering you an invitation. You can accept it or reject it.

***

NURSE JEN

I was in a local hospital recently trying to get someone to stop a severe nosebleed that hit me out of the blue. I was in the waiting room for many hours, but nobody did anything to stop the bleeding. I looked like a one-man atrocity with blood all over my clothes and blood all over the floor. They did nothing to stop the bleeding and I was actually worried that I might bleed to death. That, kind of, describes the confidence that I had in the nurses and doctors there.

The bleeding eventually stopped, but when I woke up the next morning, my nose started bleeding again. I went back to the hospital and another doctor came to see me again and this time he stopped the bleeding. He also recommended an ear, nose and throat specialist who I should call.

The next day, I visited that specialist. He put some freezing in my nose and then he put a camera up my nose. Thus, I could see what the camera was seeing in the computer monitor. I was amazed when I saw that there was a huge amount of puss at the top of my nasal passages. The specialist told me that I had an infection in my nose, something that I had never heard of before. He prescribed some antibiotics for me then I went on my way.

The next day I went to my pharmacist and he fulfilled the prescription and the anti-biotics actually stopped the bleeding. In any case, the whole experience was very unpleasant.

On that first full day that I was in the hospital a male nurse took pity on me and got a doctor to look at me. It was awful having to deal with the triage nurse at the hospital. She wanted me to fill in forms and take tests while, in the meantime; the blood was flowing out of my nose like a river and going all over the floor. My clothes were also soaked with blood. I wanted them to stop the bleeding before I did anything else, but they would not listen. It was obvious that thy simply did not know what to do.

They were nurses in an Emergency ward, but they did not seem to know what a real emergency was. It was a hospital with a huge staff and millions of dollars to spend, but they could not stop a simple nosebleed. I was aghast.

I was grateful for that male nurse and I told him so later. It was so good to finally talk to a medic who was able to break away from that 'idiocy epidemic' that was prevalent in the rest of the hospital staff.

***

On the second day, the bleeding had stopped, temporarily anyways. In the meantime, while I was lying in a bed I watched the other busy nurses tending to their patients. One nurse who caught my eye was a very friendly nurse named Jen. I noticed her especially because she laughed a lot and **she also had a beautiful smile**, which she displayed frequently.

After a few hours, I began to talk to Nurse Jen. I told her that I was a writer and that I was putting together a book of original essays. One of my essays was going to be called **'Anatomy of a Smile'**. I said that I would like to ask her to answer a few questions for me.

That got her attention right away. It seemed like she had a few moments to spare so I asked her pointedly why she smiled so much. She said that she meets a lot of people, and many of those people have their own troubling issues and might find it difficult to smile, but for her, personally, she knew that smiling was a choice. She told me that she could either choose could either choose to smile or else choose to 'wallow in sadness'. She told me that she decided to choose to smile.

"Everyone has a choice to do that", she said. "And choosing to smile is what makes the big difference for me."

What a great answer.

She went away to tend to some other patients, but later on I sought Nurse Jen out and asked her if she had to remind herself to smile several times a day. She said 'no', but said that she had become "very used to smiling and now she just saw it as a natural part of herself."

THE RATIONAL GOSPEL

Another great answer.

She didn't have any more time to talk to me, but I learned a lot from her in the short time that we talked and I have not forgotten our conversation. That experience also taught me that there are some good people in the world we can learn a lot from those people, but **sometimes we need to just come right out and ask them 'what makes them tick'.**

My nosebleed cleared up, but I was still a little traumatized. I had never experienced anything like that before and I had never even heard of anything like a nose infection. I don't know what happened to Nurse Jen, but I will thank her now because she taught me something about smiling at a time when I was in no mood to smile.

Chapter 20.

NO BEER by Bob King (2p.)

(I interrupt this serious book to bring you a few moments of levity. Nothing wrong with that. There is also some political satire in the song. Nothing wrong with that either. I wrote the first part of this song many years ago. I called it 'NO BEER'. I recently changed a few words around and people seem to like it even more now, so lately I started singing the song again.

1.
Well I had me a dream just the other night.
I dreamed that all the breweries dropped out of sight.
They said that in the evening they were all here,
But come the next morning they had all disappeared.
And there was no beer. NO BEER. NO BEER. NO BEER.
There was just no beer. NO BEER NO BEER NO BEER

2.
Well the people didn't know what to do at all.
Cause there was just no more alcohol.
I walked into a tavern or some such place.
The people were sitting around looking at each other's face.
Because there was no beer. NO BEER. NO BEER NO BEER
There was just no beer. NO BEER. NO BEER NO BEER

3.
Well I called up the prime minister. I said he should be ashamed.
His name was Justin Trudeau, He was a man of little brain.
He said, "Hey Bob. I don't want to be a stinker

But I think its time we clamped down on those no good beer drinkers."
So I just outlawed beer. NO BEER NO BEER NO BEER
Canadians don't want beer. NO BEER NO BEER NO BEER

4.
I said, "Mr. Trudeau, I just don't understand
How could you stop beer from coming into this land?"
He said, I'd gladly bring beer back into this nation.
You just have to donate some money to the Trudeau Foundation.
Then I can get you some beer. NO BEER NO BEER NO BEER.
Then I'll be happy to get you some beer NO BEER NO BEER NO BEER

(NARRATIVE: Well, a little earlier I said in this song that Mr. Trudeau was a man of little brain. I felt bad about that so I made another small change. That is because I recognized that **our Prime Minister is not just a man of little brain. He, in fact, he doesn't really have any brains at all.**

(The chorus starts out softy but then gets louder)
NO BRAINS NO BRAINS NO BRAINS
NO BRAINS NO BRAINS NO BRAINS.
He's got nothing upstairs.
NO BRAINS NO BRAINS NO BRAINS
Yes, the old brain cupboard is bare
NO BRAINS NO BRAINS NO BRAINS

He's got no grey matter
NO BRAINS NO BRAINS NO BRAINS
Yes, He's as mad as a hatter
 NO BRAINS, NO BRAINS, NO BRAINS NO BRAINS.

21. THE SPIRITUAL OVERVIEW (67P.)

SUBTITLES

Spirituality and Being Clean; Freedom of Religion; An Unseen World; Liberty, Bondage and the New Covenant; Organized Religion; Religion Causes Wars?; Good and Evil Spirits; The Salt of the Earth; Spiritual Roots; How to Spot An Evil Spirit; Religion and Spirituality; The problem of evil; Absolute Morality and Relative Morality; Evil Forces and levels of understanding; Levels and Being Above Board; Wisdom and the Comforter; Good Religion and Bad Religion; Religion and Knowledge; My Soul and its Inclinations.

***

I wanted to write a spiritual overview as a part of this book, partly because in it I would address some of the criticisms that skeptics and naysayers level against Christianity in general. Such negative people, I have found, are not really as informed or educated as they pretend to be. They usually just want to make a splash by trying to 'burst a Christian's bubble by presenting their biased opinions and criticisms in public. That would include many schoolteachers who are always guaranteed to have a forum made up of a 'captive audience' and/or who have some kind of axe to grind.

The problem is that, as I just said, they are rarely fully informed about the issues. Aside from that, they can cause a lot of mischief to take place in the minds of their students, especially young and fairly innocent students, but then that kind of thong is what they enjoy doing the most. The power of the Spirit that is talked about in the Bible is seen by them as non-existent.

Aside from that, I thought that many students would be more interested in hearing facts, and learning many things about the Spirit world that are rarely discussed in detail by anyone. It would be healthier for any student of any age to hear words that are spoken by a man or a woman who was a genuine and devout Christian. One of those Christians would be myself, so I welcome that opportunity today. I admit though that I do not know everything about the scriptures, but I have studied them for many years and I can say that I do know more things about the gospel (good news) of Jesus Christ than most other people.

As well, I would venture to say that I have some views of the gospel that are definitely unique and that might even be unheard of by some biblical scholars. I do not apologize for that however and if there is anyone who wants to challenge me about my beliefs, I would take that challenge to debate me at anytime.

***

Theoretically, the object of science is to find truth. As it happens, that is also the job of religion. Science, it seems to me, has the job of finding truth that can be seen, while religion has the job of finding truth that, mostly, cannot be seen. That is because all things are made of matter and there are some kinds of matter that are so tiny that they cannot be seen or identified.

Emotions and feelings like love and hate and kindness are examples of this. I think this job of religion is quite valid because I believe it to be the height of conceit to think that everything in life must be 'seen' in order for it to exist. There are many examples of things that are unseen, but actually exist. Love is one. Faith is another. In a physical sense, electricity is something that is real, yet unseen.

I also believe that unseen spirits exist. That includes our individual spirits, or the intangible spirit or a joint spirit' like 'team spirit' where the spirit can be a collective thing. There is also 'spirit of goodwill' that exists when people share feelings of fellowship. Another kind of spirit would be a spirit 'entity' or a disembodied spirit that we cannot see. I also believe in Holy Spirit who is the third member of the Godhead and the most active Spirit on the earth at this time.

Spirits, whether we perceive them or not, are an unseen part of our lives. I believe that all things are made of matter and that spirits are made of very fine matter that can last even beyond this lifetime. I also believe that our personal spirits have cognitive abilities. These abilities are not easily recognized because, in this physical world we live in, the cognitive abilities of our physical brain and our five senses are the ones that are always immediately before us and they always command our attention firstly.

We will be somewhat more aware of our spiritual cognition when we try to lead spiritual lives, that is, live lives of cleanliness. The full awareness and consciousness of our spirits will only become clear after we are dead and our brains cannot function anymore. In that case, our spirit, which has cognition, will do the job that the brain once did, only this time, it will have much more accurate information to go on. That is because the powers of heaven are highly organized and have much power that is not available to mortal men and women.

That is when we will come to know the nature of our spirits and even of all spirits, and know why and how they have been with us throughout our lives, even when they remain silent and unseen.

We are all pretty much useless creatures without the influence of the Holy Spirit in our lives. It doesn't matter what our talents are. Only the Holy Spirit can properly fill the contours of hard reality and give us comfort when we need it. God knows us all very well, and His Spirit, when we invite Him in becomes an active part of us, and has the power to comfort us and guide us in the ways of truth.

The main element of the Holy Spirit is truth and truth is the prime factor in everything that is of value, so we must be in tune with the truth if we wish to be of any value. That is because the Holy Spirit, or the Comforter, is of an Eternal nature. God will help us to be in tune with the Spirit, but without a strong <u>desire</u> for us to be in tune or connect with the Spirit, all efforts to do so will be fruitless. The truth is pure. You cannot mix purity with a half-truth, or something half pure.

The Holy Spirit is custom made for you and for me, but **only if we choose to partake of that Spiri**t. The Holy Spirit is also suspended in time. The Holy Spirit brings spiritual life to you and me and causes our own smaller spirits to be 'quickened'. The Spirit has been called 'living water' and is self-cleaning. The Spirit is a gift, but He will only be given to us at certain times. Those times will be chosen by the giver of all precious gifts and will also be given according to the faith of the person who asks for that knowledge and studies it out.

SPIRITUALITY AND BEING CLEAN

There are two kinds of thinking. There is cognitive thinking (with the brain) and non-cognitive thinking of the Spirit. When we die, our brain will die too. That will be the end of cognitive thinking. Spiritual thinking, however, will not die or end with death because the human soul is spirit and Spirit is never ending.

When we die we will not think in the same way as we do now and we will not remember many things from our mortal lives, nor will we want to remember many of those things. We will remember spiritual things though, and that is because spiritual things are eternal and are apart of our souls. They are therefore, of greater worth than other kinds of thinking.

Spirituality is mostly about becoming clean in body and mind. God is clean and pure and I think that <u>we could have difficulty worshiping a God who was not clean and pure</u>. Therefore, in order for God to take us into His home or allow us to enter into His presence, I would think that God would place 'being as clean as we can be' as a requirement for that.

Thus, our highest thoughts should be clean thoughts. Those are surely the only thoughts we would want to take with us into the eternities. Spiritual people desire to have cleanliness in spirit, as opposed to becoming involved in the dirt and chaos that is found in the mortal world. That would include things like sin, covetousness, people pleasing, scheming, etc.

The goal of a twelve-step group like Alcoholics Anonymous is to help people become 'clean and sober'. That's a nice phrase. The word 'sober' generally means being free from the influence of alcohol, and that is good, but I think the first word is even more important. 'Clean' means being free from everything that would stain us. It means that we are free from lusts, secrets, anger or aggression, guilt, fear, selfish thoughts, pride, and things that put us in bondage. I think it would means being free from all the things that would stain, or scar, our souls.

Some people don't mind being stained. Some people even relish the idea. Some people don't like being stained, but cannot resist the temptation to indulge in 'dirty' things; much like the pig returning to it's mud puddle (2 Peter 2: 22). And then, there are some people who feel that they are already clean, but they could easily be stained in ways that they cannot see.

Obviously, men and women in their natural physical state are not clean unless they make efforts to be so. Physically, they need to bath regularly or they will begin to look, and even smell, unclean. This is the way things are. Thus, I ask, 'is the natural spiritual state of human beings clean, physically and morally?' Or do we not need to somehow bath, in a spiritual sense? I equate this sense of bathing in the Spirit with the process of **repentance**, or discarding any immoral or wicked thoughts or feelings or attitudes.

With true repentance, we can wipe away any toxic thoughts that might have oozed out of our mental pores, and then discard them down an invisible drain in order to prevent them from clinging to us? God has surely created us, but in this world, I think that we have been given a 'maintenance contract' to go along with that? Thus, He has given us the great 'gift' of 'repentance'.

If I could choose one word that would describe the nature of the Godhead, (Father, Son and Holy Ghost'), that word might be 'clean'.

> *"let us <u>cleanse</u> ourselves from all filthiness of the flesh and spirit, perfecting holiness in the fear of God."*
> *- 2 Corinthians 7: 1*

God knows what will stain our spirits and what will not stain our spirits. We humans do not know this with exactness until we learn the actual importance and the actual delight in 'being clean'. Only after we heed His counsel and obey his laws will we find out the truth about all things through our spiritual observances, cleanliness included.

Our mortal experiences are often just not enough for us to learn what we need to know about being clean. We are all born amongst stain-causing people and stain-causing circumstances and we do not always have an awareness of who, and what, those people and circumstances are until we reach a stage of spiritual maturity.

To be clean, we also need to **associate** with clean people, read clean books, listen to clean music, watch clean movies and mainly, stand in Holy places whenever we can. When we do these things, and acknowledge and appreciate the goodness that is found there, those 'good' habits can become second nature to us. And they will become habits that will be enough to allow us to avoid getting involved in anything that would stain us.

How should we treat other people who are in an unclean state? If you see a person who is drunk and dirty and staggering down the street using foul language, should you reject that person? Perhaps yes, and perhaps no. That depends on the circumstances, but in any case, you should **reject** the state they are in.

If a person is in an unclean state on the outside, the chances are high that they will be in an unclean state on the inside, whatever that may consist of. Thus, if we really want to help someone to be clean again, we must put our focus on what is going on inside of him, or her.

We will need to get them to realize that a lack of cleanliness is an inside problem. An inside problem is an unseen problem, or even a spiritual problem. It is a problem of 'inner' uncleanliness. When the inside problem is solved, the outside problem will be solved much sooner, and then we can feel free to proceed down our chosen path.

Being **unclean**, inside and out, is something that we are all guilty of at some point in our lives. That is why we need to be purified. Purification must be total. We cannot be partially pure or 'partially clean'.

> ***"Doth a fountain send forth at the same place sweet water and bitter?"***   ***- James 3: 11***

We can only do this with divine help. Being clean in a verbal sense is being 'clear' and 'honest' too. You can access the Holy Ghost when you are clean and the Holy Ghost will make thoughts and manners clear in your mind through transferrable thought/feelings.

Being clean is also being clear headed. Clear thinking is clean thinking. Dirty thinking is when ideas become impaired and perceptions of goodness will not be fully available to us. Without clarity of thought, despite our best intentions, we will never progress. We will 'fall' backwards and land in the swamp.

The gift of repentance is a great gift. It will wash you clean when you exercise that gift in the name of Christ. That is the reason He was sent here. As well as cleaning yourself, it is also good to clean your bathing area should bathtub rings start to form. Abrasives (or tough love) may be needed for this. So choose a 'good' bathing environment. **Your first concern in that department should be your home**.

FREEDOM OF RELIGION

Freedom of religion is part of the first amendment of the American Constitution. It is also guaranteed in the constitutions and charters of many other countries. I believe that freedom of religion is the most important freedom in any constitution. It could also be called freedom of belief, (to believe what one chooses, or freedom of thought, (to think what one wants to think.)

Without freedom of religion the totalitarians of the world, (people who seek total control) will be telling us to believe all the things they want us to believe, and trying to force us into believing them through legislation and, subsequently, through the physical force of armies. I am not talking about the totalitarians coercing us to believe in God. On fact I am talking about the opposite. The totalitarians hate the notion of God. That is the way the world is going. **They totally believe that they are the 'woke ones'.**

Many people who are dedicated to freedom, however, will be prepared to lay down their lives in defense of freedom of religion. That means they want to protect people's right to have their own opinions, and especially opinions on what is right and wrong. Religious freedom allows people to set their own standards, and to worship what, or whom, they will, even if it's a person who happens to worship a fencepost.

The word 'religion' could be defined as 'whatever is the ultimate thing in a person's life'. For some people money is ultimate, and that, according to this definition, is their religion. For others, friendship may be the ultimate thing in their lives. For others, work, sports, art, music or sexual fantasy might the ultimate thing in their lives. That would be their religion, by the previous definition.

Religion is something that goes beyond the common, or 'normal', things in life. It is of a spiritual nature and not of a materialistic nature. I may not have a perfect knowledge of spiritual things, but I know they exist and I do have some knowledge about that 'spiritual world' which runs parallel to ours.

These beliefs are backed up by testimonies of knowledgeable prophets, who write and speak by Divine inspiration. Jesus Christ is the ultimate example of that and the stories about Him back up that notion. Thus, His life and His words are worth investigating.

He is a person who is considered by millions to be the Savior of the world who wants to lead people to a final resting place that is a place of peace and love and much intelligence. This is something that cannot be proven empirically, but it can be proven in a person's heart and that is what is most important.

In any case, I would always defend the right of people to believe what they believe, even if their beliefs are very different than my own. If they can persecute one religious group, they can persecute any religious person or group of people and history has shown that they will do that.

AN UNSEEN WORLD

People who doubt the existence of spirit will ask, 'Why is this hidden spirit world not evident to our five senses?' The short answer is that we came from a world made up of higher spirits. When we came to earth, we came through a veil that hid that higher world and left us in a lower world where we would have to struggle and experience many different things, both good and bad. This was called a probationary state and it was necessary for the sole reason that it would help us in gathering knowledge and help us to advance as human beings. We now live in a separate world from our former and higher world of spirits. Our world here is in a 'fallen' state. Our physical eyes have replaced our spiritual eyes, for our purposes here.

The Earth is fallen because it seems to be in our basic human natures. According to the 'Garden of Eden' story in Genesis, it seems to be a fact that our nature is to defy authority, specifically, defy the authority of God, who is our

Maker. But, someone might say:

"yeah, but Satan was there to tempt Eve to eat the fruit, hen is not doing that today.

Isn't he? Don't be a fool.

> **And the days if the children of men were prolonged according to the will of God, that they might repent while in the flesh; wherefore, their state became a state of probation,   - 2 Nephi 2: 21**

Thus, God desired for us to learn the consequences that inevitably come from exploring this inherent duality in our personalities, and by learning about it, overcoming the negative parts of it. This learning can be difficult, but it is good because it is only for the sake of our eternal happiness.

This life is the time for us to learn from our experiences here in this fallen world. This is so that we can know the right ways to live and which are the best ways to show love. That is of ultimate importance.

As we live on this planet, we will learn where independent attitudes can lead, both in a good sense and in a bad sense. They can range from being either extremely simple, or extremely complicated, depending on our personal decisions and our devotion to the good and the amount of self-discipline that we have.

The major thing we will need to learn is what happens when we believe that we are capable of attaining a permanent state of happiness without any help from God. Keep in mind that I say this as a man who has nothing but praise for individual initiative. Nevertheless, there is an important aspect of individualism that we can tend to overlook, and that is **to firstly, to recognize the blessings that our Creator gives us and secondly, to show gratitude for those blessings or favors. And thirdly, don't just think that Satan is nothing but a cartoon character who doesn't really have any power. Just go out into a downtown street and watch the drug addicts begging for money as their eyes are practically falling out of their sockets.**

Humility and gratitude are not signs of weakness. They are signs that we are <u>free</u> from the prideful ways of the secular world and free from the traps of evil forces, like having too much pride.

We cannot find happiness all by ourselves. That is like a football trying to inflate itself after it has become deflated. We need to receive the invisible 'breath of life' from another source, a higher source. Otherwise, we will only be a counterfeit image of an inflated football.

We need to know what lies <u>beyond</u> our physical faculties of seeing, hearing, feeling, tasting, and smelling. If we can discover something beyond these things, even get just a glimpse of it, then a whole new world opens up to us, and we will then begin to learn about life on a different level.

I cannot see a spirit. I cannot hear one. I can only feel a spirit while it is upon me. I am like Helen Keller. Helen Keller was a courageous woman who lived in the mid 1900's and who eventually became a world famous inspiration to millions of people. Helen became blind and deaf when she was a child. She was angry and rebellious when she was young, but then one day, through the help of her care worker, she became very excited when she discovered that she could actually communicate with people through other means.

Basically, she learned to talk by touching the throat of her care worker and making simultaneous sounds. The discovery of this power changed her whole attitude and her whole life. I compare this to a similar experience that might be had when someone becomes aware of the power of the Spirit that is within us all.

The word 'spirituality' can be a difficult thing to define. It is like defining the word 'love'. There can be many connotations to certain words. Nevertheless, it is good for people to learn as much as they can about the different categories of spirits, both in an intangible way and in a practical way, so we will come to a better understanding about everything.

When I refer to spirits in the sense of being a non-entity, I mean, for example, that we can be said to be in high spirits when we are in a good mood and we can be said to be in low spirits when we are not in a good mood. This is a common thing and quite observable.

When talking about spirits in this context we can further ask the question, "Can we change the status of our own spirits by willful means, that is, actually lift our spirits or 'expand' them simply by choosing to think more positively and with faith?" Or will we just be forced to be subjected to whatever mood that a particular spirit dictates how we should feel at a particular time? We will discuss this further in later chapters, but for now let us look at spirits in general, both spirits that are individual separate entities, and spirits that are just feelings or moods, but have a kind of life force to them.

LIBERTY, BONDAGE AND THE NEW COVENANT

As far as freedom in spirituality goes, some people might say if they decided to 'serve' God, then that would limit their freedom, because they were being subservient to another being. This is true in a way, but not true in another way, and is more important way.

Connecting with the source of all truth can actually enhance our freedom because it is, in fact, a legitimate 'connection' with the ultimate freedom. The God-man relationship is not a master - slave relationship. It is a Heavenly Father/son relationship or Father/daughter relationship, or even a Heavenly Mother/daughter relationship. We all need to <u>connect</u> with something good because we all need good and reliable reference points. Otherwise, we would literally go insane.

God is our ultimate connection. He is our literal Spiritual Father and we are a part of His family. He is a free being and we too can inherit that freedom when we show that we can safely handle it. His freedom will be

THE RATIONAL GOSPEL

our freedom.

> *"The spirit itself beareth witness with our spirit, that we are the children of God; And if children, then heirs; heirs of God, and joint heirs with Christ"*
>
> *- Romans 8: 16, 17*

God instructs us not because He wants to exert His authority over us, but He does so out of <u>love</u> and a desire that we might <u>learn</u> in the best and most expedient ways. This is so that God and His children can become 'partners', even ultimate partners who will pledge to support each other in a righteous cause even until the end.

God and Jesus and the Holy Ghost are the ultimate teachers. Nobody else comes close. They are ultimate teachers because they have reached the ultimate level of perfection and they desire, by the power of love, to share it with you and me and everyone else who wants to be a part of it and is willing to obey the commandments.

Some people love to learn about ultimate things and they will be taught those things and be given many spiritual favors because of that. Other students don't like to learn and as a result they can become lazy or distracted or rebellious. They will manage to maintain their character flaws strictly by choosing to maintain them.

Without being connected to the Spirit of truth, we will be

connected to untruth. Being connected to untruth is not freedom, although it might claim to be so. In fact, it is bondage in every sense of the word. This is because, with untruth, or relative truth, the rules are always changing. The powers behind those changing rules are the spirits of untruth.

Those spirits will always try to get us to do their will so that they can rule over us in this world and even in future worlds. Thus, we will be driven by an agenda that has been set by liars and deceivers, many of whom unite under the banner of some kind of special interest group, a group that always claims that claims to be people of virtue, or claim to be people who have superior intelligence. In other words, they sometimes call themselves 'woke' people.

To become aware of the implications of those deceivers and to be aware of how they use their persuasive powers, we need some kind of connection to truth. We also need to cherish quality of liberty.

> *"Where the spirit of the Lord is, there is liberty."*
>
> *- 2 Corinthians 3:17(emphasis added)*

Because we are a Christian organization, we believe in the new covenant that Jesus brought to earth. That new covenant is explained in the New Testament in various places.

> *"he is the mediator of a better covenant, which was established upon better promises."*

- Hebrews 8: 6

The new covenant came in to the world when Jesus came into it. It means that we will have to endure some suffering in our lives rather than be aggressive at every opportunity. Jesus was the exemplar and the spearhead of that new covenant. Most Christians will try to have forgiveness and longsuffering instead of violence and revenge. For our eternal purposes, it is the best way.

ORGANIZED RELIGION

To be fully affective, the message of the new covenant that Jesus brought to the world needs to be spread throughout the world. We cannot do that without some kind of organization. Some people say that they do not believe in organized religion, but I say we need it to create more solid information, upon which, spiritual knowledge is built. The more solid information we have, the better we will be prepared for any surprises. Presenting us with surprises is an important part of Satan's mission.

While God may speak to us individually, he needs to communicate with us as a people, His people. The entire Bible bears witness to that principle. We are His people. As the 'family of man' we all need reconciliation with our Spiritual Father. To be able to receive those communications from that Higher Power, we need to be organized and 'of one mind' regarding sacred things.

Religion is an ideal. God is an idealist, but at the same time He is also a realist. Because He is all-knowing, He can manage both of these qualities at the same time. He is the **only** being who is both and has the authority and wisdom to tell us what is real and what is important. That is because God has achieved a state of perfection. Thus, His <u>true</u> church will be a <u>perfect</u> organization designed according to our needs and abilities.

Some people feel that they have found the true church and other people are waiting for it to appear, but in any case, God's house is a house of order, not a house of chaos. And as prophesied, it is, or will be, present on the earth one day and will be a permanent thing.

> ***"And in the days of these kings shall the God of heaven set up a kingdom, which shall never be destroyed and the kingdom shall not be left to other people, but it shall break in pieces and shall consume all these kingdoms, and it shall stand forever."***
>
> ***- Daniel 2: 44***

In the spiritual hierarchy of Christian churches, the Godhead, consisting of the Father, Son and Holy Ghost, is at the head. Next in line are the prophets of the church, both ancient and those living today. Are there prophets living today on the earth? I do not see why God would withhold prophets from us, although the Bible says there will also be many false prophets on the earth.

> ***"For false Christs and false prophets shall rise, and shall shew signs and wonders, to seduce, if it were possible, even the elect."*** ***- Mark 13:22***

THE RATIONAL GOSPEL

Reading the further words of Paul, it seems that there will also be <u>true</u> prophets on the earth, as is verified in Ephesians.

> ***"And he gave some, <u>prophets</u>; and some evangelists; and some pastors and teachers"***
> ***- Ephesians 4:11***

God said that He would pour out His Spirit upon us in the last days, (Joel 2: 28) so why would He withhold prophets? We would be wise, I think, to seek out such prophets and figure out by reasoning, and by a Spiritual witness if they exist.

The gaining of the knowledge that I speak of requires three basic things. It requires prayer (communicating with God and with our higher self), the study of scriptures (learning) and fellowship with like-minded people (love).

Some people claim that they are spiritual in their own way, but they do not believe in organized religion. I do not blame people for that because the <u>true</u> church is not known about by a large number of people. Nevertheless, many of those people have given up on finding it. In that sense, it can become hust another 'cop out'.

Christ organized His church in His day and instructed His apostles to go out and preach to people, and to organize churches throughout the world according to the teachings, and the Spirit, of Jesus. Although Jesus spoke often to individuals, most of his talks were given to large groups of people. Large groups of people can be effective <u>only</u> when they are organized and with a gifted organizer at the head.

God's words and Jesus' words were intended to be spoken

to the world as well as to individuals, and if God is organizing His church, you can be assured that, even though the people in it might be faulty, the organization itself, in His <u>true</u> Church, will <u>not</u> be faulty.

Jesus commanded the Apostles to go out and teach the word to the Gentiles, to Rome and Corinth and Galatia and elsewhere, which they did. The 'organization' of the spreading of the gospel was an integral part of it all. If that was not the case and the skeptics of organizational religion could, conceivably, have a point. If they did have a good point, then, the many Apostles who died painful martyr's deaths would be very disappointed to hear that all their attempts to teach and organize and convert, even to the laying down of their lives, were not really necessary. That would be an extreme tragedy and I could not believe for a minute that God would allow that to happen.

In the comfort of our living rooms on a Sunday morning, it is sometimes easy to believe that all religious belief is personal and those various groups in their meeting halls are incorrect by preaching the gospel to every man woman and child. But God is aware of the weaknesses of all of the churches and the people in them. All churches are made up of people, and people are <u>always</u> fallible.

But no matter what the armchair theologians think, **the actuality of a 'true' church is real**. His church will be established and stand forever as was previously cited.

God speaks to his people as a whole because they are all descendants of our first parents and we are all His children. He does not want any empty chairs at the bargaining table. He holds no favorites and speaks to us all, at least, to 'those who have ears to hear'.

In the end it is vital that the most righteous, kindest and most intelligent people among us should stick together to support each other. That is why it is so important for us to be 'organized'.

RELIGION CAUSES WARS?

In order to promote clarity in my own mind, as well as in the minds of others, allow me to try to dispel a few myths that I have heard about religion over the years. Firstly, I have heard too many people say that organized religion is harmful because it is responsible for more wars on the Earth than anything else in history.

This notion gives skeptics a perfect excuse (one they were most likely looking for) to dismiss religion (and accountability) in general.

Many people who hear this opinion accept it as a true statistic, but, in fact, <u>it is a lie</u>. It is a myth that is perpetuated by people who are either too lazy to look up the facts or too prideful to look at another side of the story.

The vast majority of wars are fought over property disputes or political disputes. In the twentieth century, all of the big wars that took millions of lives were territorial wars like the Boer war, World War I, World War II, Korea. Other wars were political wars, like the Spanish civil war and Viet Nam. Religion had nothing to do with those wars.

Historically, the only exceptions I can think of would be the killings perpetrated by Charlemagne, who was tyrant from out of the 'dark ages' and only used Christianity as a justification to pillage. And there were some other other isolated incidences, like a few 'hot heads' over in Ireland about fifty years ago.

Even the Crusades, which happened centuries ago, and which many skeptics are fond of pointing to as evidence of a religious war, was actually a property dispute that arose when the Muslims 'kicked the Christians out of Jerusalem' and claimed the city as their own. Again, it was a property dispute, or a land grab. It wasn't really a religious war. Thus, it is plain to see that we can't believe everything we hear.

That is not to say that any church is perfect, not by a long shot. History tells us that the Catholic Church definitely fell into apostasy in the dark ages and after that, and some terrible things were done in its name. If we want to talk about examples of priests who became corrupt and disgraced their church, the critics will have lots of ammunition.

Such things are always a disgrace, but it does not prove the general doctrine of Christianity to be false, it only proves some of the people in the church to be false or that 'grievous wolves have entered the flock' as was prophesied.

> ***"For I know this, that after my departing, shall <u>grievous wolves enter in among you</u>, not sparing the flock.***
> ***— Acts 20:29 (emphasis added)***

The actions of corrupt people who do evil things under the name of a church will always go against the original tenets of that church and thus, those people should not be permitted to enter into a Christian church. So we must be careful not to throw out the sacred baby with the unsacred bathwater.

It was never said that the church would be perfect, in fact it was prophesied that it would not be so. So, if we want to talk about corrupt priests that may be fair game, but wars? No, not as often as people who like to revise history would have us believe.

And as far as defending those deviant priests go, I would be the first one to vote 'yes' to a death sentence on any one of them who was found guilty on charges of child molestation. So while I might defend the original Christian church on some occasions, I would not defend it on many other occasions, and I certainly would never defend corrupt priests.

Thus, I say that, despite its faults, organized religion is a legitimate thing for the simple reason that mankind was, in the beginning, supposed to be one big family who should always gather together in a spirit of unity. Yes, families can have faults and, yes, some families will contain deceivers and traitors and apostates along the way. We must be prepared for that and one way to prepare ourselves is to pass laws that are made to ex-communicate anyone who promotes the acceptance of sin.

The anti-Christians, and there are many of those, will constantly remind us of the abuses of the churches through the media and through the universities. Thus, I say that without revelations that come from God, through inspired leaders, the success of any church will be limited.

God loves all mankind and speaks to all mankind, not only just a few. So the problem then becomes not – 'is organized religion valid?' That question comes about because religions' doctrine often differ between churches. So <u>which one of the organized religions is true</u>?' I say that because their doctrines differ and sometimes contradict each other, only one can be completely true. Which one is it?

The heads of churches are human beings, and as such are fallible, and even corruptible in some cases. It is too much for people to demand that their 'all too human leaders' be perfect and know all of the answers.

Thus, a church whose doctrine may have some unanswered questions in it can still be comprised of good people who do good things, and they are not all to be condemned if one member of that church should commit transgressions.

So if there is only one true church, because of all the conflicting doctrines, does that mean that the others are all false? No. Some churches have the basic doctrine correct, but they err in minor ways of thinking and for various reasons. It does not mean that they are evil, but it could well mean that they simply do not know enough to represent the 'highest of the high'.

If I ever come to believe my church is not in sync with the truth, I always have another option. I can resolve to search diligently to find the true one. The scriptures contain many references that can provide a light for us in our search. This scripture is one of many:

> ***"For the kingdom of God is not meat and drink; but righteousness, and peace, and joy in the Holy Ghost. For he that in these things serveth Christ is acceptable to God, and approved of men."***
> ***- Romans 14: 17, 18***

THE SALT OF THE EARTH

"Ye are the salt of the earth: but if the salt have lost his savor, wherewith shall it be salted? It is thenceforth good for nothing but to be cast out."
- Matthew 5:13

Jesus believed that the guiding principle in life should be the love of truth and the seeking of it. The truth came not by sticking with beliefs that came from because of family traditions. Jesus came to cause people to break free from a religious tradition like 'waiting for the Messiah to come'.. There is a good reason for that. It is because the Messiah already came. He, of course, knew that it would be a cause for contention among the people.

"Think not that I am come to send peace on earth. I came not to send peace, but a sword."
- Matthew 10: 34 - 36

He also came as a sword to divide certain families that were too locked into traditions, including his own family. On one occasion Jesus was teaching His followers and He made it clear that He chose to preach to His followers who believed the same things as He did rather than visit with the family of His birth.

"And He stretched forth His hand towards His disciples, and said, Behold my mother and my brethren. For whosoever shall do the will of my Father which is in heaven, the same is my brother, and sister, and mother."
- Matthew 12: 49, 50

Strong language? Yes, but Jesus was a very string person with very strong beliefs, like it or not.

SPIRITUAL ROOTS

Physical beings, like plants, have physical roots, but <u>spiritual beings have spiritual roots</u>. What happens when people's roots are not strong enough to allow them to grow to the point where they can fulfill their potential?

Like a plant will die if it does not have physical roots, a spiritual being will also die without spiritual roots. So what does a person do make their roots strong enough so they will not die in a spiritual sense? Fortunately, their Creator has devised a way whereby people may gain those strong roots if they do not have them.

A wise gardener can rescue a tree with weak roots by grafting it on to another tree with strong roots. God, our Creator, **grafts** us (those who are willing) on to the tree of life Revelations 22:14, which is the tree of Jesus Christ and has the strongest roots of all. It provides all of the nourishment a spiritual being needs to grow spiritually strong. By this spiritual grafting, a man, or a woman, can become a stronger spiritual being with the capacity to be worthy of eternal life.

I do not necessarily believe that spiritual roots come from family traditions or from cultural traditions or the fact that you were baptized in a church when you were a baby. Spiritual roots take hold when you gain what is called a personal testimony. A testimony is a personal witness of the truth. Thus, a person can gain a testimony at eight years old or at eighty years old, but it is a personal thing and has nothing to do with outside influences, other than the gaining of correct information.

Gaining a testimony of the truth is the most important thing that will happen to you in your life. It will happen when you are introduced into the reality of the Spirit just enough for you to know that the Spirit exists. No matter who you are, when you gain a testimony of the reality of the Spirit, your whole life will change. It cannot help but do so. When we gain that testimony of the Spirit, we will see that it is wise to attend to it and leave behind strong attachments to the physical world. This principle is at the core of Christianity.

We can only be redeemed spiritually by finding, or seeking for, a testimony of the truth. As human beings, we are all capable of finding this testimony. Some will seek for it and some will not. It is our own free choice to do that. Even in the seeking, a man, or a woman, can take on stronger spiritual roots by learning true principles along the way.

GOOD AND EVIL SPIRITS

Then again, there are spirit entities, spirits who have identity, or a certain character about them, that can work for good or for bad. Good spirits influence us in positive ways, and bad spirits influence us on negative ways. The main spirit that works for good is the Holy Spirit, or the Holy Ghost. He is at one with God's purposes and authority and is sent from God and Jesus to influence us. This can only happen when we invite Him in to do so.

I believe in the power of the Holy Ghost that was promised in the scriptures. When Christ refers to the Holy Ghost as 'He', that means 'He' is a male personage. He also refers to Him as a 'Ghost'. That means He is a personage of Spirit. Jesus was not vague with His words. We believe that God spoke to prophets through the Holy Ghost in ancient times and that, because He does not change, He also speaks to us today by the Holy Ghost.

The following scripture is vital to understanding the physical nature of the Godhead.

> **"The Father has a body of flesh and bones as tangible as man's; the Son also; but the Holy Ghost has not a body of flesh and bones, but is a personage of Spirit. Were it not so, the Holy Ghost could not dwell in us.**
> **Doctrine and Covenants 130: 22**

It makes sense that the Holy Ghost is much more likely to be active in a person's life when they desire to have a relationship with Christ and have a reasonable knowledge of His gospel. We will never be able to live our life with the Holy Ghost, no matter who we are, if we never acknowledge Jesus Christ nor seek out his instructions for us.

> *"Abound in hope through the power of the Holy Ghost"*
> *– Romans 15:13*

The Holy Ghost, firstly, testifies of Christ. We must gain a certain amount of knowledge of the workings of God and Christ and we must come to know gospel principles, as they apply to us as individuals, and as they apply to us as a part of mankind in general. This is necessary if we are to come to a solid understanding of what the Holy Ghost is testifying of.

As individuals, we each have our own spirits and spiritual nature, although those spirits may be in the early stages of development in our mortal state. One of the main reasons we came to Earth was to have a place where our spirits would be allowed to grow. Because of all the circumstances we experience in this mortal life, both good and bad, this might be no easy task. Nevertheless, when we accept the blessings of the good Spirits and of angels and of Jesus Himself, the task, I can assure you, will become much easier.

There are opposites in everything in life. In this book I talk about evil spirits and good spirits. Unless someone is spiritually blind, it should be obvious that there is good and evil in the world. This applies to the spiritual world as well as the physical world. Some evil spirits are independent of us and some are of our own making.

God, the Father, is at the head of all good spirits, but it is the spirit of evil, sometimes called 'Satan', who is the head of all evil spirits. Good and evil have always been at war and, like it or not, this mortal sphere we are on today happens to be the prime battleground.

Evil spirits are invisible, and their plan is to work against us humans, from within and from without, to ensure that we will not have success in life. They work for our destruction instead of our 'construction'. There are many examples of evil spirits in the Bible. One example comes from a story told by Jesus in Luke 11, verses 24-26. It says:

24 "When the unclean spirit is gone out of a man, he walketh through dry places, seeking rest; and finding none, he saith, I will return unto my house whence I came out.

25 And when he cometh, he findeth it swept and garnished.

26 Then goeth he, and taketh to him seven other spirits more wicked than himself; and they enter in, and dwell there: and the last state of that man is worse than the first".

This passage tells us some things about the nature of evil spirits. It says that they literally have the ability to live in our personal realms (mind/body). It tells us that there can be more than one spirit that can occupy the same space. It also tells us that some evil spirits are more powerful than other ones.

It seems to me that evil spirits could be compared to 'hackers' who try to infect the computers that are our minds, and infect it with a virus. To get rid of a computer virus, we must have a computer expert clean it out and when that is done, we should follow a plan of protection so that we do not get infected again.

Note: **Jesus is the best Technician we will ever find for ridding our brains of spiritual viruses**. Harmful viruses of all kinds flee from Him because they know that He will ultimately bring about their destruction.

Evil spirits do not have any power to influence us <u>unless</u> we make the mistake of inviting them into our spheres of influence. There will always be spirits who exist who are at odds with us, or who hate us. It was that way from the beginning.

They are entities who remain hidden, but who are lying in wait for us to expose our weaknesses, so that they can use our weaknesses to attack us and say that those weaknesses are the main part of who we are.

Gullible people, perhaps out of guilt, will accept those accusations and forget God's promises that forgiveness is available for all who desire it and who are willing to live by the rules.

It will always be that way unless we are prepared to defy the evil ones. Thus, all people, unrighteous or righteous, had better be watchful at all times andeven able to repent on a daily basis.

I do believe that there are good spirits in this world, also unseen, who love us and want the best for us. These good spirits always have one thing in common. That is, when given an opportunity, <u>they will all testify of Jesus Christ</u> as the Redeemer of mankind. If you should ever visit a spiritual medium and that spiritualist claims to commune with spirits, ask him or her if those spirits have a testimony of Jesus Christ. If they do not have that testimony, they are not good spirits. Stay away

from them. Even if they do say that they have a testimony, it is still possible that they could be liars.

These are some of the things that we talk about at the **CHURCH OF THE RATIONAL GOSPEL**. You will not find that in any other counseling agency.

That is why we are independent of any government programs and seek our clientele out of people who have some kind of understanding of what we are talking about in matters of the Spirit.

It does not matter how much education they have, most lawyers who work within the justice system and social workers who work for the government have no idea what the implications are of evil spirits in the world and how those spirits will try to contribute to that society's very demise.

It is not in their social or financial interest to believe in such things. If they do happen to believe in spiritual forces and express their beliefs, most of the time they will not be allowed to express their opinions in a court of law, which will always dismiss their ideas as irrelevant.

HOW TO SPOT AN EVIL SPIRIT

In the normal course of events, if a tempting or disturbing image shows up in your mind and it did not come from you, then where did it come from? It surely could not have come from God because only good things can come from God. Thus, if it did not come from you it must have come from another invisible spirit, and quite possibly an evil spirit.

As it says in the Bible such entities do exist, whether we like it or not, or whether we know it or not. I do not believe though, that they can influence us unless we permit them to do so. We can permit them not only by direct invitation, but by occupying our time looking at provocative and harmful images like ones found in pornographic videos for example. Such images always have an underlying harmful and degrading influence on our minds and our spirits, especially young minds.

Spotting, or discerning, an evil spirit can be either a very difficult or a very easy thing to do. It can be very difficult to distinguish the influence of evil if you are not living a clean life. Any foul images or influences put into your mind by an outside source will just get mixed in with your own lusts as you carry on in covetous ways.

If, however you are trying to live a clean life and you are seeking the Holy Spirit, then evil outside influences will be easier to recognize. Even if you recognize them as evil, that will not matter unless the person who has had their mind invaded tries to fight against such things. Thus, I say again, stand in holy places, think Holy thoughts and seek and appreciate friends who live clean lives.

Evil images come from evil spirits and it is their presence that gives them away, if not immediately, then eventually. When such an influence comes into your mind, it should be recognized as the wide end of a very dangerous funnel.

As such, it should not be explored, but should be immediately rejected. If a person has a problem doing that, THE NAME OF JESUS CHRIST MAY NEED TO BE INVOKED.

That is a powerful name and a cleansing name and evil spirits fear that name. Along with the using of His name, faith in His power will also be necessary to use it and with authority. In circumstances where one is continually distracted by the things of the world, Singing a good hymn can be a deterrent, or a favorite scripture passage can be brought to mind, or whatever helps you to change the direction of your thoughts.

It is important to note that although an evil spirit might present an evil word or thought into our minds. When we are immersed in a carnal environment, there are times when such thoughts can come from directly within us with <u>no</u> outside influence. Thus, remember that we are all accountable for our actions and our thoughts. I believe that evil spirits can project evil images into our minds with no outside influences other than certain memories from the past or from the sensationalist media.

RELIGION AND SPIRITUALITY

If we really want to be friends with someone, we should know them well or that friendship might come tumbling down one day. IE: if we should learn that there are fundamental differences in the moral codes we choose to live by.

I made a list of certain questions that might be asked of people regarding their spirituality when and if the topic should come up and assuming they are open to talk about such things. Personally, I am confident about my own beliefs and would not mind anyone asking me questions about them, so I hope I am not being too presumptive in assuming that others feel the same way. Here are some questions that one might ask another person, not for purposes of judging, but for the purposes of understanding, clarity, and perhaps, even learning.

Do you believe in a God or a Creator?

Do you worship that God?

Does that God have feelings or is He (or She or It) without passions?

Did He (She, It) create us?

Does that God love you? Or Me?

Is there room in your doctrine for resurrection after death? Is it a physical resurrection or just spiritual resurrection?

Do you have Holy writ or scriptures that were given to you by your God? These could also be called 'revelations.

Does your God testify to you of Jesus Christ? How?

Are there any people who you regard as having spiritual authority?

Do you pray or meditate on your spirituality? How often? Once a day? Once a week? Once a year?

Do you get together with other people to discuss spiritual things or is it a solitary thing?

If it is solitary, it must be difficult at times to get motivated or to find encouragement or comfort, or counsel. So what do you do to get encouragement?

Does your spirituality entail an actual higher spirit, separate from your own spirit, who can come into your life and influence you when called upon?

People who claim to be spiritual usually have, to their credit, a moral code they live by. Do you live by a moral code? What is it called? Is there a source for that moral code other than your personal opinions? If so, what is that source?

What are the spiritual references points you use in your brand of spirituality? (IE: images, books, symbols, rituals, personal spiritual experiences, etc.)

***

Getting to know the truth about religious/spiritual matters is important. Even if I personally find some perceived lack of logic in some other people's beliefs, I still maintain that everyone should have the <u>freedom</u> to believe as they choose. On yet another hand, we have some people who say they belong to a certain church, but never go there and never carry on the practices recommended by a church (IE: prayer and scripture reading). They attend only out of family obligations such as funerals or weddings or even because they have a 'just in case' mentality.

Such people in my opinion, can automatically be tagged as hypocrites because they do nothing for the expansion of their church. If a church should claim that their beliefs are absolutely true for everyone, wouldn't they have an obligation to try and fill that church with as many people as possible?

A person's latent belief system might be seen by them as an 'ace in the hole', but that is tantamount to 'gabling with a sacred belief system and is not awise thing to do. Jesus wants to believe the best in us, but be aware that He will not be fooled. He was quite direct about calling out people who were religious hypocrites in His day. Faith needs to be consistent and righteous and lived everyday, or else it is useless.

> ***"These people draweth nigh unto me with their mouth, and honoureth me with their lips; but their heart is far from me."***
>
> *– Matthew 15: 8*

Let me say that the laws of the Judeo-Christian God are firm because they are based upon truth and if a law was not firm, there would no point in having it. Nevertheless, God has the power and the wisdom and the love that is necessary to offer mercy to those people who sin out of ignorance IE: because they know not what they do. I think it could be a different story ifa person rebelled out of direct disobedience. I go back to the scripture that says that 'no unclean thing can enter in to the Kingdom of Heaven', as was quoted earlier in this book.

When a person comes to realize the great value of true principles, they cannot help but come to love those principles. God's laws may be steadfast because they are His will, but there is also room for mercy according to His will.

When the law of Jesus Christ came to the earth, it

superseded the Mosaic law of "an eye for and eye and a tooth for a tooth' mentality. Jesus demonstrated this by His Atoning sacrifice. Thus, the laws of love and mercy are higher than the strict and rigid laws of the Old Testament. The spirit of the law is higher than the letter of the law and we should be glad for that.

"delight in the law of God after the inward man."

- Romans 7:22

THE PROBLEM OF EVIL IN THE WORLD

People who are skeptical about religion almost invariably point to the problem of evil in the world as the reason for their doubts. Many people will question, not only the existence of God, but the actual 'goodness of God'. They will ask why God created the world with such evil and cruelty in it.

The short answer is, He did not create the world that way. We human beings made it that way. In the beginning, He created the world with the Garden of Eden, which was a veritable paradise. That didn't work out too well because of <u>natural</u> human disobedience and the influence of Satan. The world we have now was, and is, the alternative to the Garden of Eden. So here we are, stuck in a world of selfishness, foolishness, debauchery, murder, etc. and we, typically, look for someone else to blame for it other than ourselves.

Aside from the corruption and suffering that is a part of life, death is always imminent for everybody. Does God <u>cause</u> people to die? I don't think so. All people die. That is a fact of life. I will die one day and you will die one day. The tragedy seems to come when people die before their time. Thus, if a child should die, from natural causes or from unnatural causes, that is always a great tragedy.

It is also a tragedy when people die slow and painful deaths. I do not believe God causes this to happen, but mankind can cause it to happen even in hospitals. It is an inescapable and sad part of mortal life.

It is my belief, however, that God can, not only bring about healing, but that He can, and will, bring dead people back to life someday when it is the right time. That is sometimes called the 'resurrection' IE: Lazarus.

That point has been made even more clear by the story about the death and resurrection of Jesus Christ, Himself, the only begotten Son of God. In other words, spiritual redemption, and physical resurrection are a part of the plan and those two things have been around from the beginning. God is not the cause of a loved one's death, instead He is the only hope we have of ever seeing that person again.

For those sad people who have suffered the tragedy of a deceased child or loved one who has passed on, it is good for them to consider this information, which has been a source of hope and comfort for millions of people.

The resurrection is the answer to the problem of evil in the world. It is the miracle in this life. We all have a choice as to whether we will accept that miracle or not. The little child who dies a painful death from cancer will choose the miracle. I believe that He or she will be all right in the end. How about you?

I was talking to a friend once who was a member of the Church of Jesus Christ of Latter Day Saints and I posed the question about the problems associated with explaining the deaths of young children. She admitted that she did not have all of the answers, but she came up with an explanation that I had never heard before and I found it very powerful. She said she believed that Jesus would come again to the earth and proceed to rule on the earth for one thousand years. This millennium reign is a point of doctrine that is accepted in most Christian churches and is evident in Revelations 20:4. It would be a transition period for everyone. The resurrection of all souls who have ever lived on the earth will take place during that time, if they have not taken place already.

This woman also said she believed that the young children who died on earth would be resurrected at that time and would be <u>raised</u> in that millennial period. This means that a child will not be raised in the world in its corrupt state, but that **he, or she, would be raised in an environment free from any and all evil influences**.

Thus, this woman believed the child would grow to be a more righteous person and an exemplar and perhaps a leader in his or her family line. The child would, in effect, be preserved in a more glorious state than he, or she, would

THE RATIONAL GOSPEL

have been had the child lived.

This whole idea is not common knowledge, but I will say that it is the only positive answer to this problem that I have ever heard. I think it might very well be true, given the scripture that says 'all things are possible with God'. (Matthew 19. 24)

So what do we try to teach our children about the nature of this world we live in? It seems we must either lie to them and tell them the world is good place, when we know it is not, or we must tell them it is <u>not</u> a good place, but we must try to make it a good place by combating evil when we can and standing up for what is right whenever we can. Even though that may sometimes be a difficult thing to do, God will be at our side when we have the courage to do that.

God does not cause suffering, but He does allow nature to take its course. I think that is because it is expedient, in most instances, for us to see the consequences of wicked human actions played out in full measure. He wants to make sure that, in the afterlife, we will have no desire to go back and live in a natural and cruel world such as this one. This is for <u>our</u> good that He desires this to happen, not for His good.

A man once said to me that if God does exist, He seems to have a non interventionist approach towards the world and to the people who He created and he found that disconcerting. He was implying that God didn't really care because He did not actively intervene in man's affairs.

I told him this: "the bottom line is that, either God intervenes constantly in the affairs of the world or He does not intervene at all. Which alternative would <u>you</u> prefer? If we would prefer intervention we had better get used to living in a state of dependency with little growth. If we prefer non-intervention, or little intervention, we will be free to seek our own levels of understanding, even if there are some growing pains attached to that. Thus, if we prefer the latter, we should 'stop belly aching, stand tall, and do something about it'.

We will not have God to protect us at all times, but we have been given instructions so that we can protect ourselves. If we follow those instructions, and have faith, we should not suffer too badly from the consequences of any personal misfortunes that come our way, and, in fact, we can even learn from those misfortunes. The Great Promise Keeper has given us the promise of the resurrection. That is enough for me.

The world may be cruel, but life is good, even though it is not always easy and not always fair. Once we accept this idea, we will all need to deal with the various obstacles that come our way in whatever way we can, while not forgetting to love God, love our neighbor and to 'be of good cheer' because He has 'already conquered the world,"

ABSOLUTE AND RELATIVE MORALITY

Many people think that morality is all relative, 'Relative' as opposed to being 'absolute', Relative thinking people live their lives according to vasryiong circumstances. In other words, they might say that what is bad for one person might be good for another person and vice versa. If two people do not make clear where they stand on that point, they could end up talking about the same subject in two totally different contexts and there would then be no resolution. Thus in a world of relative morality there is nothing definite. In a world of absolute morality there are many things that are definite.

When we believe that morality is relative, it might follow that everything is relative. If we think that because a murderer was brought up badly and that is why he killed his innocent victim, then following this pattern of reasoning, we might think it was not really his fault. We might think that that murderer should be held blameless and he, or she, did not really sin, but it was a result of his, or her, upbringing. It is true that some people came from underprivileged backgrounds and dysfunctional families, but I do believe that everyone has a basic notion of what is right and wrong.

I also believe that Jesus Christ, because of his sacrifice and his crucifixion on the cross, has literally conquered death and can also redeem us from any sins from the past, if repentance is there.

Personally, I am an absolute thinker and I believe that there is a definite right and a definite wrong in life. Otherwise, I am afraid that there would be no point to life. I also believe that people in general, have some kind of understanding of this notion inherent in them, with perhaps the exception of people who have been brainwashed, or have been determined to be clinically proven psychopaths (that is people who have no conscience).

Even if someone was abused when they were young, everyone is still able to recognize this truth in their moments of clear thinking: that some things are morally right and some things are morally wrong. They might not adhere to it, and there might be circumstances that make it difficult to adhere to it, but we all recognize right and wrong at some level and have an opportunity to 'choose the right'. There are millions of people who come from backgrounds of poverty and neglect and even abuse who grew up to be good people as well as happy and successful people. To think that underprivileged people are not capable of making good moral choices is a form of bigotry and prejudice.

In an <u>ordered</u> universe absolute right and wrong must exist. If we do not have absolute morality, or a universe that is one of order, then it is true that we are a total product of our environment, in which case, <u>we have no freedom of choice.</u> A Father who loved us would not give us a universe like that. He also would not leave us with a million questions and no answers. The answers are there. We only have to choose to look diligently for them for them.

Evil spiritual entities want to destroy us will always try to take away our freedom of choice and will promote such ideas such as relativism. Through their philosophies, they will try to convince all people that morality is relative and thus, that some sin is acceptable, or even that all sins are easily forgiven. This is attractive to sinners, (which we all are to some degree), but when we think morality is relative and not absolute, then choice becomes irrelevant. This is because there are no longer any moral standards, and when here are no standards by which to measure anything, so nothing really matters.

God provides an absolute system of moral standards to make our purposes more clear and our lives happier. Not only do we all need a good system of ethics and good people at our sides, we need God Himself. In that way, we are all beggars, every one of us. There are only two kinds of people in the world - those who need God and know it and those who need God and don't know it.

I do believe that the spirit world exists and that it is invisible to our physical senses because it is made up of very small and very fine matter. Sometimes, some people might even call it the supernatural.

> ***"all spirit is matter, but it is more fine or pure and can only be discerned by purer eyes; We cannot see it, but when our bodies are purified we shall see that it is all matter."***
>
> *– Doctrine and Covenants 131:7, 8*

Although it may be invisible to the human eye, I believe that my eternal spirit will continue to exist in the spirit world after I die. As well as existing after we die, our spirits also existed before we were born. The realm where we were spiritually created first is often referred to as the pre-existence. The Bible refers to this in the book of Jeremiah:

> ***"I knew thee before thou wast formed in the belly."***
>
> *–Jeremiah 1:5*

There are good spirits and there are bad spirits. Spirits do not influence us on earth in obvious ways, but they do have various subtle means of influencing us. Both good spirits and evil ones can influence us. The important thing to know is that the good ones will be aligned with Jesus Christ and testify of Him. The bad ones will not do that.

The spirit world is very close to this one, but it is made up of fine matter, as I have said, and cannot be detected by our physical senses. The existence of this fine matter I speak of is not provable using the scientific tools of our world because such tools are useless in a world where matter is of a different substance than the matter (or instruments that are used to detect it.) The fact that it exists though is evident, not only in the scriptures, but in the various experiences of millions of people who have credible stories to tell about their own 'after death experiences' and often those stories have an amazing amount of commonality or correlation.

Thousands of people have borne witness that their spirits entered into another dimension, saw a bright light, and then came back after a short period. Many of these witnesses were well-educated and professional people. Were these thousands of unconnected people all liars telling the same lie? I don't think so.

EVIL FORCES AND LEVELS OF UNDERSTANDING

Many people think that if a person is a Christian, then they should be free from evil influences and they should be perfect examples of good character. This assumption may be correct in certain ways, but in other ways it is wrong. Christians, in fact, can be prime targets for forces of evil that operate in the spirit world.

I suppose it might be possible that there are some people in the world who are good people, but who do not go to a church every Sunday. Fair enough. On the other hand, I know that there are other people who do need to go to church every week; and I happen to be one of those people. Nevertheless, I do believe that anything that we should ever achieve in this life, in no matter what field, will be worth absolutely nothing in an eternal sense, unless that sacrifice that was made 2000 years ago is properly acknowledged.

> *"I am the way, the truth and the life. No man comes unto the Father but by me."*
> *- John 14:6*

Evil is a reality. We can see it every night on the evening news. We can see it in the vacant stares of hopeless drug addicts on the streets whose only sins were making a few wrong decisions. We can see it in a myriad of places. We can, at times, even see it in ourselves. This must be fought against, in ourselves firstly, and in others secondly.

LEVELS AND BEING ABOVE BOARD

We must strive to think at a 'higher level' of consciousness and even to exist at that level. I call it being above board, (or 'above bored'). It involves embracing a state of being that is:

1. Feeling positive about life and your spirituality.

2. Feeling caution about doing wicked things.

3. Feeling enthusiastic about doing good.

How do we do that? By doing that, we rise from one spiritual level to a higher level and then higher levels after that. We start by gaining knowledge. We seek out all the wisdom we can find. We recognize it, accept it, rejoice in it and give thanks for it. We then use that knowledge for purposes of virtue and thus, become more accustomed to it. As we gain more virtue, we rise to a higher level and while at that new level, we gain more knowledge and then more virtue and then more knowledge and so on.

We do this until we get to a highest level we can achieve within the bounds of our capabilities. And then, through exercising of our new knowledge, and having a spiritual witness of it, we make it part of our being and, hence, we <u>become</u>, what could be called, 'a new creature'.

We need to always 'follow up' on becoming a new creature and evaluate our progress. When we discover new things that are to our benefit, then we must accept and recognize the notion that we are experiencing life at a <u>higher level</u> than our former selves. You should not worry about being called an elitist snob by some people when you accept any legitimate knowledge.

God has many ways of causing us to be humble, so snobbery is not in the equation for a true Christian. We are not being elitist by thinking elevated thoughts. We are simply striving to become the best person we can be and that should be the duty of all men and women, with no exceptions.

When I talk about levels I am not necessarily talking

only about up and down levels. I could be talking about levels of intensity or levels of light or levels of expansion. An expanded level is a bigger level. There is more room to move around. The spirit causes our mind to expand when we experience feelings of peace instead of stress; feelings of joy instead of sadness; feeling of humility instead of pride, feelings of honesty instead of self-justification. We find peace and confidence by obtaining a good self-image and it is only having a sacred belief system that we will gain that better self-image.

To achieve positive spiritual change, we will need positive spiritual help; both help from God, and as well, from spiritual people who know where to find God. Because we all sink into a lower realm at least once in our lifetime, **that is evidence that every one of us has, or will have, the need for change in our lives at one time or another, and even for 'help' in our lives.**

> *"Because of the word of God... your understanding doth begin to be enlightened, and your mind doth begin to expand."*   *- Alma 32:34*

WISDOM AND THE HOLY GHOST

The Holy Spirit, also called the Holy Ghost and the Comforter, is the third member of the Godhead and is a personage of spirit. He has the power to enter into our minds and to give us confirmations about things that are true. As it says in the scriptures, He will "teach us all things and bring all things to our memory". - John

14: 26

After Jesus died and was resurrected, He ascended to His Father in Heaven. He had done His job. So His mission was fulfilled. He was, and is, the Savior and Redeemer of the world. Our relationship with Him is the same relationship that we all can have. It is the same for you and me and for every man, woman and child living in the world, <u>if</u> we will accept it.

Even though Jesus now dwells with the Father in Heaven, He <u>sent</u> to us, as He said he would, the Holy Ghost who would be here to comfort us, to guide us, to teach us all things and bring all things to our remembrance. Near the end of his mission, Jesus said these words:

> *"It is expedient for you that I go away: for if I go not away, the Comforter will not come unto you; but if I depart, I will send Him unto you." - John 16:7*

Jesus means what He says. He never talks in empty words. So it appears to me from reading the scriptures that the Holy Ghost became the most active part of the Godhead as far as we are concerned today. The Holy Ghost, or Comforter, is referred to as **'Him'** in the same scripture, so I would think that Jesus is talking about a male personage. Because He refers to the Holy 'Ghost' I assume that means that the Holy Ghost is a personage of spirit. He is a spirit who can and does guide each of us, in the spirit, in our daily lives when He is invited to do so.

The Holy Ghost will always testify of Christ and both Jesus and God the Father and that is why He is named as a full partner in the Godhead. There are many theories about the actual nature and organization of the Godhead and even many priests and commentators from various Christian churches will admit that they do not know exactly what it is and so they tend to just ascribe it to the 'mysteries of God'. Nevertheless, it is knowable.

> *"Unto you it is given to know the mysteries of the kingdom of God: but to others in parables; that seeing they might not see, and hearing they might not understand."*
> *- Luke 8:10*

The Holy Ghost is not observable to us, so it seems that He must be felt in the spirit. Personally, when I perceive that the Holy Ghost is with me, I feel different things at different times. I have felt warmth about me on some occasions. I have felt an increase of light around me on other occasions. I have felt a slight reverberation of sound on other occasions when certain words come into my head. Most times I feel, what I can describe only as a prompting, or a confirmation, or an expansion, of something that I am already thinking about.

When I am actively doing something, I feel that my timing is working at its best when the Holy Spirit is with me, and thus, my mind and my language skills are at their best. My overall energy is increased. My timing is better and timing is always critical in the achievement of our goals.

If we wish to be as 'perfect' as we can be, it only stands to reason that we must be connected, in some way, to the most perfect being, or beings, that we can find. That should be a sacred goal. A connection to a 'pure and living being' gives us the opportunity to learn about true spiritual principles. For me that pure and living being is evident in the words, and the works, of Jesus Christ.

The upper spiritual levels in life are the levels where the Spirit of God is more accessible. We all have our freedom to choose to accept the gift or not. If you read the scriptures that I quote here in my book, I suspect that you might start to feel your mind churning.

IF SO, THAT DOES NOT MEAN THAT YOU KNOW EVERYTHING, BUT IT DOES MEAN THAT YOU ARE ON THE RIGHT TRACK AND THAT YOU MAY EVEN BE STARTING TO FEEL THE HOLY SPIRIT WORKING IN YOU RIGHT NOW.

In my church, we believe in the value of searching for the truth, not a relative truth, but an absolute truth. We believe the spiritual infrastructure was put into place a long time ago that will enable us to do this and it begins with study and prayer. When we pay heed and listen to the promptings of the Holy Ghost and come to know Him and how He works, we will eventually come to know the truth and the truth will 'set us free'.

How long that will take depends upon how much baggage we need to sort through and how much perseverance we have, but in the end, our goal of freedom and happiness, can be attained. It can be attained in a physical sense, a mental sense, in an emotional sense and in a spiritual sense.

Statistics show that 'people of faith' are generally happier than people who do not have a faith. There is always a danger though that a person might think they are better than other people if they have faith. But this is something that scriptures have always warned people about. (Luke 18: 14)

To avoid the actual danger of becoming elitist, we must give any credit we receive because of our new knowledge to someone else; a parent, a mentor, and ultimately, to Jesus. We must point to the source of our gifts and humble ourselves at all times, and perform works of charity for the less fortunate whenever we can. Our humility is not false modesty or virtue signaling. It must be a fact.

What a great relief it is to be able to point to someone else as the source of your faith. It absolves you from the responsibility of performing monumental tasks. It eliminates the tendency to point to perceived enemies and accusing them of holding you back, or doing you wrong. We need to always hold ourselves accountable.

It stands to reason that when we attain a higher level, either we accept it and gain from it, or else we deny that higher status and sink back into the mud of mediocrity and accept the standards of the bottom feeders. It is our choice.

Heaven is a higher level than hell. That should be obvious. they are equal worlds only to soul-less people who have no desire to progress. If one wishes to deny that and say that every human soul will receive the same rewards in the end, despite the decisions they made in this life, it is their privilege to do so.

As for me, I would like to live with God after this life is over and I am told in the scriptures that no filthiness can be 'received into the kingdom' of God. Although we are all saved by grace, we shall be known by our works.

(James 2: 17)

The level we live at in the life after this one will probably be somewhat of a reflection of the one we lived in our last life (the mortal one). In this life, we can become locked into bad behavior out of pure habit. Intentions may not have anything to do with it. But we can become yoked with undesirables and dwell, in a de facto sense, when we insist on living at the level of the lowest common denominator.

Personal communication is an important aspect of living in today's world. One would think that with the social media, so prevalent in our culture, that communication would be a piece of cake, but it is not so. Social media can be a format for a superficial kind of communication based upon many assumptions and superficial opinions, even fraught with a mob mentality, one that is usually seen as politically correct, of course.

Our most powerful communications are not only in our words, but in how we present ourselves. Unless we are truly wise, words are often overrated. Words can sometimes mean anything a person wants them to mean. The devil himself knows how to use words very well and He uses them for purposes of deceit.

There will come a time in our lives when we must choose between principles that are true and a person we care about, but who does not happen to share those principles.

That will be just one of the tests we face on this mortal sojourn that we call life. Such things are tests for us, and sometimes a certain amount of grief can be involved in those tests. So if we must inevitably face such serious decisions.

We should be prepared for them as best as we can by learning what actually constitutes true principles and what does not do that. That is because you can be sure that there will come a time when we will be called upon to use those principles in a way that will reveal to all people who you really are.

There are also some people who believe it is too late for them to change or that they are too old to change. This is not true. I say that it is better to walk ten feet in the truth as an old person than to walk ten miles in untruth as a young person.

If we are a people of character, we must face the fact that the issue of morality is unavoidable. We should try to be the best person we can be. Success in our job, or anywhere else, is secondary to our success as decent human beings. Jobs are always temporary. Character is, pretty much, permanent.

GOOD RELIGION AND BAD RELIGION

Let me first make the observation that, aside from any bad or coercive religious practices taught in a church, moral principles, in all cases, need to be taught in the home first. Most churches teach good principles, but I have seen too many fathers rely on the church (or even the schools) to teach their children, but it is the parents who need to spend time teaching good principles to their children, teaching by word and by deed.

Many people who relied on the church to teach their children and assumed that their children would receive the doctrines by some kind of osmosis have been disappointed when they learned that, as the children grew up, they fell away, or even turned against religion.

Regarding coercive religion, I have also observed that when spiritual beliefs are forced upon a person and rituals are followed only out of tradition or intimidation or heavy handed persuasion, it will, more likely, be restricting to a child's personal growth rather than edifying or supportive. False beliefs are based upon false, or flawed, information. <u>This is as opposed to personal understanding and an awareness of the truth. True teaching needs to involve a spirit of love.</u> Even if a principle is true, if that principle is not taught with a spirit of love, it will probably not 'take hold'.

Being coerced into a false belief system is something that people will either accept or rebel against. If a false belief system is imposed upon someone, then it <u>should</u> be rebelled against. Who would wants to commit to a religion that doesn't hold up to the truth and liberty in every way?

Experiencing false, or coercive, religion in one's youth is something that can cause a person to be bitter, controlling, stubborn and prideful, later on in adulthood. Those generations, and the generations that follow them, can suffer from someone holding on to a religion that has no appeal to one's spirit, but only has rules. So the question becomes – are these beliefs, which were told to us, really true, and how can we find out if they are true?

I have met many people who say that for them to believe in God, God must follow certain guidelines. For example, a person might say, "I could never believe in a God who is against abortion, or a God who is against homosexuals getting married. I would not believe in a God like that."

In such cases, <u>that person has closed himself, or herself, off from learning,</u> no matter what the issue was. And thus, they can never come to know the real God for the reason that they rejected the idea of learning something different. They 'lean to their own understanding'.

> *"Trust in the Lord with all thine heart and lean not unto thine own understanding.'   -   Proverbs 3: 5*

People who do that are, I think, worshipping a God of their own making. Thus, they limit their chances for any kind of progress or enlightenment. This is not because the principles they believe in are wrong. They may not be all wrong. It is because those principles are coming from a very unreliable source, which is the 'natural human mind' that works in 'natural human configurations'. To say that our opinions supersede God's will in any situation is prideful and automatically disqualifies us from having anything of importance to say on anything.

Even if people are well intentioned and even if they are accurate in 'some of their perceptions' on 'some' issues, they will still have nothing to offer anyone because 'some' of the sources of their information are flawed. Such people who do not wish to make sincere inquiries about the 'absolute' nature of universal **truth** should stick to talking about other things, like football or baseball.

> *"For my thoughts are not your thoughts, neither are your ways my ways, saith the Lord."*
> *   - Isaiah 55: 8*

If we feel we have a legitimate grievance against God, we

will all have an opportunity to air that grievance at some point, but to create a God of our own making, and to sustain that perception amongst our family and friends, is a foolish mistake.

We are all free to conceptualize about God, but for you or me to state absolute ways that He, or She, must be, according to our opinions, and which are often confirmed by like-minded friends, is a foolish thing to do.

The good news about religion and spirituality is that, while a false sense of the spiritual can lead to confusion and emotional swamps, a true grasp of spirituality will provide the best way out of all deceptions that are in our path.

True religion and spirituality will eventually lead us into the light and the fresh air and into a state of liberty. Spirituality, along with courage, faith, and a love for the truth are the main things that will combat and defeat all of the enemies of freedom and personal happiness. Discovering truth and listening to the still, small voice of the Spirit has been instrumental in setting free millions of people from different kinds of bondages and different kinds of addictions.

Again, if a person is to learn and grow in this life, they will need to become connected to the spiritual side of life. If one does not try to connect with that, they will be missing out on the very reason their souls were sent here to this planet.

I know a playwright who is a good writer and successful at his craft. He has a knack for writing plays that have a lot of humor in them and he develops characters that are always interesting. I know, however, that the man is not acquainted with the spiritual side of life. He has never read the Bible, as far as I know, and has seldom had discussions about Bible principles with another person who is sensible about religion.

I do not say it, but I sometimes feel the urge to tell this man that, although I enjoy watching the characters in his plays and his comedic repartee, and although I have found his plays very entertaining, I have never found any ideas in them that I would consider to be truly profound. Because of that I would speculate that his career advancement will only go so far.

I say these things because I love this man. He is a good man who is a good thinker, but because he basically just does not know about that other side of life, he limits himself in his own thinking and seems to default to a politically correct form of intellectualism whenever he can. He gets some acclaim in his profession and that increases his self-esteem, but that might just simply be because he is, without knowing it, a people pleaser, but still, a man whose observations have nothing to do with absolute truth.

I am not recommending here that my friend join a particular church at this point, but I do suggest that he needs to become more acquainted with the Spirit and he needs to understand intelligent religious people better in order that he might gain a different kind of understanding. Without the knowledge of the unseen spiritual half of life, I am afraid that a person will never be more than half a writer or a half a person.

To gain a basic knowledge of what sensible religious thought consists of, a person needs to talk to sensible religious people. If you do not know of any sensible Christians, you should seek them out. Ask them questions. If they are good people and feel that they have something good to offer to others, I know they will be eager to share their thoughts with you.

Also, search for a theological doctrine that is both intelligent and practical; one that has love, humility, forgiveness and compassion at its core; one that is simple and yet, very spiritual; one that explains the plan of salvation <u>from the beginning to the end</u>, from the pre-existence to the Second Coming of Christ. These are things that God wants us to know about, and information about these things is accessible to us.

We each have our own beliefs based upon our many years of experience and we are entitled to hold those beliefs. It is a good thing, however, to seek out other realms of experience that we have never been privy to and try to discern the truth about them. If we investigate a certain doctrine, but cannot maintain a heartfelt belief that it rings true, then we can ignore that specific doctrine for the time being and investigate another one that is more intriguing.

A church that we, perhaps, once showed interest in should not mind if <u>we do not</u> join up with them, because if we don't believe their doctrine and we cannot and should not accept it, the <u>people in that church should not even want us to be in their church</u>. They should realize that our involvement in that church would not be in their best interests, nor in ours.

On the other hand, if the doctrine makes sense and feels right and we gain a <u>spiritual witness</u> of its validity, then, we should not be afraid to accept it or just to proceed further along in our investigation of it. It's that simple. Thus, we can come to know better what our spiritual options are. Like it or not, the basic knowledge of things spiritual is the most necessary component of personal growth. Thus, we should never be afraid to ask questions of anyone.

RELIGION AND KNOWLEDGE

<u>God is not unknowable</u>. We <u>can</u> come to know the ways of God. As Jesus once said to his disciples:

> *"Unto you it is given to know the mysteries of the kingdom of God."*   *- Luke 8: 10*

It will take time and study on our part, but the answers will come. Some people want all the answers immediately, but that is simply not the way that knowledge works. In short, God does not dispense the truth on demand because we are just not ready to receive it in its full measure.

Sometimes it can take a devout student of the gospel many years to fully realize one essential principle. When that is learned and recognized, however, it will become embedded in that person's heart and soul. This does not all happen overnight.

> *"For precept must be upon precept, precept upon precept; line upon line, line upon line; here a little and there a little:"*
>
>   *- Isaiah 28:10*

Most knowledge is usually a cumulative kind of knowledge; here a little, and there a little. Conversion rarely happens in one sudden moment, although that is still possible. If we choose to utilize a spiritual mode in our personal operating system, as opposed to a secular mode, we must always begin at an entry level and that involves a 'learning curve'. It is a 'spiritual' learning curve.

Learning is usually broad based and certain conditions apply in different situations, but the basic principles of knowledge are constant. We cannot understand the whole structure of Divinity at once. It is impossible. We must proceed in stages and in different levels of understanding as we become accustomed to the feelings of the Holy Spirit. This Spirit is found among righteous saints (followers of Christ) and can be transferable and felt by anyone who is interested in fellowshipping with them through the mutual contemplation of the truth.

If we do not have a basic knowledge, higher principles can still be learned, but they will not always be retained. They are likely to lose any power they have because they are not built upon a firm foundation.

Without a firm foundation, any knowledge that was gained would likely be 'spilled upon the ground' over time. There is a learning process to be followed, and when truths start to become involved in the process, that process will not be seen as a chore, but as an exciting adventure.

> *"Seek ye first the kingdom of God, and His righteousness; and all these (other) things shall be added unto you."*   *– Matthew 6:33*

MY SOUL AND ITS INCLINATIONS

Because of the word of God...Your understanding doth begin to be enlightened, and your mind doth begin to expand." - Alma 32: 34

THE HUMAN SOUL, WHEN LEFT TO ITS OWN IS A GOOD THING. IF IT HAS BECOME CORRUPTED IN IT'S DEPTH, IT WILL NOT BE A GOOD THING.

I BELIEVE THAT OUR MINDS, WHICH ARE HOUSED BY OUR SOULS, HAVE THE CAPACITY TO SHRINK OR EXPAND ACCORDING TO OUR OWN RIGHTEOUS DESIRES AND OUR UNDERSTANDINGS AND OUR PERCEPTIONS AND OUR CIRCUMSTANCES AND MAINLY TO THE VALUE SYSTEM THAT WE HAVE ASSIGNED TO OURSELVES IN OUR HEARTS, MINDS AND SOULS.

THAT VALUE SYSTEM THAT WE WILL EVENTUALLY ASSIGN TO OURSELVES WILL BE THE MOST IMPORTANT ASSIGNMENT (OR DECISION) THAT YOU OR I WILL EVER MAKE IN OUR LIVES AND IT WILL COME FROM TOTALLY WITHIN US AND WILL NOT COME FROM SOMEWHERE ELSE. THAT IS HOW IMPORTANT THE QUALITY OF INDIVIDUAL INDEPENDENCE AND INDIVIDUAL THINKING IS.

There are many good experiences we can encounter everyday that will act upon our spirits and cause them to <u>expand</u> (feel good) or to <u>shrink</u> (feel not so good). Let us make a partial list of some of the things that can cause our spirits to shrink.

1. Angry or resentful thoughts (for obvious reasons)

2. Worry, financial or other (for obvious reasons)

3. Guilt (for obvious reasons)

4. Physical things. Have we ingested too much sugar or too much salt or too much caffeine? Caffeine may make us feel good at first, but used to excess, our thoughts can become more unfocussed.

5. Paranoia. Fear can cause our spirits to shrink. Some fears are legitimate and some are not. Sometimes just remembering the things that caused us to fear in the past will be enough to actually make our spirits shrink all over again.

6. Feelings of unworthiness or inferiority. (for obvious reasons)

7. Boredom. When one is bored, one tends to look around for some outside stimulus to give them a kick-start. They often fantasize and deceive themselves, which compromises their integrity and diminishes their character. Fantasy always has lethargy as a companion, and even cowardice too.

8. Greed. Ambition is good. Greed is not good. Greed may contain ambition, but that makes that kind of ambition illegitimate and it will cause your spirit to shrink. It is carnal by nature, as is lust and covetousness.

9. Sin in general. *(see the Ten Commandments)*

For married people, I think the most important factors that affect our spirits are the factors involved in the spiritual relationship between spouses. In a marriage, the couple should share everything. That is what marriage is. It includes sharing their emotions, their beliefs, their concerns, their finances, their schedules, their joyful moments, their sad moments, their problems, and most important of all, their spiritual states. If a marriage is on a downslide, the spirits of the people involved will also be on a downslide and tend to shrink.

Marriages should be based upon sacred and agreed upon principles. If those principles are ignored or forgotten then it is unlikely that that marriage can survive a direct assault. There needs to be a joint effort to sustain the original principles behind the institution of marriage.

Sometimes, in some marriages, it is not uncommon for selfish practices and attitudes to enter into the marriage and take hold. One spouse might try to belittle the other spouse and cause his or her spirits to shrink either knowingly or unknowingly.

A person, male or female, who desires to be in control, will have their own ways of being abusive, other than physical ways, and that can cause the spirits of the people to shrink. The spectrum of abuse applies evenly across the board with both men and women. Some people just do not realize the damage caused when they try to belittle one who is close to them by insulting their personal worth. They use it as a tactic and, no matter who is the instigator, it is always bound to wreak havoc because the spirit can only shrink for so long, and then it either rebels or it dies.

> *"the tongue is a fire, a world of iniquity." – James 3:6*

Then there is the other kind of person, the <u>codependent</u> kind, who wants another person to have control over their spiritual state and hands over their free agency to them because they feel an obligation to be subservient out of infatuation, or fear, or a need to be dependent.

Such situations may be extreme, but when they happen. They are always harmful, mainly because they are 'freedom destroying'. Some people are not proactive enough to make a relationship work so they turn it into an emotional contest or a dominant/submissive relationship where one spouse can give the other spouse the impression that they are not as much worth as they might think they are. They might see that kind of relationship as being better than having no relationship at all.

Thus, such people might decide to put their faith in misplaced emotions instead of spiritual feelings of tenderness. Tenderness is not usually a natural way of behaving. It is a learned and a valuable human quality.

Harshness or constant resentment is a twisted way of thinking. If a person's twisted sense of security can actually find some comfort and/or resolution in self-created drama, as chaotic as that may be, they will be in for a disappointment if some kind of resolution for that is not found.

Unfortunately, this mutual and super charged emotional manipulation happens to certain couples because it is the only way they know how to relate to each other. Over time, the results are never good and are often disastrous.

Thus, new learning, and change, will be called for under such circumstances. New learning can lead to a new perspective. That is a good thing and also, frankly discussing the issues involved can, by itself, actually improve the communication between a couple.

The people involved in abusive situations are not usually aware of how they are affecting each other, and there is seldom no frank discussion or corrective process in place , whereby they can actually see what they are really doing in the big picture and correct it.

That strategy should have the specific goal of trying to make two people support each other and try to expand each other's souls. When bad emotions take precedence over the Spirit, it can only lead to bad results.

THUS, I SAY THAT PRINCIPLES SHOULD ALWAYS RULE OVER PASSIONS.

22. DRUGS (11p.)

Subtitles: An eighty three year old Religious Man's Experience with Morphine; A Horrific Phone call; Is There Anything Wrong with Wanting to Feel Good?; Murderers Among Us

AN EIGHTY THREE YEAR OLD RELIGIOUS MAN'S EXPERIENCE WITH MORPHINE

I have a friend named Ken who is a very spiritual man. He is eighty- three years old and his approach when talking about gospel matters is intelligent and unique and always interesting. Last year Ken had a fall and broke one of his hips. A doctor did surgery to repair the hip and then prescribed some drugs to help Ken deal with the pain as he was recovering from the operation. One of the drugs that the doctor prescribed for Ken was Morphine, which is an opiate that can produce feelings of euphoria, on the downside however, it can produce hallucinations in the mind and also bring 'fogginess' into a person's thought process.

Ken noticed some of the effects of the drug right away. Most of those effects being bad ones like a tendency to not be clear headed and to be unfocussed a lot of the time. He did not like the tricks that his mind played on him when he was under the influence of morphine. One thing that he said to me was – "I don't believe that you can feel the presence of the Holy Ghost when you are under the influence of opiates." That, to him, was a traumatic thing and a major attack on his peaceful and very rich life.

When he spoke to me, he also said, "when you can't feel the influence of the Holy Ghost in your life, then your life becomes horrible."

***

A HORRIFIC PHONE CALL

Receiving a phone call from an old friend can be a very pleasant experience. Sometimes though it can be a horrendous thing.

I received a phone call recently from an old friend who lives far away from me. She informed me that her twenty nine year old son died just a few days ago. The cause of death was an overdose of the drug Fentanyl.

It was very sad. He was her only child. She knew her son was in trouble, but it seemed that there was nothing she could do about it. She spent a lot of money trying to get him straight, but it was no use. The pull of the drugs and his so-called friends were too much for him to resist.

That friend I just spoke about was a very good nature and even a jolly woman. When I visited with her and her family in the past, I noticed that their house was usually filled with much laughter. That alone might make them good parents, but there are other factors to consider. The humor they practiced was not a lower class if humor like telling dirty jokes. Their main kind of humor seemed, to me, to be the humor of happy people who liked to make funny scenes, or skits, that were played out by them as they created funny cartoon like characters. It was very humorous and nobody got hurt by the humor. I silently applauded them for that. Still, the main effect of that was that **everybody felt good** about what was going on.

I admired them for that. I thought that they were excellent parents. Now, after their tragedy, I was prompted to ask myself if there was something missing in their quest for 'laughter'.

IS THERE ANYTHING WRONG WITH WANTING TO FEEL GOOD?

Most children admire their parents and want to be like them. Is that a good thing? Perhaps yes, and perhaps no.

It is said that everybody loves to laugh and that everybody loves a clown. Are those good things? Perhaps yes, and perhaps no.

Recently I asked myself, "Why are strong drugs so attractive to certain people?" One answer to this question came into my mind. Although it might be controversial, and although some people might be offended by it, I would like to share it with you. The answer was this:

A family who is always laughing and clowning around, even laughing at humor that was clever, might seem to be a good thing. A young person who has a certain disposition can see that 'joking around' and laughing is just a harmless activity that allows them to FEEL GOOD'. That causes the influence of the young persons 'fun loving parents' to be credible. They might think that that is what a family ought to do or that it is quite harmless and it can be fun and even joyous.

THE RATIONAL GOSPEL

At the same time, if a young man or woman takes a strong drug and it makes them feel good or even ecstatic, is there anything wrong with that?

THE THING THAT ALL PEOPLE NEED TO REMEMBER IS THAT 'HAVING FUN' MAY BE A GOOD THING, BUT IT SHOULD <u>NEVER</u> TAKE THE PLACE OF SERIOUS CONCERNS. I SAY THAT BECAUSE I BELIEVE THAT LIFE IS FIRSTLY, A VERY SERIOUS BUSINESS. HAVING FUN IS A GOOD THING, BUT **'FUN' SHOULD NEVER TAKE THE PLACE OF VIRTUES LIKE RESPECT, PRUDENCE, INTELLIGENCE, (REAL INTELLIGENCE AND NOT ACADEMIC INTELLIGENCE), FREEDOM, SELF - RESTRAINT, KINDNESS, AND MANY OTHER GOOD VIRTUES.**

The problems come when a youth starts to take drugs on a regular basis and does it mainly just to 'feel good'. They can easily dismiss the virtues that I just talked about and 'go for the yuks' and the fellowship of their peers or fellow druggies. When that happens, it can become compulsive behavior, and even dangerous behavior and even more dangerous in today's world.

If a drug taking youth sees the damage that drugs can do they might think that principle does not apply to them or that they are invincible, or they can just say to themselves. "Hey, I just want to feel good. What's wrong with that?" What is wrong with that is that the exquisite feelings that a strong drug can give them can be too strong to resist as life goes on and a tragedy like death could become the end game.

Most young people in their reckless moments might just ignore warnings about the 'dangers of drug use'. Thus, the 'I just want to feel good' philosophy will rule the roost. They can also get self-assurance when they say to themselves 'youth is on my side and it always will be on my side.' MISTAKE. But many youth will just move along as passengers on their pleasure train, not concerned about how worried their parents are about their son or daughter's future.

***

MURDERERS AMONG US

I watched a show recently about drug usage among young people in Vancouver. In that show, a drug dealer was interviewed. Everybody knows that fentanyl kills people, thousands of them ever year. The dealer, who was on the show, tried to give the impression that she was one of the 'good guys'. She did that because, even though she sold fentanyl she did <u>not</u> cut it with other harmful substances that make it fatal much more often and faster than taking it in its pure and uncut state.

So that dealer was not really one of the 'good guys' after all. Fentanyl, in whatever state, kills people. This woman was no better than a psychopath and a murderer and she should be put in jail for a long time to prevent her from killing other people.

This tragic incident that happened to my friends son, brought home a problem to me that I have ignored for a long time.

The days when I dabbled with drugs are well behind me now and I definitely do not miss those days. It did bring home to me the bad things that are happening in our society today due to the usage of hard drugs and opiates, especially among young adults.

These things are not pleasant for me to dwell on or talk about so I will only say one thing more. Those dealers can be much more than problems, they can be literal 'horrors' for everyone who is involved. It is a cruel thing for our legislators to allow harm and even death to come to the young people in our country. Also it is criminal of the justice system to let other criminals freely sell 'poison' to young people and allow them to get away with it.

***

This is how traps get set. The drug trap is similar to an animal trap that has 'iron jaws' that can take a hold of an animal's leg and not let go. This does not happen with human beings though. With humans, as opposed to animals, the trap can take a hold on a certain part of an addicts brain. after some time, the addict will feel totally at the mercy of 'the trap, even though they <u>still</u> might not acknowledge the deadliness of the trap. By then it might be too late to 'break free'.

TO SUM UP, A PERSON MUST LEARN ABOUT IMPORTANT LIFE PRINCIPLES, PRINCIPLES THAT WERE NEVER TAUGHT IN SCHOOL. ONE OF THOSE PRINCIPLES GOES SOMETHING LIKE THIS:

"DON'T PUT TOO MUCH FAITH IN 'FEELING GOOD', BECAUSE EVENTUALLY THERE WILL COME A TIME IN YOUR LIFE WHEN YOU DO NOT FEEL GOOD AT ALL. THEN YOU WILL BE ON A SLIPPERY SLOPE AND THE ONLY SOLUTION WILL BE A DEDICATED EFFORT TO MAKE USE OF 'GOOD SELF-IMPROVEMENT STRATEGIES". THAT IS A CERTAINTY.

THUS, IF YOU ARE A YOUTH WHO IS ATTRACTED TO DRUGS OR OPIATES OR EVEN ALCOHOL, I BEG OF YOU – PREPARE YOUSELF TO FIGHT THAT BATTLE <u>NOW</u>, BECAUSE IT COULD BE THE BIGGEST BATTLE THAT YOU WILL EVER FACE.

Let us look at spiritual meditation and compare it with the 'high' that comes from using mind-altering drugs, even so-called recreational drugs.

Where does drug usage usually lead? Under the influence of drugs, it will lead to a hodge-podge of incoherency and meaninglessness. It becomes like a dreamland where nothing is real and, in most cases, nothing is really that important.

In this life, things that are <u>not real</u> have no value. It is a zero sum situation. In the beginning, the intensity that is felt on a drug high might seem like a thrilling experience, but, in reality, it never leads anywhere and, in the end, it always leads to a zero. Zero times a hundred is still zero. If nothing is real in your world, your world is worth nothing except for some insignificant physical sensations. Any relationship that starts out with faulty perceptions will always be doomed to failure.

If a drug user's personal relationship is not working, I think that he, or she, over time will realize this and stay away from using their drug high as a tool to influence others. Hence, they will focus more on the physical sensations that come with the chemical high that they experience.

OTHER PEOPLE SOON BECOME IRRELEVANT IN THE MIND OF THE DRUG USER AND 'HIGH' FEELINGS BECOME THE GOAL. IF THE HIGH FEELINGS ARE NOT REALLY EARNED OR LEGITIMATE, THE PERSON WILL NEED TO ACKNOWLEDGE THAT FACT AND KNOW THAT DRUG HIGHS ARE REALLY NOT DEPENDABLE AND CAN LEAD TO MANY MISPERCEPTIONS ABOUT MANY THINGS.

WHATEVER THE ATTITUDE, LET US NOT BE DECEIVED INTO THINKING THAT WHILE A PERSON IS HIGH ON DRUGS, THEY ARE NOT EXPERIENCING SOME MYSTICAL TRUTH THAT THEY WERE BLIND TO BEFORE. THEY ARE EXPERIENCING A PSYCHOLOGICAL ILLUSION, ONE THAT IS ONLY PROPELLED BY THE PHYSICAL SENSATIONS THAT THEY FEEL.

IN MATTERS OF TRUTH, AND EVEN PERSONAL SUCCESS, SUCH PHYSICAL SENSATIONS ARE OF NO REAL VALUE TO US, OR TO ANYONE ELSE, OTHER THAN PERHAPS PROVIDING US WITH A CHILDISH SENSE OF GIDDINESS.

<u>REALITY IS TRUTH</u> AND TRUTH IS NOT NEGOTIABLE. THERE ARE OTHER TRUTHS THAT WE CANNOT SEE, BUT REALITY IS ONE TRUTH THAT WE CAN SEE, AND SO IT IS ABSOLUTELY ESSENTIAL THAT WE HOLD ON TO IT AS OFTEN AS WE CAN.

THAT IS BECAUSETHE TRUTH MAY GET TWISTED IN OUR MINDS IN OUR LIFETIME AND WE WILL MISS THE SECURITY AND SAFETY THAT TRUTH AND REALITY HAVE TO OFFER.

THE TRUTH OF OUR UNIVERSE IS OFTEN REFLECTED IN THE NOTION THAT GOD ALONE IS TRUTH. THAT IS A GOOD THING TO ME BECAUSE OUR CREATOR IS, INDEED, THE EMBODIMENT OF TRUTH AND HE HAS PROVEN HIMSELF TO BE GOOD MAINLY BY THE LAW OF SACRIFICE (THE ATONEMENT) WHICH TOOK PLACE TWO THOUSAND YEARS AGO.

THE SECOND ASPECT IS THAT THE TRUTH CREATES FEELINGS OF UNITY AMONG OUR FELLOW TRUTH SEEKERS AND FEELINGS OF UNITY ARE FEELINGS OF LOVE.

WHO WILL WE ULTIMATELY LOVE? WE WILL ULTIMATELY LOVE THOSE WHO ARE UNITED WITH US IN A RIGHTEOUS CAUSE AND WILLING TO SHARE THE GOODNESS OF LIFE RATHER THAN TRY TO HORDE IT, OR USE CHEMICALS TO REPLACE IT.

THE THIRD POSITIVE ASPECT OF TRUTH COMES ABOUT BECAUSE OUR TRUTH, AND HENSE, OUR LOVE, UNDER GOD'S WATCHFUL EYE, IS AN ETERNAL LOVE

THE HIGH THAT COMES BY THE SPIRIT IS IMPORTANT, BUT IT IS ALSO FAIRLY SIMPLE. IT IS ABOUT DISCOVERING THE GOOD PRINCIPLES OF ETERNAL TRUTH AND LIVING THEM AND SHARING THEM. THOSE

TRUTHS ARE AVAILABLE TO US ALL THROUGH THE SCRIPTURES.

IT REMINDS ME OF THE TIME RECORDED IN THE BIBLE WHEN OUR WHEN OUR CREATOR FIRST SAID, "LET THERE BE LIGHT." AND THEN HE SAW THE LIGHT AND SAW THAT IT WAS GOOD. THUS, WE CAN ALSO CONSIDER THE IDEA THAT 'LIFE IS LIGHT'. AND IF WE VIEW LIFE WITH A PROPER, GOD-LIKE PERSPECTIVE, WE WILL SEE THAT IT IS **GOOD**.

A DRUG HIGH, OR EVEN A HIGH FROM SEXUAL FANTASY (WHICH MAKES USE OF BRAIN DRUGS OR HORMONES) CAN HAVE EXCITING BEGINNINGS, BUT IT NEVER HAS ANY SOLID CONCLUSIONS. IT IS LIKE AN OLYMPIC DIVER SPRINGING UP HIGH AS CAN BE OFF THE SPRINGBOARD, BUT LANDING WITH A BELLY FLOP.

THE LEARNING EXPERIENCE IS ALL-IMPORTANT IN LIFE AND COMING TO CONCLUSIONS ARE THE MOST IMPORTANT PART OF THE LEARNING EXPERIENCE. WITHOUT SOLID CONCLUSIONS, WE ARE ONLY CREATING DOODLE ART AND FANTASY. DOING DOODLE ART AND FANTASY MAY BE HARMLESS, BUT IT IS ALSO NEVER PRODUCTIVE. THUS, MAYBE THOSE THINGS ARE NOT REALLY HARMLESS AT ALL.

THE DRUG EFFECT HAS NO VALID CONCLUSIONS TO IT MENTALLY, PHYSICALLY, EMOTIONALLY OR SPIRITUALLY. I HAVE PERSONALLY OBSERVED THAT PEOPLE WHO HAVE LITTLE FOCUS IN LIFE OUTSIDE OF THEIR IMMEDIATE NEEDS (THEY ARE SOMETIMES CALLED 'SPACE CADETS') ARE NOT PEOPLE WHO

EVER FIND SELF-FULFILLMENT. THOSE PEOPLE ARE FAIRLY COMMON AMONG DRUG USERS.

THUS, ABSTINENCE IS AN IMPORTANT KEY IF A PERSON WANTS TO BREAKFREE FROM THE 'DRUG TRAP'.

IF YOU CAN THINK OF A BETTER WAY, YOU ARE ALWAYS FREE TO GIVE IT A SHOT. MY OPINION HOWEVER, IS THAT WITHOUT SPIRITUALITY, YOU WILL BE LIKE A DOG CHASING ITS TAIL. THUS, MISPERCEPTIONS ARE FUTILE AND FUTILITY WILL BE THE FINAL RESULT.

SO PLEASE REMEMBER MY EIGHTY THREE YEAR OLD FRIEND KEN WHO I SPOKE OF EARLIER. SEEK THE SPIRIT OF GOD, EVEN A SMALL PORTION OF IT. AND WHEN YOU FIND IT, DON'T FOOL AROUND WITH IT. LET IT LINGER. EXPAND ON IT IN YOUR MIND. YOUR MIND CAN BE A WONDERFUL COMPUTER IF IT IS PROGRAMMED CORRECTLY.

LET YOUR CONFIDENCE IN THE SPIRIT BE YOUR PERSONAL IDENTIFICATION CARD. THUS YOU CAN CALL ON A HIGHER POWER WHEN YOU NEED HELP AND YOU CAN USE IT TO HELP YOU SAY KIND WORDS TO OTHERS AND DO KIND THINGS FOR ALL PEOPLE.

WHEN YOU DO THAT, IT WILL NOT FAIL YOU.

Chapter 23

A BETRAYAL AND THE SPIRIT OF GENTLENESS (9p.)

There is always information traveling around the various media outlets and performance venues. There is also information, good and bad, true and false, passed on in school classrooms and among friends who occasionally gather together and discuss current events or a thousand other issues.

The most important information that we can receive however, will come to us by the Powers of Heaven, namely the Holy Ghost.

The only conditions there is that our minds must be at ease and be prepared to receive that information or personal message. If the Holy Ghost is sending you a message, which is something that He likes to do, you can bet that that message is one that applies directly to you, and it will be good for you to know.

Early in the morning is a good time to receive those messages. Your mind might not be totally clear, but it is clear enough that you should get the gist of it and you should be able to round up more details from the message if you are in the mood.

Some of the information we receive from 'upstairs' might not be important. No problem. Dump it. The spiritual wastebaskets in your house are numerous. They are there to take care of spiritual spam mail. Feel feel free to delete those messages.

Yes, the devil has his own salesmen and saleswomen and he has his own phone marketers. His call center is in hell and it is very active. Even though most of the time their phone marketers get 'hung up' on, but there are still a few calls that get through to naive customers.

If that message is really coming from the Holy Ghost, there should be some evidence there that there is something good there, even something that has a 'good feeling' about it.

Just remember that the Holy Ghost is a Heavenly being and that is good. He is a part of the Godhead along with the Father and the Son. He is not there to sell you something or fool you or to entertain you. Also, He knows you very well and He is aware of the things that you need the most. Also, know that He also has no time for people's idle curiosities.

My point is that sometimes, on occasions that can rarely be predicted, we will receive good and new information. That special information can be received in many specific ways. Those are ways that will touch our minds or our hearts. They will always be to our benefit and that is why they are important.

Your heart is your control center for receiving messages from the Holy Ghost. When there are signs that a message that you receive is relevant, that message should be investigated. If the information strikes you in your heart, it can come through inspired teachings in the artistic realms, or in religious realms, or in some other realm that activates our inner feelings and our desires to know what is true.

Personally, unless that message does not make any sense, I pay attention to it, or even just scan it a few times and see it fits in with any important concerns that I have in my life on that day.

Again I say, 'watch out' because there are a certain amount of 'tricksters' in the spirit world that mean us no good.

However, if an imposing spirit is aware that you are cautious and have some good knowledge about religious principles, they might just decide to 'back off and leave you alone', rather than have their foul intentions exposed by a person who actually has some knowledge about righteous principles.

***

MONDAY, MAY 15, 2023

Recently, I felt betrayed by a close family member. The incident caused me much anguish because she was once a very beloved member of my family, and there seemed to be no good reason for the betrayal and her cutting me off from having communication with her.

This morning, I was lying in bed and I received some comfort concerning my situation. I can't explain exactly how or why, but 'real comfort 'was something I needed at that time and it was something that I actually received, even though it was not expected. I believe that those feelings came because the Holy Ghost came into my room and His presence was felt by me.

Even though I could not see Him or talk to Him, I could feel a higher presence in my room at that time and it was unique to me because it, (He) was a Spirit of noticeable 'gentleness'. In retrospect, that conformed in my mind the reason why one of the other names of the Holy Ghost in the scriptures is 'THE COMFORTER'.

The feelings and ideas that come from the Holy Ghost are pure feelings. That is because the source of those ideas and feelings is <u>PURE</u>. Thus, those ideas are capable of touching our hearts. In any case we must still be aware that the devil is sly and has the ability to present ideas to us that are actually counterfeit ideas.

'Feelings', however are much more difficult to counterfeit than regular ideas that are expressed in words alone. Keep that in mind when you experience good feelings and do not know where those good feelings are coming from. This is why true learning about righteous things can be a deterrent to being 'taken on' by false doctrine and frivolous desires.

WHAT ARE SOME OTHER WORDS BESIDES 'GENTLENESS' THAT MIGHT DESCRIBE THOSE GOOD FEELINGS? HOW ABOUT WORDS LIKE 'MELLOW', OR 'LOVING' OR 'PEACEFUL'? I WOULD EVEN ADD TO THAT A WORD LIKE 'CONTENTMENT'.

IF YOU SHOULD FEEL THE PRESENCE OF THOSE FEELINGS, THEN PAY CLOSER ATTENTION BECAUSE THAT WOULD MEAN THAT THERE IS A BETTER CHANCE THAT THE MESSAGE THAT YOU ARE 'RECEIVING' IS LEGITIMATE AND COMES FROM EITHER A DIVINE SOURCE, OR FROM A SOURCE THAT

EXISTS ON A 'HIGHER COGNITIVE LEVEL'. IF YOUR MESSAGE IS FROM A DIVINE SOURCE THAT MEANS THAT THERE IS MORE THAN A GOOD CHANCE THAT YOU CAN EXPAND ON THAT MESSAGE WHEN YOU HAVE THE TIME TO 'MULL IT OVER'. THE REWARDS OF EMBRACING THAT MESSAGE IF COMFORT WILL BE OF GREAT VALUE FOR YOU, EITHER IN THE FUTURE OR RIGHT NOW.

IS A HIGHER COGNITIVE LEVEL SOMETHING THAT YOU CAN TRUST? NOT NECESSARILY, BUT THE ONLY TRUE SIGN OF TRUSTWORTHINESS WILL COME FROM A MYSTERIOUS, BUT REAL, CONNECTION TO A SPIRITUAL AND HOLY SOURCE LIKE THE HOLY GHOST, OR PERHAPS EVEN FROM JESUS HIMSELF.

Be aware though that, from my experience, Jesus does not spend too much time on trivial issues. He deals more with actual 'life changing' issues. The first job of the Holy Ghost is to testify of Jesus. Therefore, you can bet that His expertise is in the contemplation of 'life changing' issues.

In any case, the revelations that we receive from the Holy Ghost, or the Comforter, are the most important revelations that we can receive, even though it may not always be easy to discern exactly where they are coming from. Thus, 'learning' becomes a big part of hearing, or feeling, what the will of God actually consists of in your particular life.

How important is the Comforter on our lives? Here is a quote from the book of Matthew in the New Testament. The quote came from Jesus Christ. In other words, just be thankful and try to feel the peace and the strength that is near you.

***

"ANYONE WHO SPEAKS A WORD AGAINST THE SON OF MAN IT SHALL BE FORGIVEN HIM, BUT WHOEVER SPEAKETH AGAINST THE HOLY GHOST IT SHALL NOT BE FORGIVEN HIM, NEITHER IN THIS WORLD, NEITHER IN THE WORLD TO COME."
- MATTHEW 12: 32

Many times Christians have been accused of being over-tolerant, or wimpy, or namby-pamby. The person who made the above statement was definitely none of those things. This was a very fiery statement. Jesus Christ made it so we had better pay heed to it. He was saying that that is how important the Holy Ghost is.

Again, just be careful about accepting SPAM notices that try to distract you or convince you to buy some kind of miracle cure. Also, remember to pray that God will allow you to connect with Him so that He can give you some verification through the Comforter about the truth of the messages that you are receiving.

Sometimes correct advice from an understanding and trusted friend can be valuable, but just make sure that your trusted friend has some kind of belief in the spirit world, or they might not take you that seriously, and might just think that you have 'flipped out', or, heaven forbid, that your mind has been 'brainwashed by aliens'.

"Trust in the Lord and lean not to thine own understanding." - Proverbs 3:5

TECHNICALLY, THERE ARE TWO METHODS BY WHICH INSPIRED INFORMATION CAN BE TRANSFERRED TO US HUMAN BEINGS. ONE METHOD IS THE VERBAL METHOD AND THAT CONSISTS OF SAYING THE RIGHT WORDS AT EXACTLY THE RIGHT TIME. THE OTHER METHOD IS THE SPIRITUAL CONTEXT THAT COMES WHEN THERE IS AN HONEST AND LOVING AND EVEN A HOLY SPIRIT BEHIND THE DELIVERY OF A PARTICULAR MESSAGE. THAT WOULD BE A MESSAGE THAT YOU CAN <u>FEEL</u>.

IF A BENEVOLENT SPIRIT IS INSPIRING THE MESSAGE THAT YOU ARE RECEIVING, IT WILL BE ACCOMPANIED BY GOOD FEELING THAT CONFIRMS THAT THAT PARTICULAR MESSAGE IS GOOD. THAT IS BECAUSE THE SPIRIT WHO GIVES YOU THAT MESSAGE KNOWS EXACTLY WHO YOU ARE AND IS ALSO VERY NEAR YOU.

THOSE FEELINGS WOULD BE FEELINGS LIKE THE ONES THAT I MENTIONED A LITTLE EARLIER. THUS, IF AN INSPIRED MESSAGE COMES TO US, IT WILL USUALLY COME BY BOTH THE BEST WORDS, AND BY THE SPIRIT OF THE COMFORTER.

KEEP IN MIND THOUGH THAT FOR A FRIEND OF YOURS TO TAKE SERIOUS NOTICE OF WHAT YOU ARE SAYING WHEN YOU SHARE YOUR SPIRITUAL BELIEFS, IT IS IMPERATIVE THAT YOUR FRIEND HAS AN UNDERSTANDING, EVEN A BASIC UNDERSTANDING, OF WHO JESUS WAS AND WHAT HIS SACRIFICE WAS

ALL ABOUT. IF YOUR FRIEND DOES NOT HAVE THAT BASIC KNOWLEDGE, THEN IT IS VERY LIKELY THAT THEY WILL NOT FULLY UNDERSTAND WHAT YOU ARE TALKING ABOUT.

That is not necessarily their fault; they have just never been privy to the righteous secrets of the universe. It is possible for them to learn about those righteous secrets, but I am saying that you should tread softly and don't give them more information than they can handle.

In the rational gospel it is our desire to send and receive inspired thoughts both verbally and in the spirit. Keep in mind however, that words are not always dependable in their exact definitions. We realize that fact and we try to view laws of truth, not by the letter of them, but by the spirit of them.

Many of the words in the Bible are sent and received in the Spirit and the writer of those words uses the best words that a wise and loving human being (*or prophet, who are by nature, wise and loving*) can deliver.

That is why most of the scriptures have been canonized as inspired. 'Canonized' means that means that it is either approved of by God or approved by an ordained representative of God.

IF THAT IS THE CASE, THEN THE MESSAGE WILL BE TRUE. AND IF ANYTHING IS UNCLEAR, WE SHOULD ASK AGAIN, AND SEEK AGAIN TO KNOW WHAT IS TRUE .

Thus, the messages we receive in our minds must be rational and intelligent. Again, we believe that is the way that the rational gospel should always work. Take note however, that if you are not used to using spiritual discernment, then most of the messages that you receive should probably be not accepted in full, unless a spiritual witness is present.

How will you know if a message is inspired by the spirit? I can only say that, from my experience, it is a matter of dynamics. When the true spirit speaks, you will be literally compelled to listen. At that moment, you will just know.

IN CLOSING, I ALWAYS ASK PEOPLE TO STAND IN HOLY PLACES, SO THAT THEY WILL BE MORE ABLE TO FEEL THE SPIRIT AND MORE OPEN TO RECEIVING IMPORTANT MESSAGES AND FEELINGS, AND INSPIRED WORDS THAT MIGHT COME YOUR WAY.

SO BE AWARE THAT INSPIRED FEELINGS **MIGHT** COME INTO YOUR HEART AT ANY RANDOM TIME, ASSUMING THAT YOU ARE 'CLEAN AND SOBER'. IF THOSE FEELINGS DO COME YOUR WAY AND THEY MAKE SENSE, THEN EMBRACE THEM, AND GIVE THANKS FOR THEM AND THAT MYSTERIOUS HOLY SPIRIT HAS TAKEN HIS PRECIOUS TIME TO BLESS YOU.

24. NOTHING GOD CAN'T DO (3p.)

(I wrote this song a number of years ago, as you can tell by the names of the wrestlers mentioned. It is about a father and son talking about God while driving in a car. The song has the element of contrast in it. It is the contrast between an innocent young boy who loves to watch wrestling on television and a father who has been through a lot in real life.

Vs. 1
I was driving around in my car with my son the other day.

We started talking about God and all the things that He can do.

Well, he's got a pretty good imagination

And he asked me some pretty tough questions.

I must admit, he almost stumped me on a few.

Like when he said, "Dad, can God beat up Hulk Hogan in a wrestling match?"

I said, "yup".

He said, "Can he beat up Andre the Giant and the Ultimate Warrior too?"

I said, "I believe so, but he wouldn't want to hurt those wrestlers, whether they are good guys or whether they're bad guys, because He loves them the same way He loves me and you."

THE RATIONAL GOSPEL

Chorus –

And He can shine upon the ones who live in darkness.

His light is always there to see us through.

If He can take a broken man and help him understand

And turn his grey skies into blue

Then honey, there ain't nothing that God can't do.

Vs. 2

He said, "Do you think God can hold up a great big building with one hand?

I said, "Sure".

"Well, can he hold up a truck and a semi-trailer with the other hand too?"

I said, "Yes, I believe so."

"Well, can he hold up a truck and a semi-trailer and hold them up or forty six days and ...."

I said, "Hold it son. I told you, there ain't nothing that God can't do."

Chorus:

And He can shine upon the ones who live in darkness.

His light is always there to see us through.

If He can take a broken man, and help him understand, and turn his grey skies into blue,

Well, there ain't nothing that God can't do.

Vs. 3

He said, "Well I God can do all those things, why doesn't he just come down and show us?"

I said, "Well first, you have to prove that your faith is true. And if you live the gospel every day and always take the time to pray, I think you'll find there ain't nothing that He won't do for you. "

Chorus:

And He can shine upon the ones who live in darkness.
His light is always there to see us through.
If He can take a broken man and help him understand, and turn his gray skies into blue,
Then there ain't nothing that God can't do.
There ain't nothing God can't do.

To see the video go to: https://youtu.be/2SyzCgRq1rs

Chapter 25.

THE DESCENDING ORDER OF FAITH (5p.)

All people need to decide, at some point, what part religion or faith will play in their lives. I believe that there are four basic options for all of us. Those options could very well fit into a quadrant, which would illustrate the degree to which they choose their level of faith.

1. Be devoted, humble and eager to learn
2. Acknowledge it, but act on it only occasionally
3. Ignore the church
4. Fight against the church

The first principle is one of complete devotion and obedience to the commandments. Here is a quote from a man of great faith that illustrates this:

> *"Perhaps the greatest discovery of my life, without question the greatest commitment, came when finally I had the confidence in God that I would loan or yield my agency to him - without compulsion or pressure, without any duress, as a single individual alone, by myself, no counterfeiting, nothing expected other than the privilege. In a sense, speaking figuratively, to take one's agency, that precious gift which the scriptures make plain is essential to life itself, and say, 'I will do as you direct', is afterward to learn that in so doing you possess it all the more".*
> *– Boyd K. Packer*

The word 'it' in the last line refers to free agency. This thought contains the idea of complete devotion, out of one's free choice, and to be obedient out of sheer humility and the acknowledgement of the truth.

***

The first item on the list belongs to God. He sets the rules and we, by our free choice, will decide whether to obey them or not. Personally, I try to be very careful when I speak about God's realm. I am simply do not know enough about it, nor do most people. I just know that it exists and is all-powerful.

To me, the second item starts a more descending pattern in matters of faith and we can see evidence of the descending pattern as we observe the situation in our world today. The people in the second quadrant acknowledge God and religion, but go to church only occasionally and do not let religion be a large part of their daily lives. Many of these people are uncertain about the nature of God and find theology in general somewhat confusing. Those are often people who claim to be religious out of a 'just in case there is a God' mentality. Then again, there are others in this part of the quadrant who have a testimony of God, but are just unwilling or unable to fully live up to it.

In the third item on the list refers to people who do not want to know about it. The main reason for that is that is simply cramps their style. Thinking that the gospel might be true would make it more difficult for them to just get drunk or have illegitimate sex. The idea of being accountable does not appeal to them at all.

The fourth item on the list consists of people who want to be in the intellectual limelight, but have no means of getting there other than to cling to myths about religion and broadcast them in public forums as a way of garnering attention to themselves and trying to make others think that they are privy to some kind of 'inside information'.

Upon close inspection, an observer can usually tell that most of the arguments of people who fight against religion have many flaws in them and totally ignore things like the higher intelligences, the power of the spirit, and the absolute miracle of the universe itself.

So the attitudes about religion will vary from person to person, which is the way it was supposed to be, I guess. Although I do have definite opinions on the subject, as everyone should, I do not condemn anybody for their views. That is not my job. However, I firmly believe that the lives of people who set their sights on eternal goals live much more fulfilled lives than those who do not.

Personal success and happiness need to be lasting in order to be legitimate. 'Lasting' means permanent. True spirituality is a permanent thing. Thus, happiness and success requires spiritual roots to keep that 'living thing' nourished so that it will be permanent. Any problems in finding spiritual happiness can be solved only by spiritual solutions, which will require going back to examine those roots.

When problems arise in someone's life it is not usually circumstances that are to blame, but the following of an untrue principle, or even the misuse, or misinterpretation, of a true principle. Trials and tribulations happen to good people and to bad people, but we will always fall short in solving them when we do not have the spiritual eyes and ears that enable us to pinpoint a problem and then have the spiritual strength to deal with it.

Before we address how we might sustain a level of 'spiritual strength in our lives, let us try to define further what the word really means. When I talk about spirit, I talk about different kinds of spirits. There are spirit entities with some kind of identity and there are spirits without any physical identity. An example of a spirit without identity is when we say something like, "there was a spirit of good fellowship in the room"; or we can talk about a 'spirit of goodwill', or a 'spirit of compassion'.

We can talk about a championship football team as having a good 'team spirit' about it. 'Team spirit' is an example of how a separate spirit can be at work can work for constructive purposes when two or more factions work together with the same purpose and with the most efficiency. A good team spirit not only makes the maximum use of each person, but there is something else that is created in the process that increases the overall effectiveness of the team. That 'something else' is difficult, or maybe even impossible, to define, In other words, it is often the case that **'the whole is greater than the sum of its parts'.**

That idea is valid, but can be difficult to explain. Nevertheless, most professional athletes will attest to the benefits of such a 'team' spirit in the experiences they have had of working effectively with their teammates. Such a spirit that comes from a well-coordinated joint effort is often intangible, but we can 'feel' it when it happens.

The late author Dr. Stephen R. Covey talked something similar in his book 'The Seven Habits of Highly Effective People'. He called it 'synergy'. He used that word to describe the process of gaining strength from unity. He used the physical example of two wooden boards holding up <u>not only twice as much weight as one board</u>, but up to four times as much weight. Extra strength is produced when the two factions work together properly.

When we are connected to something else in a united purpose, our strengths become multiplied beyond the simple mathematics of it all.

In human terms, most of us are all searching for some kind of human synergy or a strong unifying force. It might be described as a sense of belonging to something greater than ourselves, or something that is an embodiment of the best part of our existence. This is a good thing and most people seek a natural path to try to obtain that unity of spirit.

Other people will try to gain and make use of a good spirit <u>as individuals</u>. That may work or that may not work, but for me I prefer the companionship of like-minded people who are in possession of a sensible doctrine. the logistics of that doctrine is sufficient for people who are intelligent and who have a lot of integrity and who are able to work as a team without any 'prima

donnas' trying to steal the show.

Chapter 26

ALWAYS CONSIDER CONTEXT (11p.)

What is our main goal in our existence? Ultimately, religious people think it is to go to the most perfect place they can find and live there for eternity. That place is generally called 'heaven'. That is their main context. It is quite straightforward and simple, but the details of Heaven can be difficult to understand because they are a part if that higher world that we know little about. We were not ready to learn about all the details of that in the past. Hopefully, after much preparing and by the grace of our mighty God, we will be ready to learn about it in the future.

The ideal goal of any group, be it political or otherwise, is to **achieve** their best vision of their ultimate goal. That is an ideal, but it is a 'legitimate' ideal and not just a fantasy that is based upon an unreal world. But heaven is a very real world because our very real God lives there and this will be made clearer to us the more we gain confidence in our Heavenly Father and in His love for us.

We can all come into the presence of God, but to go there permanently the opportunity for that must be earned. We can only earn it be being obedient to the Eternal laws that we have been given.

> *If you love Me, keep My commandments. And I will pray the Father, and He will give you another Helper, that He may abide with you forever— the Spirit of truth, whom the world cannot receive, because it neither sees Him nor knows Him; but you know Him, for He dwells with you and will be in you."*   *- John 14: 15-17*

That is true because when something is good and beautiful and permanent, there will be certain requirements involved for us imperfect beings to be able to expand our faith and partake of the blessings that come with that faith. The happiest Christians are the ones who have a large amount of faith. Another word for faith is '**confidence**'.

Many people do not have any faith in faith.

That is because they get it mixed up with 'blind faith'. Blind faith, to me, is really no faith at all. There must be a foundation of truth in the process of being faithful or it is not real faith.

That is why, in my belief system, true faith must be found within the overall context of truth. If we were to have faith in untruth, it would make absolutely no sense. That is one reason why I ask people to consider context when they analyze people's beliefs.

To those people who have faith in God, Heaven is not a fantasy world. It is totally real and it is a promise that we should have faith in it or we just might not recognize it when it comes to us. Going to Heaven is simply about believing in a good environment and a good context as a permanent ideal. To our great God that is **not** a difficult thing for Him to facilitate. It is actually easy for Him to do, but we must be ready to receive it. In that way, it will be a joint effort and a joint effort (or a team effort) is always the best way to get things done.

Thus, in the world of the things that matter most, Heaven is fair game. Another word for faith is 'confidence'. We will need to have confidence in something if we will have the strength that we need in order to support that 'something' with all of our hearts, even unto the end.

Here is a passage in the Doctrine and Covenants, which is a book that contains many revelations from the first prophet of the church Joseph Smith. This verse contains a beautiful concept.

> ***"THE GLORY OF GOD IS INTELLIGENCE, OR IN OTHER WORDS, LIGHT AND TRUTH."***
> ***- DOCTRINE AND COVENANTS 93: 36***

Is intelligence really the most important thing in life? Let us look deeper into the context. <u>Some people might say that **love** is the most important thing in life.</u> That is a good thought and I suspect, it is a thought that has 'some' truth in it. But love doesn't always work out in the end. We just need to look at the national divorce rate to see the truth in that. <u>There can be many obstacles in matters of 'love', but only things like understanding and **'intelligence'**, patience, kindness, long suffering, and mainly the presence of the Holy Ghost, can overcome those obstacles.</u>

Intelligence, to some people, might seem to be in opposition to passion, but that is not true. It may be a highly personal matter, but still, there will need to be much consideration on that particular topic. Many examples of love gone wrong are that way because they were not well thought out. In other words they are often just not realty- based or 'intelligent' enough to eliminate all of the obstacles that might show up. Thus, I say that love must have a large amount of 'intelligence' behind it or it can go 'off track'.

Does lasting love require being more intelligent than having more passion? Absolutely.

Intelligence requires the elimination of false or confusing ideas that cause people to become literally confused or confounded when storm clouds come on the scene. Generally speaking, passion is just not smart enough to eliminate some of those daunting obstacles.

Here is a question for us to think about. Am I eligible to enter into heaven? Here is another question. Are <u>you</u> eligible to enter into Heaven? Here is another question. Do you even understand what I am talking about here? The contexts of all the things I talk about are endless, but I do believe that, sometimes, a context can be vitally important to our understanding of a principle.

Questions, questions, questions. Wouldn't it be nice just to dispense with them all? Yes, but we cannot because somewhere in the answers to those questions lies the truth, and 'the truth shall make you free'.

> "YE SHALL KNOW THE TRUTH AND THE TRUTH SHALL MAKE YOU FREE."
> – JOHN 8: 32

So we cannot dispense with all the questions unless we have one thing. That is – the correct answers to those questions.

Are those questions impossible to answer. I would say 'NO' to that. I do believe that the correct answers are there. 'The only stipulations are to diligently seek for them AND to be 'prepared to receive them once you can see them clearly'.

Can we come to know those true answers? I believe that we can. Today I will go to church. That is a place where people who have been blessed with a basic understanding of the truth gather together in a building that has been set apart for learning more with other people who appreciate the same values.

Those values are always things of a righteous nature. Simply put, my church might **not** provide a perfect environment some of the time, but if the Spirit is present there, it is a certainty that my church will 'theoretically', be the best environment for me.

Even if I have some personal issues that I will need to deal with, the first thing to consider is, 'will I be in the best place to be able to deal with them. If I am in the Lord's house, that is the best place for me. That is the <u>context</u> that will suit me best.'

The people in my church try to live by high moral standards. Those standards have been established by words from God called Holy Scriptures. In the present time that we live in, Jesus has established God's true church, and it continues to be witnessed and sustained by the Holy Spirit of God.

That means that the true church provides for an environment that is as accurate in its sensible doctrine and in its sensible beliefs and in its sensible passion. This doesn't mean that the church will be perfect. It will not be. This is because we live in a tainted world, and thus, we will probably somewhat tainted ourselves. The only thing we can hope for is to be forgiven for our transgressions and begin again with a clean slate.

By divine inspiration, or 'the Grace of God', we have been blessed by having many 'golden nuggets of wisdom' delivered to us by prophets who are under the guidance of

God and are also influenced by our personal redeemer who is Jesus Christ. There could be imperfections in any church because we happen to live in an imperfect world. It seems it is the best we can do would be to appreciate that potential ideal and do our best to help as many people as possible know what that ideal is, and to do what we can to cause that ideal to become a reality.

If we do our best to make our church great again then we should then be able to maintain a strong faith in our original righteous goals. That is all we can do.

In the meantime, we should be grateful for our lives that allow us the <u>opportunity</u> to undertake this sacred quest of searching for the truth. If we fail in this effort, we need not throw up our hands and give up. We should just repent and try again with a clean slate. Then, when we feel that we have become better people, we should actively support our church and sustain it for the entire world to see.

***

Were it not for prophets like Joseph Smith Jr. and the many faithful saints who I have met. I would never have met my wife if I had never been converted to the truth of the gospel. Thus, my children would never have been born. Hard to conceive of the notion that my beautiful children came to exist today partly because of a man named Joseph Smith, who was an itinerate preacher who lived almost two hundred years ago.

It is hard for me to conceive of the notion that my relationship with my children was solidified by 'religious doctrine', which is basically, 'words written in books'. But **the**

truth is a powerful thing and thus, it needs to be accepted and embraced in whatever form it might appear to us.

Thus, I love Joseph smith and partly because were it not for his influence in my life and his righteousness and courage, my beautiful children would not have been born. That is part of the context of my life and I am grateful for it.

Someone may mock me and I may put up with it, but I will resent anyone who mocks my admiration for Joseph, or who mocks the Atonement of Jesus Christ, or who mocks the divine nature of Jesus Christ.

I am also grateful for Joseph Smith and not because he established the church in 1830, but because he was a prophet who was ordained by God to do what he did. Not only was he a prophet, but he was a GREAT prophet. You will need to check out his writings to verify that.

The point is though that 'wise people' speak wise words. Thus, such a complicated organization as the LDS church could only be organized by many wise people who were under the influence and guidance of God, and not under the guidance of one lone uneducated man. Joseph Smith was one lone man and he only had a grade three education, but he was an inspired and gifted man, and was favored by God. It was absolutely amazing that he accomplished what he did.

Joseph also had friends who were also inspired to a large degree. Thus, if wisdom is an important context in our lives, which it should be, then we have, indeed, been blessed by our acceptance of wisdom. And we should be grateful for that.

Wise people will have a good grasp on reality. They can speak with authority about the past, the present and the future and they can do so because they have studied such things intensely and have also been blessed with the Divine guidance that they have asked for.

Since Divinity is mostly in a realm by itself. This premise will be impossible to confirm, or deny, but the strong faith that believers have will be enough to provide all observers with evidence that anyone can potentially have access to that higher realm I have been speaking about.

Thus, strong faith and proven 'wisdom' actually causes this gift of access to take place. Wisdom is an immaterial thing. I cannot touch it or feel it, but sometimes there are some people who can always 'call it up' when they need it and answers will be given to us by the mysterious power of the Spirit. Wisdom can cause the average man, or woman, to confirm 'sensible thinking'. This will come through the Holy Spirit who can live within us. If someone should ask me why I think the way I do, I will tell them about what I just said and explain that that is the context that I work in.

We can call up affirmations in the temporal world, but that is never a dependable process. As well, we could never call them up permanently, for 'all things shall pass'.

There is a caveat here however that denies the notion that all things must pass and affirms the notion that, among the faithful, **there are some things that shall not pass**. That caveat is expanded upon in this Old Testament verse from the book of Daniel :

> *"And in the days of these kings the god of heaven will set up a kingdom which shall never be*

> *destroyed; and the kingdom shall not be left to other people; it shall break in pieces and consume all these kingdoms, and it shall stand forever."*
> *- Daniel 2: 44*

Thus, we could say that, 'most things shall pass', but 'only things that have been sanctified by a sacred and an eternal god will not pass away'. I can only really possess permanent knowledge by the Holy Spirit, who is Himself, permanent and eternal. Again, my context lights my way.

> **"WITH GOD ALL THINGS ARE POSSIBLE."**
> **- MATTHEW 19: 26**

How can a relatively innocent human being tell the difference between those two ways of believing and discern them on their own as his, or her, life comes closer to the end? I say that they do that through two adjacent processes. One process is what I call '<u>sampling</u>' or 'discernment'. That means judging what is good for everyone and judging what is bad for everyone. Another term for sampling is to 'mentally prepare'.

That preparing can also mean 'experimenting on the word'. That refers to monitoring our personal experiences and then learning whatever wisdom we might gain from contemplating those experiences, especially if we write them down in a journal, and then incorporate what we have truly learned into our characters.

You can experiment on anything, but if you do not bring the word of God into the equation, your experimenting will prove in the end, to be inconclusive.

That process of experimentation can be one that uses reasonable data, even in a scientific sense, but that doesn't really matter because the main process that you should use will be a spiritual process. The spiritual process makes the spirit essential to the outcome of your experiment. <u>The physical process</u> is also very relevant for us because that is the place where we had our learning of the spiritual things that we needed to know in order that we might advance in our progression.

That was due, to a large degree, because of the LITERAL CONTRAST of the two realms, which are the Spiritual Realm and the physical realm. Thus, it seems that it might be required to experience an inferior realm, that is the physical realm, and alongside of that, also experience the superior realm that is the Spiritual realm and compare and contrast the two realms.

Perhaps God thought that it would be good or us to experience both realms at the same time so that we could see more clearly the differences between the two realms and that would help us to discern which realm was the best for us, and therefore give us more intelligence to make our choice as to where we wanted to spend our time in whatever Eternal ream we chose to exist in.

***

I am merely speculating here, but nevertheless, if what I say does not ring true, I can only say that it will not be the first time that I have been wrong. Take that for what it is worth. I am only speculating on how God might actually work. As a citizen of this world and as a citizen of this backward country called Canada, I feel that I have the right to speculate on whatever I want, that is if Mr.

Trudeau has not already made 'speculation' against the law.

I do not claim to know all about the Eternal realms. I am not that smart. I hope you will forgive me for that. I do however, like to ask a lot of questions and I hope that many of my questions will be answered and that the answers that I receive will contribute to my ongoing learning process.

Perhaps someday, I will write a sequel to this book and I will call it The Rational Gospel, Volume two. In that book I hope to tell you what my choice of realm will be regarding which one of the two realms I will choose to exist in.

I don't want to be a spoiler, but I think that most of you know by now, which one of those two realms I will choose.

Chapter 27

Bob's Obbs #2   (11p.)

As humans beings, and especially those human beings who are professional politicians, our great capacity for making wonderful discoveries that make positive contributions to society is only exceeded by our immense capacity for self-justification and making accusations against other politicians.

The mutual quest to find the truth becomes pointless or 'goes out the window' when one person deliberately tries to misrepresent the opinions of another. This principle is always seen in political debates between the different political parties, all of which are acting purely out of their own self interest..

A 'realization' of anything is a true 'intellectual event'. When any new knowledge is gained, the personal implications of it should be written down, shared and pondered. This is a 'realization event'. Celebrate it and turn it into true knowledge.

I believe that it is not those who possess the most truth and knowledge who are most favored by God. It is <u>those who make the best use</u> of whatever truth and knowledge that they have been given.

"We do not need revolutions. We need revelations."

"The truth is forever at rest. The proclamation of truth is never at rest."

"The truth is not our enemy, but our greatest ally. I am not talking about cold, hard facts, but the warm spirit of truth. If it is not incorporated into our cause, it will be outside of our cause. If we are not fighting for it, we will be fighting against it."

If you ever feel that you have found the truth, you must face the distinct possibility that truth can be a delicate thing and that many of the people you know will not accept it. Many of them will say in effect, 'your ideas are not welcome here'. This can apply to family members, friends, work associates and even to people who you may have known all your life.

Did you ever have a day when you felt really good and noticed that several good things happened to you on that day? Did you ever think that it might be possible that that was God specifically working to 'make your day'? Did it occur to you that it might be a good thing to make it reciprocal, and if you concentrated on doing as many good things as possible today, so that you might actually 'make God's day'?

Okay, I'll admit it. I am not really a very intelligent person. But that's not necessarily a bad thing. I say this because, when the truth does present itself to me, I can more easily recognize that truth because it <u>stands out</u> more distinctly from my regular humdrum way of thinking. Thus, ironically, I would say that, in a way, a lack of intelligence might be a blessing.

For some people, if they are to progress, they will need to give up certain things. Sometimes, it may be that we will need to give up <u>the thing that we do the best.</u> That can be very difficult, but it might be necessary.

The greatest talent a man or a woman could have, and a

God like quality as well, is this: to be able to **change something bad, into something good**, by friendly persuasion. That is like witnessing 'magic' in its truest sense.

A bird may fly over to the other side of a river then fly back again. That doesn't mean that they have changed. Only when a person crosses the river with their whole being and lives on the other side, does change happen. There is a big difference between personal change and personal oscillation.

Personal change starts with learning. Learning starts with wonder. Thus, the effort required to learn new things should start with a 'wonder-full' and an enthusiastic effort.

There are many times in our lives when change is desired, but there may come a time when change will be <u>demanded.</u> That will be the time when we begin to dislike ourselves because we have come to realize the full extent of our personal weaknesses.

It is a wonderful thing to be able to change something that was considered second rate into something first rate. Nevertheless, it is better all around to settle for second best in reality than accept first best in a fantasy.

It is good to ask yourself at the end of the day, "Was this a day that I would want to take into eternity with me?" If it was not, ask yourself what you can do tomorrow to make it so?

Age does not determine worthiness or unworthiness. Let your experience work for you instead of against you. The world has lots of problems that have never been solved. You cannot solve them all, but perhaps you can contribute something to solving a few of them. Speak kind words. Make people smile. Tell funny stories (even if you have to make them up).

Some older people refuse to accept the responsibility of evaluating their own personal character. For those who do though, there comes a time when intellectual meandering is over. You have had enough time to think. The evidence should be in, and hopefully, you will have chosen the right path. If not, it is not too late to change your mind, as long as you can still breath.

Be of a forgiving nature. You cannot really isolate the emotion of bitterness to a certain compartment of your brain. It has a way of spreading itself through your whole body and coming out in ways that you may not have expected.

The road to happiness is open when four things come together in harmony. Those things are: freedom, unity, correct order, and passion."

Try to be <u>active</u> in the pursuit of things that are good. Forces of evil are real and will try to prevent you from doing that, but in my time, I have learned about a weakness that the devil has; that is that - HE CANNOT HIT A MOVING TARGET.

The biggest problem facing mankind today is not cancer or heart disease or war or malnutrition. It is spiritual blindness. That is something that leads to the aforementioned things.

It is a good thing to create laughter and smiles, but we must always recognize that life is, firstly, a serious business. Smiles are a sign of unity among people and that is good, but unity <u>at any cost</u> is not the end goal. Moral responsibility, or obedience to God's laws comes first. The smiles and laughter and unity come second and, as a consequence, those smiles will be more meaningful than they ever were.

A person should see himself or herself as one 'whole' person. The parts of their psyches should not be held together with hooks, strings, tape or velcro.

In the morning, if you have been doing things right, you should feel good about at least one of the four aspects of your life, either the physical, the mental, the emotional or spiritual realm. Focus on that aspect that is presently running on all cylinders and run with it. Don't always try to correct the one that is not working properly. Sometimes you should choose the best one, go with it, and the other three should catch up soon. <u>Go with what you know you are good at first</u>.

A question one might ask at the beginning of the day is: "Do I have the strength to deal with the things I expect to encounter today without resorting to indulgence, resentment, escapism or emotionalism?" When I spend my morning time cultivating good thoughts, those good thoughts and the feelings that go with them are likely to follow me around for the remainder of the day.

Some people set goals for themselves that are inherently unachievable and they feel a sense of failure when they do not achieve them. Ironically, this can be used to one's advantage in the search for happiness. This is because <u>if</u> you can still find contentment without having achieved your original goals, romantically or financially or otherwise, then it shows that you have greatly increased your own personal independence. Thus, you did not need help from outside worldly circumstances in order to become fulfilled as a person. You will be, spiritually speaking, 'independently wealthy'.

Always go first rate; first-rate friends; first-rate conversation; first-rate music; first-rate literature, etc. If you settle for second rate, it can easily become a habit. First rate does not need to be expensive or complicated. It can be simple. As long as it is clean.

Society is still about dogmatism, except that the main players have changed over the years. Years ago, the churches told everybody what was right and wrong. Now it is academia and government ideologues who tell everybody what is right and wrong and most of the time you aren't allowed to argue with them.

I make it a point in my personal philosophy not to give opinions about things that I know very little about. I also make it a point in my personal philosophy <u>not to listen</u> to people who give opinions about things that they know very little about.

Don't get discouraged by the bad things in the world. Bad things can happen to good people, but when those good people rise above those bad things, they become even better people.
          - Bob King from the book 'The Hat's in the Ring'

When I consider the three realms we all live in – the mental, physical and emotional, I never underestimate the physical. I compare it to a game of football. You can have the best game plan in the world (mental) and you can have all of the confidence and team spirit that you need (emotional), but if you do not have the ability to <u>(physically)</u> drag the ball over the goal line, you are not going to score any touchdowns and you are not going to win any games.

Is tolerance always in our best interests? What about tolerating the ideas of stupid people, or people who never take moral factors into consideration? Do their opinions matter? We may tell them that their opinions matter so they don't feel left out and so their feelings won't be hurt. But do those opinions really matter in truth? No. So let us not waste time with the ill informed or the uninformed or the wild eyed idealists around us. Let us seek out opinions from those who are informed and have thought things out fully. Thus, too much tolerance should not be tolerated.

Timing is everything when it comes to effectiveness. Like a disciplined army, sometimes we must hold back or even retreat, but there will be times to press forward; to engage; to emerge; to advance, or even to just wait.

Always bring God into the equation; and Christ too. God made our spirits, but Christ has given those spirits substance and meaning. In that way, He has spiritually begotten us and is the never-ending source of all goodness. Understanding and experiencing goodness is not possible without considering the source of all goodness.

The wisdom of the natural man is child's play to God. What we need to do every day is try to be as wise as we can be. And when we reach the highest point we are capable of, pray that God might lift us up just a little bit, so we can enter, even slightly, into the realm of the Holy.

Good advice may be welcome, or unwelcome, but good companionship is always welcome.

If we want to have high quality and trustworthy friends, then we need to be of high quality and trustworthy ourselves.
    - Bob King from the book "Freedom ,Bondage And The Human Experience."

I think that making children laugh is more important than buying them expensive toys.

You do not need to be all things to your children or to your spouse. It is more important just to <u>be there</u>.

An important aspect of raising children is finding a balance between protecting them, which includes invoking discipline, and empowering them, which includes letting them take certain risks.

Sometimes children resent parents because they see them as not knowing how to have any fun. Sometimes, the children may be right in their assessment.

Parents, be a light to your children, not a dark mystery.

Giving birth to a child and living with them in the same abode may be enough to be able to call yourself a parent, but not enough to call yourself a 'good' parent. That title of 'good parent' needs to be earned.

I think that we will all desire to spend our time (and eternity) with those people who we genuinely care about and those people who genuinely care about us. In eternity, filial obligations for their own sake will no longer exist. In a spiritual sense, that part of life is over and a new life has begun.

We all experiment with different ideas in life and that can be a good thing. There comes a time however when we reach a certain age that the data from our experiments will be in. That is when a <u>conclusion</u> needs to be reached in our experiment.

If there is no room for free expression, walk away. Some people might allow you the freedom to speak, but will not allow themselves the freedom to hear you.

Anger can be passed on from parent to child. The parent may express their anger in one way, but the child may develop their own unique way of expressing their anger and some parents will not understand that.

It may seem unfortunate, but there will be times in life when we will be forced to choose between sacred principles that we believe to be true and people we love who do not share those principles.

It is okay for a person to be fierce when his fierceness is controlled and it is for a good purpose. When it is not controlled, however, fierceness by itself is unstable and dangerous.

The battles in life often seem like 'guerrilla wars'; that is, hide and seek at an extreme level. Camouflage is often needed. When you show anger, in whatever form, you draw the attention of your enemies to yourself. You give away your position. The enemy, who is the devil, knows exactly where you are and he can then 'pick you off', or strike you from any flank he chooses. You will be an easy target. Thus, I say, be 'battle wise', for we are all in a battle and, hopefully are on the side of the good.

Freedom (liberty) is a sacred thing. When I was in my twenties I investigated a certain church. They believed in a one-world government. How foolish I was to even consider joining it. A one-world (globalist) government means that that government will have full control over everything. Even if it appears benevolent at first, in time it will become corrupt. Then there will be no turning back. You and everybody else will then be 'owned'. You will be trapped in an intricate spider's web and there will be no escape.

Here is my response to a rebellious teenager who doesn't like to hear about gospel truths talked about in our home. "I am your father, and as your father I have a solemn duty to tell you about things I have found to be true in my own lifetime. Whether you want to hear those things or not, I will tell them to you anyways. That is because I feel that is my duty as your father to do so. If you don't want to hear about them that is your choice, but know that I am secure in my knowledge that I have done my job."

Having a strong family means having a collective wisdom, love, and the courage to protect each other. Families also need a spirit of gratitude, and a set structure for learning. Good spirits will attend you when your family commits to developing those things.

In the early morning spam messages may infiltrate my mind for hours at a time, but if I am aware, at some time I might hear a whisper of just a few words. They might just last a few seconds, but if they ring true, then I will know that are coming from the Holy Spirit. That is that time I will say to myself, "YES, THAT IS WHAT I NEEDED TO HEAR.

Purity, however difficult it may be to attain, is the ultimate human quality. When you enter into any worldly situation, unless guided by religious beliefs that are pure and kind, you will always be entering into a tainted world. Any relationship entered into, unless it is driven by a friendship that is 'pure,' will be tainted to some degree.

If you are looking for a spiritual adventure, I say, try journal writing. Journal writing is an adventure because if it is honest then it will be challenging in a good way. Honest self-analysis is always challenging and it allows for much learning. If you don't find a challenge in journal writing, I suspect that it is because you are not doing it properly. There are always things that you can write about and find pleasure by just doing that.

Detaching from a bad situation without feeling any resentment may be difficult to do, but bitterness in the mind can be superseded by having good feelings in the heart. Those good feelings can only come as a gift from the Comforter. Those same feelings were given to you in the very beginning. Ask God to help you to recall those feelings and thoughts and He will do that, but He will do it with His own timing.

May the worldly things that you were once obsessed with become <u>less</u> important as time goes by, and may beautiful, but forgotten, beliefs from a distant past begin to touch your heart once again.

Freedom (liberty) is mostly in the mind. That makes it within your grasp. If it is within your grasp, what are you waiting for? Reach out and grab it.

Chapter 28

THE FINAL GATHERING (10P.)

> "THE GATHERING OF ISRAEL IS THE MOST IMPORTANT WORK TAKING PLACE ON EARTH TODAY. ONE CRUCIAL ELEMENT OF THIS GATHERING IS PREPARING A PEOPLE WHO ARE ABLE, READY, AND WORTHY TO RECEIVE THE LORD WHEN HE COMES AGAIN, THESE WILL BE PEOPLE WHO HAVE ALREADY CHOSEN JESUS CHRIST OVER THIS FALLEN WORLD, A PEOPLE WHO REJOICE IN THEIR AGENCY TO LIVE THE HIGHER, HOLIER LAWS OF JESUS CHRIST".
>
> *- Russell M. Nelson, the president and prophet of the Church of Jesus Christ of Latter Day Saints*

President Russell M. Nelson has declared the gathering of the children of God. Those who always believed in God and still do, will be assembled and begin to set up a mighty and glorious kingdom that will last forever. This Kingdom will include all the righteous people of the world who live today, or have lived in the past, and lived by the laws of our spiritual Father who abides in Heaven.

Not wanting to over-generalize about the problems of families of various faiths in nations around the world, I begin with the state of my own family and I asked each member in that family to consider what will happen when the chaos of the world is finally, eradicated and peace and sensibility and the prudence of Our God and our Savior will rule over the whole earth.

These solutions will not be according to value-less psychiatrists, pill popping doctors or authoritarian scientists, but the solutions will come from the mouth of God, our perfect and invincible creator who has personally and successfully gone through the steps to ultimate self-fulfillment according to the master plan. That plan was one that he set in motion from the beginning. Evidence of His wisdom and His Spirit came from His mouth and the mouths of His assigned prophets who were given a portion of His Holy Spirit when He called them to assist Him in His work.

This decision of the Father was made with a Holy determination to 'set things right' after allowing men and women everywhere to make their own choices or in other words to 'do things 'their own way', if they insisted on it.

That 'allowance' was a strategy that was often froth with error, pain and suffering. That pain was allowed, I believe because human beings, it would appear, needed to be shown, literally, that the natural way of doing things would not work. The errors of the people needed to be played out until the end, so that all people might learn from those errors.

Considering the alternatives, I surmise that this was the only way that human beings could undergo 'true learning' which is something than is needed if men and women will actually progress in their journey.

Human beings needed divine guidance and that was something that needed to be proven, and eventual was proven, thanks to the wisdom and the love that God had for His children. End of story.

The rebellious nature of human beings had been obvious throughout the earth's early history. God knew that total freedom of choice would not work for achieving self-mastery or self-fulfillment. Too many mistakes would be made. Those

THE RATIONAL GOSPEL

mistakes would need to be corrected under the true guidance that only God and His prophets could provide.

Our Father, along with His Son Jesus, gave us many gifts. The main gift that He gave us was the Great Atonement. Another great gift that he will give us very soon will be when He 'backs off' from allowing human beings to have license or 'carte blanche' to do whatever they want to do in a moral sense.

That 'backing off' will be be a corrective measure that realigns the forces of the world itself. This is so that the divine purposes of our God will be fulfilled, and so that happiness and harmony will be realistically attained. That will happen when we will be able to teach everyone that **all families will need to be raised in righteousness and raised with true learning.**

That aspect of the progression of mankind will be covered in the final days when the teachings of God will come directly from God Himself. Given the often-ineffective state of raising families in this day, this active re-entrance of God and His love into our world will be welcome news to most people. Those people will then begin to give our good God the credit that He deserves for His understanding and His patience.

The people would also witness the great leaders from the past who became resurrected beings who came back to Earth and gave their testimonies about the Holy work that was to be done when the final gathering happens.

It is a recorded in the Bible that resurrected beings like Moses and Elias appeared to the inner circle of Christ's church in Jesus' time on what is called the Mount of Transfiguration (Moses 17: 1-8)

So why would these historical figures not appear in such a great event as the final gathering that I am speaking of? I say that they did appear, and I would guess that they <u>will appear again</u>. I can think of no reason why they would not appear.

Furthermore, why not include in this exclusive group, Jesus Christ Himself, who had the main job of bringing forth righteous men and women of the world who want to do the will of God for all of the people of the world to see and witness. The children of God would come together in a righteous movement that would 'bind the hearts of the parents to the hearts of their children'. This verse is the last verse in the old testament.

> ***"And he shall turn the heart of the fathers to the children, and the heart of the children to their fathers, lest I come and smite the earth with a curse."***
> *— Malachi 4: 6*

I suspect that when Jesus does reveal Himself to His people He will also reveal the scars that were left in His hands and feet as proof of His great sacrifice. This would be in the same manner as Jesus showed himself to the Nephite children when He revealed Himself to the Nephite tribe in the book of Mormon. (3rd Nephi 11: 13,14)

In the beginning, moral freedom was ultimately given out of love and trust, but was taken away at a time when God, and only God, felt it was appropriate for Him to do so. That decision proved to be a just decision and that act also

THE RATIONAL GOSPEL

proved to be for the benefit of all men and women. That was mainly so the great Christmas message of "peace on earth and goodwill towards men" will finally become a reality.

In this current year of 2023, this gathering has not yet been fulfilled, but the message of my story is that <u>this mighty quest has at last begun</u> and will one day soon be completed. Thus, I say, 'Rejoice'.

In the past, our God knew that the beautiful gift of free agency would also facilitate any reckless ideas that certain people might have, and which would lead to a major contamination of the world itself. Those ideas would be to our detriment, but they would also be necessary for the growth of human beings. He saw clearly that the former policy did not do anything good for men and women in general, but human beings must see their plans, however foolish they may be, played out until the end and the final results are reported. On a righteous human level, those final results will probably never be a pretty sight.

This new restriction of the law will be welcome in our world and in the minds of the fellow citizens in our world. These new laws will be according to the **'laws of ultimate correction'**. All laws are restrictive and there are reasons for that. One of our earthly jobs is to come to understand why there should be restrictions or 'commandments' among the Children of God. Having no restrictions leads to disobedience and rebellion and those things are <u>always orchestrated by the devil and are always destructive</u>.

Like a wild animal, who must be tamed to be of use, God saw that giving mankind free reign was a policy that ended up bringing forth no good results. Good results in the human situation could only come from obedience and allegiance to whatever is good and <u>whatever has proven to be good</u>. This was obvious and was undeniable to all reasonable human beings. Thus, we make corrections and then we move forward.

Hallelujah!

> ***"The glory of God is intelligence."***
> **- Doctrine and covenants 93: 36**

This scripture verse may be simple, but it is personal evidence to me that the gospel teachings that are found in this church are truly inspired. I have tested them out and found them 'not wanting' It is for this reason that I named this book – THE RATIONAL GOSPEL.

That is basically because those same principles that Jesus gave us should be good for any thinking man's, or any thinking woman's, philosophy. That is because the principles all make sense. They make sense because they are 'true'.

The assignments that the Lord gave to his followers were given out of love and given at a time when He felt it was most appropriate. If the people wanted signs, they would get signs, but first it as necessary for them to learn about which signs are most relevant by their own experiences. It seems that there was no other way that things would effectively work.

The gospel message was to be spread to millions of other people and families, and will, I suspect, be spread to millions more. I believe and hope that I will be preserved myself to watch it happen and to encourage people to get involved in it.

I am a little bit nervous of some of the idealistic concepts that are spoken about in the Bible, but after due study, I can say that but I have faith in God and I have much trust in Him, enough trust that I will try to make my eye **'single to His Glory'**.

For example, let me say that I would not assume that my relationship between my wife and myself would be a perfect example of marital bliss and Celestial glory. God, who has all understanding and knowledge, will be the judge of those things. I await his final and righteous approval for all of the important matters in my life for now and in my future.

***

The Holy Spirit is quite capable of naming life's problems, big and small, and addressing those problems and finding the correct solutions for them in the clearest of terms. People who live under the laws of God in unity can address specific problems by utilizing 'the powers of heaven', or even 'the power of faith', to assist us in the undertaking of those noble goals.

I speak here not of business or of romantic quests, or of worldly quests, but I speak for quests concerning the mass healing of millions of families and individuals who once decided to sincerely commit themselves to following the laws of our Heavenly Parents and who will decide to do so again when this gathering, or this 'second chance' comes around. This will be for the mutual benefit of all concerned.

We also understand, however, that in our secular environments we will often be tempted by agents of evil who will attempt to 'water down' the righteous commandments that have been given to us. I do, however, have faith in the wisdom of God in all matters, and I will hereby be resolved to sustain his judgments.

In other words, my personal dreams of grandeur consist of not much more than standing in a clean and beautiful temple while living under a covenant, to give service to our God, and I might add, with our beautiful smiling children standing at our side, possibly even our grandchildren. I view such a dream as a very beautiful thing.

That Temple, or chapel, that I mentioned would be a Holy place that has been dedicated for learning and for gaining knowledge. There are also many good and pure feelings that will comfort us during our trials and those good feelings are a vital part of our remarkable religion. It is a religion that seeks for the unification of all of the Children of God, and a religion that will finally see the fulfillment of all the sacred prophesies that have been made by our God throughout history. This is the only way by which 'literal salvation' can happen.

In the Great Gathering the edicts that prohibit alcohol and tobacco in our lives will also apply to drugs. Pharmacists and doctors may be smart, but the Lord is smarter. While some drugs or substances may alleviate pain, they can also lessen the power of our Spirits. Those blessed spirits of ours have graciously been given to us by our Heavenly Father

Under the 'wrong conditions', the power of the human Spirit can be severely 'watered down' in our fight to preserve a totally pure and wholesome spirit that can bring to people joy, wisdom, and genuine peace when God's commandments are observed and followed.

"But where there's hope inside, true love will reside, and where mortals fail, true love will prevail."
   - Song: "True Love Will Prevail" by Bob King

"The secret to happiness is freedom and the secret to freedom is courage." - Thucydides

SOME OF MY RELATIVES:

Personally, as I was writing in my journal, I made a list of some of my relatives who I would like to see working to make the world a much better place and a much happier place.

In the beginning the main players for me in this 'gathering project will be the families of: Faye King and Jimmy King; Robert and Leanne King, James and Jean King, Catherine and Herbert Armitage; Megan King and Liam Holman; The Gordon and Joanne Thomson family; James King junior; David King; Jean and Stan Menzies; Winifred and Hugh Macdairmid; May and Bill Johnson; Joyce and Robert Albert King; Charles and Kaye Armitage; Alan and Marge Armitage; Keith and Murial Armitage; Ivan and Irene Armitage; Mary and George Dodds.

There may be other family member who are either added to this list or deleted from it. I don't know, but I am sure that will not be for me to make any ultimate decisions on those matters.

This list of families would also include members of those families who somehow lost their connection to their original family, whether it be through divorce or apostasy or something else. They would still be included in the Great gathering if they wanted to be, and agreed to be loyal to the Lord's cause, which is evident to us mainly in the scriptures and will be expanded upon by people who have the authority to preach the full gospel of God and Jesus Christ.

I use my family as a prime example of this gathering not out if a personal bias, but I do that because the next world will be a world of resurrection, which would apply to all the consenting families and consenting peoples in the world. I think that my family would want to be a part of that. I also believe that the joining together of husbands and wives will be done with their consent. God believes in 'the perfect law of liberty' (James 1:25) and does not 'force' people to do anything that they don't want to do.

Most of the problems and difficulties that plagued some people in the earthly world will no longer exist in the new and redeemed world. Thus, through the grace of God, anyone can begin again with a clean slate, that is, if they desire to do so.

God's ability to forgive and forget is a very powerful thing and contains a lot of love and a lot if courage. We will all be able to access that beautiful place where that will happen and it will happen when the final gathering actually happens, and then there will be much cause for celebration for the 'family of mankind'.

> *"In my Father's house are many mansions. If it were not so I would have told you. I go to prepare a place for you."*
> *- John 14: 2*

CHAPTER 29

LITTLE CHANGES AND THE BIG CHANGE   (3p.)

WHAT IS THE 'BIGGEST BIG CHANGE' THAT WE CAN ACCOMPLISH IN OUR LIFETIME AND WHAT ARE THE 'BIGGEST LITTLE CHANGES' THAT WE CAN ACCOMPLISH IN OUR LIFETIME?

Let us start with the big change. The biggest big change that we can accomplish is to decide to do the will of the God, that is the God of the Bible, and to associate with other men and women who have decided to do that. It will be as simple as that.

On the other hand, many men and women in our world have a nasty habit of thinking negative thoughts; even things like sad thoughts, or vulgar thoughts, or trivial thoughts, or stupid thoughts, or nasty thoughts, or accusatory thoughts, etc. Certain substances that we take into our bodies that affect our minds can facilitate these negative thoughts. What can you do about that situation if you should find yourself in it?

As an example for me, one substance that caused me to experience bad thoughts recently was a steroid that was prescribed for me by a doctor for a skin rash. I stopped taking them immediately when I recognized that those unappealing thoughts were coming into my mind and affecting my mood in a negative way.

By that I mean that my mind was being invaded by thoughts like the ones I just mentioned earlier. I felt like those thoughts might even be 'taking over' in my mind. Thus, I got rid of them. That made room up there for the 'good stuff'.

BEING ABLE TO CHANGE OUR MOODS, AND BE RID OF THE BAD INFLUENCES THAT CAUSE THEM, IS PART OF THE BIG CHANGE THAT WE WILL NEED TO MAKE FOR OURSELVES.

What changes are the most important changes that a person makes for themselves? <u>Is it the big change or the biggest little changes?</u> To be honest, I don't really know the answer to that, but what I do know is that if you want to commit yourself to undertaking the big change then the Lord would <u>not</u> be happy if you do not change the smaller changes first. That is for the purpose of being prepared to make the BIG CHANGE.

To begin the process of change we must first make all of our changes by keeping in mind our duty to try to change a negative mood into a positive one. And make sure you are not making those changes to satisfy your own ego. You will need to incorporate those positive mood changes into your personality quietly and be resolved to do those changes every day in order to be successful in our most important quests.

Making positive changes will enable us to serve the Lord better, and to serve our fellow human beings better. I cannot speak for the Lord but I am confident in saying that making positive actions will increase our status with Him greatly.

Thus, it might be wise to keep a copy of this essay and read it when you need something that will bring you 'up' instead of keep you 'down'. The best solution however, is to regularly offer up a little prayer and ask for the Lord's advice and assistance as you go about your busy day.

The biggest 'little change' that people can make for themselves will be for the purpose of ridding our minds of all negative thoughts and replacing them with happy thoughts, positive thoughts, intelligent thoughts, creative thoughts, and beautiful thoughts. Good thoughts, like good memories from the past, or even funny memories from the past, are always welcome in my psyche.

As well, thinking about good plans for the future are always welcome in my mind and can get me personally excited about the very future that once caused me worry and anxiety.

This good 'change of thinking' can take place at any time, or in any place, or with any companions. It can even happen in an instant, that is, if the slightest will to change is there in you.

Thus, I say that you can actually change yourself from being a negative person into being a positive person and it can happen IN AN INSTANT. Please be aware that that would be a great and magical thing.

CHAPTER 30

THE MAN YOU CALL YOUR DAD   (4p.)

One night I had an idea to offer one of my songs to people who have followed my music for many years. I chose a country song that I wrote a few years ago called, 'THE MAN YOU CALL YOUR DAD'.

I never had a chance to record the song on a CD, and I don't remember if I ever played it for anyone, but I liked it a lot, and I did post the lyrics for it on face book once, and found that it got a very favorable reaction. It is about my own 'sentimental journey'.

My father was Jimmy King and my mother was Fay King. My father was a musician and bandleader in Winnipeg where I grew up with four siblings. My father was the leader of a Big Band for most of his life and he received a lot of acclaim over the years. And by the way, the song 'Sentimental Journey' was the song that he chose to be his band's theme song. The song was originally recorded by Les Brown and his orchestra in the 1940's.

I admit that I took a few artistic liberties with the storyline, but, 'Hey, I'm a songwriter and it became my policy to put out the most interesting stories that I can put out'. So here it is:

THE MAN YOU CALL YOUR DAD

Verse 1
When I was a young boy growing up, I used to look up to my dad.

I thought he could do almost anything, and I overlooked any faults he may have had.
And my mom was a woman with a heart of gold. Guess you could say I was blessed.
And my dad used to say, of all the women in the world, he was smart enough to marry the best.

One day I was playing with my toys on the floor, and I saw my mom looking at me.
She called me over and picked me up and sat me on her knee.
She gave me a kiss and a little hug and it made me feel good inside.
And I still remember how she smiled at me as she spoke these words with pride.

Chorus:
Your eyes remind me of a certain young man with a heart so true and fair.
You got his chin. You got his skin. You got his color of hair.
If you could live your life like him that would make your mama glad.
He's coming home in an hour or so, the man you call your dad.

Verse 2

Well as the years went by I grew up tall, that being a part of natures plan.
And I did the things a young man does to try to prove that he's a man.
But I was kind of shy and it took a while for me to loosen up with a girl.
Then one day I met someone very special who set my heart in a whirl.

Verse 3

She and I started spending time together. We grew closer day by day.
But when she started talking about wedding bells, I began to shy away.
So I went to my mom for a little advice, cause I didn't know which way to go.
Mom looked at me and spoke the same words she spoke so long ago.

Chorus:

Your eyes remind me of a certain young man with a heart so true and fair.
You got his chin. You got his grin. You got his color of hair.
If you could live your life like him, that would make your mama glad.
Just ask yourself what he might do. The man you call your dad.

Verse 3

Well I got married shortly after that. And I haven't regretted a day.
I've got to admit we've had our ups and downs, but all in all we're doing okay.
And in time I became a dad myself, the father of a fine young boy.
And I watched mom and dad grow old, living in a time tempered joy.

Verse 4

Then one day my father passed away. We just turned around and he was gone.
We all cried and we all prayed and then proceeded to carry on.
But my mom could never quite get used to the fact and she grew as frail as could be.
Then one day I was called to her bedside where she spoke these last words to me.

Chorus

Your eyes remind me of a certain young man with a heart so true and fair.
You got his chin. You got his grin. You got his color of hair.
If you could live your life like him, that would make your mama glad.
I'm going away to join him now, the man you call your dad.
I'm going away to join him now, the man you call your dad.

CHAPTER 31

My Testimony Revisited (5p.)

Subtitles: The Brides and the Bridegroom

As I end this book, I know that I have wandered through Bible doctrine, including the old Testament and the new Testament as well as the doctrine of the Church Of Jesus Christ Of Latter Day Saints with a desire to explain some of the finer points of it all so that people will understand the truths that were told by ancient prophets, and are even talked about by latter day prophets in the Book of Mormon and the Doctrine and Covenants. I believe that those books have been inspired by God. Inspirational words have been written in the New Testament books, and the Old Testament books and have inspired us in the same way.

My job may not be finished here, but I feel that I have done the best I can do under my present circumstances to explain this love that I feel for the Father, Son and Holy Ghost.

Any words of wisdom will come from God, or else from his loyal servants. It is the same. Those wise words can also come from latter day prophets and many of those words can be found in the in the Book called the Doctrine and Covenants. Most of those quotes in that book came directly from the first prophet of that church whose name was Joseph Smith. In my opinion, all of the books that he wrote had writings that were inspirational for people who were, and who still are, looking for a good direction in their life, or for some kind of enlightenment or a knowledge of the truth.

I can only hope that the words that I say and the quotes that I offer will be strong enough and gentle enough to touch people's hearts, even some hearts that have been waiting to be touched for many years. Those people will then know that, after all of the struggles that we all have been through, the time for the final redemption is near.

For many of us, it is actually here NOW.

I will not make demands or make promises to anyone, except to say that people should, as the scriptures advise us, seek out the truth that God is hoping we will someday accept, and from there we will live our lives with a similar love as the love that The Father, Son, and Holy Ghost have for us.

The word 'lure' is a strong word, but it has a couple of different meanings. The first meaning means 'to trick', that means tricking someone into doing something that might not be good for them in the end.

The second meaning means to 'persuade' someone into doing something that **will definitely be for their**

benefit. I may be accused of trying to 'lure' someone into doing something that will ultimately be good for them, that is, persuading someone to live by the gospel of Jesus Christ. I plead guilty to that without apology, but I have a policy of not intruding in people's sacred beliefs without being asked to do so.

People will always make the decision to do what they will do strictly by their own free choice. It is all above board and they are always free to say 'yes or no' to that. That is the way things should be done.

I hope that the stories I have told, after studying the issues for many years, will make it clear that the stories are fascinating, and the Latter Day Saints themselves are generally a gentle and kind people. The vast majority of Saints try to live by high moral principles. Again that is according to the gospel of Jesus Christ.

The rational Saints are a very 'rational people' who seek out the will of the Lord by being obedient to the words of Jesus Christ and His Apostles and then, when and if they find it, they will proceed to do it, and seek to do it by covenants that they will make in one of the many Holy temples that now dot the Earth.

This is so that they may gain the confidence, which is the faith that is required to propel their souls into the next realms with the assurance that their righteous desires will be fulfilled by living according to God's plan, which is also called the Plan of Happiness.

This will happen so that they can proceed into the next level with the assurance that our Great Creator, who is our Heavenly Father, and who is the embodiment of peace and love, will sanctify their future existence.

Another benefit for us is the excitement that comes to us when we realize that all the great truths of the universe have finally been revealed to us in their fullness and we will be shown how we can deal with all if those things in ways that the Lord will approve of.

THE BRIDES AND THE BRIDEGROOMS

The relationship between human beings and Jesus is talked about in an allegory that is found the Bible. The bridegroom is Jesus. The brides are you and me and all the people of Christ. **That includes all men and women who accept Him and invite Him into their lives, so th\at they may partake of the many blessings that God has in store for us, even certain blessings that are now beyond our comprehension.**

Is this the only way? Yes, it is the only way.

"No one cometh unto the Father but by me. "
John 14:6

I don't want to appear too flippant right now, but I would like to close with words by the famous country singer Tammy Wynett who once sang a song called 'STAND BY YOUR MAN'. You may notice that I changed one word from the original lyrics. The word is 'our' instead of 'Your'. I think that that that man who we should stand by is Jesus Christ Himself and He belongs to all of us.

> *"Stand by **our man** and show the world you love Him. Please give Him all the love you can. Stand by **our man**."*

In my mind, this woman was not singing about some rough living, hard drinking cowboy. She was talking about Jesus Christ who is 'our man' and is everybody's man.

Amen.

CHAPTER 32

GRADUATION DAY (11p.)

SUBTITLE: Our Two Choices

I think I just graduated. I woke up this morning knowing that there are some definite barriers between myself and certain people, or enemies as I sometimes refer to them, whose mission in life is to hamper my life and my personal progress. Why? Its a long story and I don't know all of the answers, but the problem is there and the only issue at hand for me is that I will need to resolve those issues in my own mind and not wait for someone else to tell me what I should do about them. As it happens, I am handling those issues quite well and I will explain how I do that, so please don't feel sorry for me.

Any bad relationships that I have are are mostly with people who are holdovers from my younger days and they know who they are. They hope that their resentments are going to curse me and do me damage, but I know who they are and I know what their game is. I am resolved that I will not let them do that or let them interfere or meddle in my life.

I cannot destroy the barriers or problems or misunderstandings between me and some other people because they are embedded the minds of those people, or enemies, and I have no jurisdiction in their realms.

However, there is something else that I can, and will do. That is, I will 'ride those barriers'. I will ride those differences. I will ride them on my 'super surfboard'. and ride them out until the barriers, and my enemies, will no longer exist, at least not in my realms. I cannot discard my enemies totally because their resentments (barriers) will still be there and that never produces a comfortable feeling.

Personal resentments are the focus of my enemies who, I suspect, belong to a certain club of men and woman that I commonly know as 'Resentments Anonymous'. The members of that club do not have any righteous ambitions at all, and besides that, some of them like to play very dirty.

That bunch gets together once in awhile and they talk about other people and may even talk about bad things that I may, or may not, have done, so that they can further smear my reputation without putting too much effort into it. I am wise to them however, and I will let them try to wait me out because I know that I will survive and be happy, much to their dismay.

Those barriers that I mentioned are like childish Merry go-rounds. They never allow anyone to go anywhere other than in the same old circle. All of the horses and all of the sights are the same and there is nothing of interest there for a person who is older than six. So as a part of life, I sometimes just go along with it and I just go round and round and around. And I wait.

I don't mind waiting anymore because I have learned that there is a trick to 'effective waiting' that not too many people know about. The trick is to find a 'good friend' who understands all the mechanics that are behind attitudes of resentment, and who are willing and able to help us overcome resentments from other people, and even resentments within ourselves.

I am fortunate because I have found such a friend to help me. That friend is a special friend because he is always near me and constantly helps me out by his instructions and even just by the influence of his presence. My friend is a person, but he is also a spirit. He was once a human being as well, for the most part at least. That is why many people refer to him as 'the Son of Man'.

In his mortal days he was a teacher, or a Rabbi, in the Jewish community. He was, and is, an extremely smart man, given his Divine heritage. He has been with me for a long time now and I have grown to love Him because of His goodness and His willingness to sacrifice things for my sake.

My friend always knows just what to do. That is because He came here directly from a place called 'Heaven'. Heaven was the first place where He went to school and where He began His learning. He had the greatest teachers that he could possibly have and He shares some of the things that he has learned with me.

I have accepted those things, and have made them a big part of my life. Thus, at present, I fully intend to ride the barriers if resentment with my friend until the barriers either crumble or just 'perish'.

***

I feel great today. I am happy. I can see clearly now. I feel that I have finally graduated. At the beginning of this story, I mentioned the fact that I **felt** that I was presently graduating from something. 'What am I graduating from' and 'what am I graduating to', you might well ask. So I will tell you.

I am graduating from a realm that I have inhabited for many years. It was not a hellish realm, but neither was it a heavenly realm. There was, however, not a lot of growth in my former realm. I know that now. I did begin to experience growth about thirty years ago when I started learning about the gospel and how most things worked.

I try to continue with that growth process today. Most times I am successful with it, but not always. Life can be tough, I will also add that, unfortunately, I, personally, can sometimes be 'not very smart'.

Over recent years though, I studied my realm at length and I think that on this day, which is July 4th, 2023, I felt, as I laid in my bed this morning, that the Great Spirit was trying to talk to me and let me know that I might be ready to advance to a slightly higher spiritual level. That would be a realm where, I assume, my Lord would allow me to spread His gospel more than I have ever done before. I call it my Graduation Day and this is going to be my song on this day:

> *"I can see clearly now. The rain has gone.*
> *I can see all obstacles in my way.*
> *Gone are the dark clouds that had me blind.*
> *It's gonna be a bright, bright sunshiny day."*
>   - Johnny Nash

It was good for me to think that I might be possible for me to see clearly all of the obstacles that are in my way. That is because I do love righteousness, and I do love life, even though it seems that sometimes life doesn't love me. That is okay. I can deal with that if I try.

Thus, I say that it is perhaps possible that, with my new positive attitude, I can now contribute something good to the world that just might cause rational thinking people to investigate that wonderful gospel message that I have found and that just might cause people to actually come to know about ..... wait for it... **the meaning of life**.

Is that a bold claim to make? Yes, it is, but then my God is a bold God, and He has said and done many bold things in the past, so one shouldn't be surprised that He is still bold today.

> ***"Ye shall <u>know</u> the <u>truth</u> and the truth shall make you <u>free</u>."***   *- John 8: 32 (emphasis added)*

There are a couple of principles in this short passage from the Book of John that people should take notice of. One principle is about '**knowing**'. Another is about '**truth**' and a third one is about being '**free**'.

All three of these things are excellent things. Good things come with a price, but excellent things come with a high price. If we want to have excellent things in our life, we must pay a high price, which basically amounts to spending a lot of time studying and preparing.

We must also have rules in our homes too, so that thieves cannot come into our homes, or into our country, and steal those excellent things. Those would be things that we sincerely believe in, like our belief in a benevolent God, and our belief in our in our core values, and in our belief in 'having the freedom to choose'. We should also believe in simple, but excellent things like hard work and in being kind to others. There are many excellent things that we can have in our lives and those things should always be preserved.

It seems that those things can only be preserved by making **RULES** and by convincing people, by <u>righteous</u> persuasion, to **FOLLOW THOSE RULES.** Many ideas have been put forward throughout history regarding ways to persuade people to follow those rules, but it seems that not all of them have worked, that is, until now.

WHY NOW? WHY IN THIS DISPENSATION OF TIME? IT IS BECAUSE THIS IS THE TIME THAT A GREAT SACRIFICE HAS BEEN MADE FOR THE PEOPLE OF THIS WORLD AND FOR THE SAKE OF THEIR ETERNAL BENEFIT. THIS MOMENT IN TIME IS THE ACTUAL MOMENT THAT WE HAVE ALL BEEN WAITNG FOR.

IT IS THE MOMENT WHEN PERMANENCE ACTUALLY ENTERS INTO THE EQUASION OF THE HAPPINESS OF MANKIND. IT HAPPENED WHEN GOD ALLOWED FOR THE SACRIFICE OF HIS ONLY BEGOTTEN SON, SO THAT THE SOULS OF THOSE WHO FOLLOWED THE SON IN THIS FALLEN WORLD COULD AFTERWARDS PROCEED WITH HIM INTO AN ETERNAL REALM WHERE THE MOST RIGHTEOUS DESIRES OF JESUS' FOLLOWERS COULD BE FULFILLED, AT LEAST THE DESIRES THAT DID NOT INFRINGE ON ANYONE ELSES' RIGHTEOUS DESIRES.

***

SO IT MAKES SENSE THAT WE SHOULD WANT TO ATTAIN THOSE GOOD THINGS AND PRESERVE THEM FOR FUTURE GENERATIONS. THUS, WITH THE HELP OF GODLY INFLUENCES, WE MAKE RULES. BUT SOME

PEOPLE HAVE A NATURAL AVERSION TO RULES AND WILL REBEL AGAINST THEM, AND WILL ALSO REBEL AGAINST RULERS, AND ESPECIALLY RULERS WHO THEY REALLY DON'T KNOW VERY WELL.

God knew that too and I think that that was one reason why He chose a very bold teaching method for His children. That method was, basically, to turn HIS children loose, but with some good instructions for them, and with a sacred sacrificial offering for them at the end of it all. That sacrifice would be the life of the Father's only begotten and much loved Son.

Then our Creator would just let the children learn from the past as best as they could, and also learn by some suffering that they experienced when they made some mistakes as they lived in the mortal realm.

This meant that faithful people would need to go through a certain amount of pain to get to a better spiritual place where they wanted to be. Undergoing that pain would cause some bitterness in the minds of some freedom loving people.

Those people knew that independence was a good thing, but what they didn't know was the fact that there must be rules put into place that would allow true independence to actually take place. What are those rules? If you don't know, I can only say, 'read the Bible, especially the Ten Commandments. That's a good start.

The Lord knew that some 'rebellious thinking' would happen among independent, but peace loving, people. Thus, after some people have separated themselves from us by their insistence on remaining bitter, things would proceed to go on as they did before. However there were some very strong admonitions given to the people about eliminating sinful behavior in their lives. IE: *"The wages of sin is death." - Romans 6: 23*

Some people who had a lot of bitterness in them decided to serve another master. That 'master' was one who was demanding and manipulative. That 'other master' often went by the name of Satan.

That decision would bring those followers of Satan their own rewards, which, in truth. were basically curses. But when people began to witness the ugliness of anger, envy, greed, exploitation, addictions, wars, etc. many of them began to understand that BITTERNESS IS DEFINITELY NOT A GOOD THING AND SHOULD BE AVOIDED AT ALL COST.

That caused some of those people, or souls, to either hate, or disregard, the God who would allow bitterness to become a part of their lives.

Personally, I have chosen to progress along my chosen path and be loyal to my Heavenly Father who set the rules in the first place. Also, I will shut myself off from the bitter people and do so with no regrets. Regrets are what those people want me to have, but I will not have them.

They flatter themselves that they are so good that they want to share with me their bitter, and unforgiving regrets, and their rebelliousness that they created for themselves many years ago. That rebelliousness was something that they mistakenly saw as 'acts of courage'.

But I will leave them to wallow in their own self-aggrandizement. They will curse me for refusing to join their club, but I don't care. That is because I have other things to do and other people to meet and other smiles to generate. Those other people who I want to meet are smart people. I know that because I have met many of them and I know that they are smart because the Spirit told me so in my heart. They are also caring and unselfish people, and I will love them because they are a part of my Eternal family.

On my graduation day, there won't be a band playing or singers singing. There won't be any square black hats flying up in the air. That is because I am the only one graduating in my realm that I am aware of. As far as I know, I will be the only one who even knows about my graduation, aside from my special friend. That is because my graduation applies specifically to me.

Do I feel isolated and alone because of that? No. I feel grateful for it, and even celebratory. My graduation ceremony was small, but it is was given to me as a gift from a very special friend, a man who saved me from some a very perilous fate. I am talking about my Savior. That makes my spiritual graduation day a very important ceremony in the Spiritual realm. Not many people know about it because it was, basically, between Him and me, and that is all. Nevertheless, I rejoice because of that.

There won't be a speaker giving a valedictorian speech on my graduation Day. That is because I am the only one who is graduating. I thought about nominating myself as my valedictorian speaker, but I decided to turn my nomination down. That was because I just did not feel like giving an emotional speech to just to myself.

***

Thus, I will continue to ride the barriers on my super surfboard. My surfboard will carry me forward to places where my special friend and my devotion and my personal ingenuity that I have nurtured over the years will stymie all resentments towards me.

To make me bitter, just like my enemies are bitter, is the gift that my enemies want to give to me. They want to give me a full membership in their 'Regrets Anonymous' group. That group says that getting a membership in their group would be for my own good, and that that it is a unanimous opinion amongst all the members.

That is because it is essential that all of the members of RA (regrets anonymous) totally rely on each other for support. That is their security blanket, but they do not know that security never comes with QUANTITY of people, or big numbers. It comes with QUALITY PEOPLE, even if their numbers are small. Thus, I will thank the bitter people for their gift, but I will politely refuse it.

That is because, like I said earlier, I have too many other things to do. I will concentrate more now on where I want to go in the future, now that I feel I have graduated to a slightly higher realm. The main thing I need to do is to proceed to do my work with my Heavenly friend as we ride the barriers until the barriers crumble, as they will surely do.

OUR TWO OPTIONS

As I end this book, I will quote again something that I said earlier regarding our two options that we will have to choose from as we prepare to enter into the Eternities.

> *"Behold there are save two churches on the one is the church of the Lamb of God and the other is the church of the devil; wherefore whoso belongeth not to the church of the Lamb of God belongeth to that great church, which is the mother of all abominations; and she is the whore of all the earth."*
>
> *- 2 Nephi 14: 10*

This scripture makes our two choices very clear. Now that you have read my book, it will probably be obvious which choice I will make for my future. **HOW ABOUT YOU?**

CHAPTER 33

EVIDENCE OF REAL HOPE AND PROPHESY (4p.)

Friday, July 14

(This is my first post-graduate revelation since my graduation ceremony last week. People who have never been in a crippled state might not know what I am talking about in this essay because they cannot identify with all the daily nuances, or nuisances, of being in a crippled state. Nevertheless I will proceed with my writing because there are, I am sure, many people who <u>can</u> identify with that state.)

I fell into a deep sleep after breakfast today. In my sleep I had a dream. I dreamed that I was walking down a hall at Muchmor lodge. I didn't have a walker. I didn't have a cane or a wheelchair. It felt very real and I was walking totally free. I can only imagine that many crippled people like me have dreams like that.

I soon woke up and realized that I was still crippled. It was like I had died, but I didn't know that I was dead.

Anyways, when I actually woke up I started to go back to feeling somewhat depressed, (that darned reality again) and I became resigned to the fact that I was destined to stay a crippled man for the rest of

my life. BUT, there was something different about it this time.

***

Post script: I think that in the spirit world, which is a different world, and sometimes a more real world than the physical world, that that dream was indeed very real to me. It was a dream of legitimate hope, and maybe even a dream of faith, or confidence.

I COULD THINK OF NO OTHER REASON WHY THAT DREAM CAME TO ME AND WHY IT WAS SO REAL. IT COULD NOT HAVE HAPPENED, IF IT DIDN'T COME FROM GOD.

THAT IS WHEN MY THOUGHTS ENTERED INTO A DIFFERENT REALM. IT WAS A REALM WHERE I COULD SEE THE FUTURE, A DREAM OF PROPHESY. IT WAS NOT A MAN-MADE FUTURE, BUT A GOD-MADE FUTURE.

I, PERSONALLY, SAW THE WAY THAT THINGS WERE MEANT TO BE SEEN. IF IT HAD TO HAPPEN AFTER THE RESURRECTION, THAT DIDN'T REALLY MATTER. THAT IS BECAUSE I SAW, AND FELT, THAT IT WAS GOING TO HAPPEN, FOR SURE, AND FOR REAL. THAT DREAM GAVE MY SPIRIT A DEFINITE LIFT. THAT WAS ENOUGH FOR ME. I THEN RESOLVED NOT TO LOSE MY FOCUS

LIKE PETER DID WHEN HE TRIED TO WALK ON THE WATER.

THUS. I SAY THAT IT HAD TO HAVE COME FROM GOD AND IT WAS MEANT TO ENCOURAGE ME, BECAUSE HE KNEW THAT I WAS FEELING DOWN. I HAD TO THINK THAT THAT SUNDAY SCHOOL LESSON WAS MEANT FOR ME. ALSO, I KNOW OF NOBODY ELSE IN THIS WORLD WHO COULD HAVE GIVE ME SUCH A POSITIVE AND UPLIFTING MESSAGE.

MY DREAM WAS SO REAL THAT I CAN ONLY SEE THAT REALITY AS VERY STRONG EVIDENCE THAT IT IS ALSO A PROPHECY. TODAY, I HAVE MUCH MORE HOPE AND I APPRECIATE THE GIFT OF THAT HOPE A LOT. I MAY NOT BE A PROPHET, BUT I AM A 'MAN OF HOPE' – THAT IS WHO I AM TODAY.

***

Post Post Script: Today I brought a root beer down to lunch in the lunchroom. When I took the first big sip, it was fizzy and delicious. I had the feeling that I was experiencing a shot of hope. Was that a sign?

I thought about my dream again. Because of my initial doubt, I figured that you can't trust dreams even when they make you feel good. I was distrustful of that dream in the beginning when I discovered that it didn't apply to my real live life. Upon further reflection, I changed my mind. I figured that that dream was more than real. It was a prophetic revelation, a revelation that someday, I was going to be healed. I just knew it.

True prophesies are very real. That dream had to have come from God because it was totally real. It was a prophecy specifically for me and my future. It told me that i would one day be healed.

It took this 'genius' a while to figure that out, but I finally figured it out. I figured that true hope with a spiritual witness is prophecy, and that we would all do well to believe it when, and if, that 'other reality' is made manifest to us.

As I further thought about it, I know that I did have to undergo some suffering when I became crippled, but that is all right because I am a better man now because I saw some evidence of my healing in my dream. With my very real dream of being healed through Christ, and through the intelligence of our Heavenly father, those feelings all caused my new hope to actually become embedded in me to a certain level. Will I be able to make use of that level or see that level increase in its scope? We shall see.

***

I had learned the truth about hope and about the truth behind prophecy. I felt it would be foolish of me to deny it. It may be true that most people will never learn in this life. That is that <u>true hope can be true prophesy. And especially when there is the evidence of a true vision behind it.</u>

Post Post Post Script.

Sunday, July 16:
A member gave a good lesson on personal change in a Sunday School class today. He talked about Paul after he became converted. His conversion was a major change in his life. Then he compared Paul's inadequacy with Peter's inadequacy, when Peter tried to follow Jesus' example, and walk on the water, but failed. Peter began to sink and Jesus had to pull him back up again. This was as an example of a minor change in Peter's life.

A very smart woman, who I knew, was present during the lesson, and she commented about Peter's failure to walk on water. She summed up the lesson in 'three words'. She said that Peter failed because **'he lost focus'**. Good comment. Could that apply to myself at certain times?

I thought more about that later and I felt a little guilty because I had to admit that last week, I lost some focus myself in my desire to have more confidence in talking about the gospel with others. I was still felt good about the dream (prophesy) but I seemed to have lost a small amount of confidence as a 'doer of the word', a confidence that I had glimpsed about a week before.

After that Sunday school lesson, I was then resolved to get my focus back, get back on the right path, and then STAY ON IT.

***

In any case, I say that if it is truly a prophecy from God, then it will surely come to pass one day. I will keep you informed about my progress on this matter.

Praise the lord and His wisdom. – B. K.

CHAPTER 34. LETTERS FROM A FRIEND (5P.)

Dear Bob:

I just finished reading your new book for a second time and I found that I discovered even more insight out of it. I was quite impressed by your last essay in it called on 'TRUE EVIDENCE OF HOPE IS PROPHESY'. I noticed that in a previous essay of yours called 'BETRAYAL AND THE SPIRIT OF GENTLENESS' you had a similar theme in that essay. I was wondering why you did not combine the two similar themes into the same essay?

Yours truly,
 PW. Doodle

***

Dear P. W.

The answer to that question is a simple one. The Holy Comforter is the spirit who can freely give us comfort in our lives when we need it the most. I always, sort of, knew that was true, but until recently I did not fully understand the great extent to which that wonderful principle actually applies to each of us. (shame on me.)

It just did not really 'click in' with me in the past, but I have since realized that powerful prophecies that come into our hearts and into our minds as gifts can actually change a person's whole outlook on life.

WHEN A BEAUTIFUL FEELING IS STRONGLY FELT IN A PERSON'S SOUL, THEN ALL THE RIGHT AND GOOD FEELINGS, INCLUDING A STRONG SPIRIT, OR SPIRITS, WILL BE THERE. THEN THEY SOMETIMES WILL

SPEAK,ON MASSE, AND THEY WILL SAY VERY QUIETLY: "I HAVE SOME GOOD NEWS FOR YOU. DO YOU WANT TO HEAR IT? IF SO, LISTEN VERY CLOSELY."

How many of us will then trust in the unknown and listen, (if you have 'ears to hear', to a still small voice that is speaking to you.)

And how many people will disregard that gift that we all potentially have. Why do they do that? Maybe God knows why, but I don't. So maybe I am just not that smart. Nevertheless, I do love my God and I do trust my God and I intend to declare that to the world.

IN ANY CASE, THOSE GOOD FEELINGS THAT ACCOMPANY A PROPHETIC MESSAGE IS THE PROOF THAT WE NEED THAT A <u>PROPHESY FROM GOD IS GOING TO COME TRUE</u>. IT CAN'T MISS,

WHETHER IT HAPPENS IN THIS LIFE OR IN THE NEXT LIFE AFTER THE RESURRECTION, THAT DOESN'T REALLY MATTER VERY MUCH. IT WILL HAPPEN AND YOU WILL FEEL THOSE GOOD FEELINGS ONCE AGAIN, EVEN OFTEN.

THAT IS BECAUSE A PROPHESY FROM OUR ETERNAL GOD ALWAYS STANDS, EVEN FOREVER. IF THAT PROPHECY DOES NOT CHANGE A BAD ATTITUDE ABOUT LIFE THAT YOU MAY SOMETIMES HAVE, THEN IT SHOULD, AND IT WILL, DO THAT.

***

Thank you, Bob:

I agree. I was reading some interviews with some astronauts on the Internet. Seeing that they did some fantastic things as a part of their jobs, I just thought they might be a little more profound when they talked about those kinds of things. Perhaps they should have taken a course on literacy that they could find useful after their space adventures were over, and they were talking to journalists about those wondrous adventures. Then they might be more interesting people to talk to.

Perhaps Neil Armstrong was given a script for his famous sentence when he took his first step on the moon, which went:

"That was a small step for a man, but a giant leap for mankind."

I thought that his quote was a good one. It did sound a little contrived, but maybe it was legitimate. Again, I don't know.

In any case I think that your ideas about the prophecies and the pleasures of Eternal life are much bigger than the vague destiny that Mr. Armstrong predicted.

In fact, I think that your revelation was miles ahead of his, and I would even say that your prediction is makes his 'giant leap' sound more like a simple 'bunny hop'. I do maintain though that your quote is about Eternal life and thus, is much wiser and more relevant to us humans who live in this mortal world.

***

Dear P.W.

I think that we are on the same page here. Why didn't NASA send somebody interesting up on those space flights with the astronauts? How about somebody like David Letterman, or Yogi Berra, or Joan Rivers. Isn't it true that the media and its professional clowns really run the world?

No. Don't take me seriously P.W. Life is about serious business. Entertainment is not.

<u>I did not write that essay to draw attention to myself. I only wanted to offer all people a confirmation that many good things are going to happen in the coming years, and even in the coming eons ahead of us.</u>

As long as we continue to learn things about God, we will be okay. Whether those things are related to our present worlds or whether they are related worlds beyond us. Whether they are literal worlds or physical worlds or worlds with a different chronology, they are still going to happen.

The point of that essay was <u>not</u> about receiving messages from colorful people in the entertainment world. <u>It was about receiving important life-giving messages from our kind and loving and magnificent creator and forcing ourselves to allow those messages to help us become better people, and to help us ease our sufferings, and along the way, motivate us to actually find joy in the things that we love the most.</u>

Good things will happen someday. Prepare for that. Also, remember that <u>hope</u> really does spring eternal. Be prepared for that too, and try to accommodate it as best as you can when it shows signs of coming true.

If this life that we are living is to be a success, we have got to love it and accept it. We cannot force ourselves to do that. We just need to decide to do it, and then <u>do it</u>. Then we need to practice forgiveness and charity, and then seek out the truth. As we seek out the truth, we must seek out the best mentor and exemplar of that truth that we can find, and then follow that person in their ways of righteousness.

After that, we can just <u>relax</u> and allow the chips to fall where they may, and be resolved to go forth with freedom and with peace, and with the learning of true principles. And, as well, do those things with joy, love, courage and gratitude in our hearts.

"From my experiences, the witness of the Comforter will always leave us with a feeling of complete satisfaction and even a feeling of bliss. Such a feeling does not come easy for us and that is why I identify that feeling as the literal evidence of the truth".

Thank you for your letter. I wish you well, Mr. Doodle, and I hope to meet you in person one day.

- Bob King

***

In closing, I would just like, with all sincerity, to say thank you to all of my readers out there, and say **'may God bless you'**, and never forget your 'shining moments, and if you don't have any shining moments, pray to God that He may help you to remember some of them and even create more of them.

– Bob King (bob.sandwiches@gmail.com)

www.ingramcontent.com/pod-product-compliance
Lightning Source LLC
LaVergne TN
LVHW081537070526
838199LV00056B/3688